VIOLENCE IN INTIMATE RELATIONSHIPS

VIOLENCE IN INTIMATE RELATIONSHIPS

XIMENA B. ARRIAGA
STUART OSKAMP
editors

The Claremont Symposium on
Applied Social Psychology

SAGE Publications
International Educational and Professional Publisher
Thousand Oaks London New Delhi

For information:

SAGE Publications, Inc.
2455 Teller Road
Thousand Oaks, California 91320
E-mail: order@sagepub.com

SAGE Publications Ltd.
6 Bonhill Street
London EC2A 4PU
United Kingdom

SAGE Publications India Pvt. Ltd.
M-32 Market
Greater Kailash I
New Delhi 110 048 India

Printed in the United States of America

Library of Congress Cataloging-in-Publication Data

Main entry under title:

Violence in intimate relationships / edited by Ximena B. Arriaga
and Stuart Oskamp.
         p.   cm.
    Includes bibliographical references and index.
    ISBN 0-7619-1642-3 (cloth: alk. paper)
    ISBN 0-7619-1643-1 (pbk.: alk. paper)
    1. Family violence.   I. Arriaga, Ximena B.   II. Oskamp, Stuart.
    HV6626 .V554   1999
    362.82'92—dc21   99-6256

99   00   01   02   03   04   7   6   5   4   3   2   1

Acquiring Editor:	Jim Nageotte
Editorial Assistant:	Heidi Van Middlesworth
Production Editor:	Denise Santoyo
Typesetter:	Christina M. Hill
Cover Designer:	Candice Harman

Contents

Acknowledgments vii

PART I: NATURE OF VIOLENCE

1. The Nature, Correlates, and Consequences of Violence
   in Intimate Relationships 3

   Ximena B. Arriaga and *Stuart Oskamp*

2. The Controversy Over Domestic Violence by Women:
   A Methodological, Theoretical, and Sociology of
   Science Analysis 17

   Murray A. Straus

3. A Typology of Male Batterers: An Initial Examination 45

   *Amy Holtzworth-Munroe, Jeffrey C. Meehan,
   Katherine Herron,* and *Gregory L. Stuart*

4. Limitations of Social Learning Models in Explaining
   Intimate Aggression 73

   Donald G. Dutton

PART II: CORRELATES OF VIOLENCE

5. The Interpersonal and Communication Dynamics of
   Wife Battering   91

   Sally A. Lloyd

6. Alcohol Use and Husband Marital Aggression Among
   Newlywed Couples   113

   Kenneth E. Leonard

PART III: CONSEQUENCES OF VIOLENCE

7. Women's Responses to Physical and Psychological Abuse   139

   Ileana Arias

8. Health Consequences for Victims of Violence in
   Intimate Relationships   163

   Phyllis W. Sharps and *Jacquelyn Campbell*

9. Physical Aggression and the Longitudinal Course
   of Newlywed Marriage   181

   Thomas N. Bradbury and *Erika Lawrence*

Author Index   203

Subject Index   209

About the Contributors   213

ACKNOWLEDGMENTS

We would like to acknowledge the assistance of many individuals and institutions who made possible this volume and the symposium upon which the current contributions are based. We are grateful for the financial contributions from Claremont Graduate University and the other Claremont Colleges in support of the Claremont Symposium on Applied Social Psychology last year. We appreciate the efforts of the CGU student assistants (Suzanne Blaisdell, Katrina Bledsoe, Todd Blickenstaff, Mary Ellen Dello-Stritto, Sam Gilstrap, Alison Stolkin, and Phelan Wyrick) and the hard work of staff members Gloria Leffer and B. J. Reich in preparing for and holding the successful conference, and the assistance of Douglas Wiegard and Chris Agnew in preparing this volume. We especially thank the authors of the chapters in this volume for their stimulating presentations and careful revisions. To all of these contributors who were essential in making the current volume possible, we express our sincere gratitude.

PART I

Nature of Violence

The Nature, Correlates, and Consequences of Violence in Intimate Relationships

Ximena B. Arriaga
Stuart Oskamp

One of the greatest contradictions of human nature is that some of the most personally injurious behaviors occur among loved ones. Rates of physical assault between intimate partners are disturbingly high. Estimates of the percentage of couples that engage in behaviors such as hitting, pushing, or shoving–what has recently been labeled "common couple violence" (Johnson, 1995)–range from 12% (e.g., Straus & Gelles, 1990) to 57% (e.g., O'Leary et al., 1989) and even higher. Sad to say, more severe forms of assault against women, resulting in physical injury and even death, are also not uncommon. Indeed, women in the United States are more likely to be killed by a male intimate or acquaintance than by a stranger (Federal Bureau of Investigation, 1993).

Perhaps because violence in intimate relationships can have such devastating consequences, this has been a topic of long-standing interest and great concern for behavioral and social scientists. The last three decades have seen substantial research on the dynamics of violent relationships–research that has promoted and will continue to advance the development of effective programs to end violence. More recently, concern over the prevalence and severity of domestic violence has become widespread in the U.S., leading to an increased sensitivity among the general public. For instance, law enforcement officers are less likely to treat instances of domestic violence as "private affairs" and more likely to arrest batterers; public officials are implementing tougher laws against convicted rapists; and funding institutions increasingly seek to support projects on intimate violence. Even public perceptions regarding relationship violence have dramatically changed. Previously, there was a widely shared belief that domestic "incidents" should be kept secret, for fear they undermine a family's image of public respectability (Gelles & Loseke, 1993). Today, the public endorses open discussion of domestic violence as an important topic to be addressed in talk shows, newspaper cover stories, and even movies (e.g., "What's Love Got To Do With It?" Gibson, 1993).

Despite the general acknowledgment that violence in intimate relationships is a serious problem and despite a widespread desire to eliminate it, there is little agreement over how to effectively and permanently end such violence. Many controversies have plagued the field of interpersonal violence (cf. Gelles & Loseke, 1993). Researchers have disagreed, for instance, about what constitutes violence as well as who inflicts and who sustains violence. Despite such disagreements among scholars, much has been learned concerning the nature, correlates, and consequences of violence. This volume brings together the recent work of leading investigators on these topics.

In this chapter, we provide a foundation for understanding research on violence by describing key facts about the nature of violent relationships. We also outline the approach taken by each of the authors to address particular aspects of violent relationships, and we underscore ways in which these chapters individually and collectively contribute to documenting, understanding, and ameliorating violence in intimate relationships.

THE NATURE OF VIOLENT RELATIONSHIPS

Describing the nature of violent relationships can be a difficult task, primarily because several distinct conceptualizations of violence have been used in the professional literature. For many family researchers, behaviors such as pushing, slapping, and shoving constitute violence (also referred to as "abuse" and "physical aggression"), albeit mild forms thereof (O'Leary, 1993; Straus, Gelles, & Steinmetz, 1980, pp. 20). Criminologists adopt a different standard, categorizing incidents as "violent" only when they lead to physical injury or can otherwise be considered a crime (cf. Straus, this volume). Yet another perspective on relationship violence has been adopted by feminist scholars, who have suggested that such violence involves male attempts to overpower and terrorize female victims. This view makes severe psychological abuse and intimidation as much a component of violence as is physical assault (Yllö, 1993).

These different conceptualizations have resulted in discrepant reports concerning societal rates of violence, the reciprocal versus one-sided nature of partner violence, the underlying causes of violence, how it escalates, and most importantly, what might be required to end it (Johnson, 1995; Straus, this volume). For instance, whereas researchers studying relationship vio-lence may view couple therapy as an important step to ending violence, others focusing on criminal behavior may point to jail as the solution, while those focusing on power dynamics may see a primary need for resources to aid in removing women from their batterer's control. These disagreements over conceptualizations of violence have contributed to bitter debates over how to end violence in our society.

Only recently has it become increasingly clear that there are different types of violence, which call for different types of interventions (cf. Emery & Laumann-Billings, 1998; O'Leary, 1993). In an analysis of the nature of violence, Johnson (1995) has begun to resolve these disagreements by stress-ing that extreme, life-threatening behaviors are dramatically different from hitting or pushing behaviors, and that these two types of behaviors constitute distinct phenomena (see also Straus, this volume). The first of these phenom-ena comprises physically assaultive behaviors that occur when, over the course of a conflict, couple members "lose control" and consequently hit, push, or kick a partner. Such common couple violence rarely escalates into more injuri-ous or life-threatening behaviors (Johnson, 1995; cf. also O'Leary, 1993, p. 19). Moreover, many of the couples who display it do not persist in violent interaction patterns over time (cf. Bradbury & Lawrence, this volume).

On the other hand, a different type of violence stems from deeply-rooted "patriarchal traditions of men's right to control 'their' women" (Johnson, 1995, p. 286). In addition to physical abuse, this violence involves economic subordination, extreme coercion and intimidation, isolation, and a host of other control tactics–a form of violence that Johnson (1995) refers to as "patriarchal terrorism." Moreover, severe batterers tend to escalate the sever-ity of their violent acts over time (Johnson, 1995). Whereas couple violence, in a majority of cases, is instigated by both partners (Bradbury & Lawrence, this volume), extreme psychological and physical abuse is a pattern perpe-trated almost exclusively by men (Johnson, 1995).

Mild or moderate forms of violence occur in a larger number of house-holds than do severe forms of violence, such as those resulting in injuries that require medical attention (Johnson, 1995; see also Strauss this volume). However, the frequency and intensity of attacks by severe batterers are much greater than are the frequency and intensity of violence in common couple conflicts. Research has shown that, in couples where both members engage in less severe forms of violence, the partners assault each other an average of six times per year. In contrast, male batterers who engage in extreme psycho-logical and physical violence assault their wives an average of 65 times per year (Johnson, 1995). Thus, at least two serious social problems can be identified: (1) For a large number of couples, it is not uncommon to engage in violent behaviors–behaviors that should not be labeled "harmless" (see Straus, this volume); and (2) a number of men inflict much more serious physical assaults and severe psychological abuse on their partners–a more critical social problem, which deserves immediate attention lest the rate of women killed by male partners increase even further.

Recent research has led to an increased understanding of the factors that are correlated with each type of violence. In an important early effort to document factors associated with dating violence, Sugarman and Hotaling's (1989) review of the literature yielded an extensive list of factors associated with being the target or perpetrator of violent behaviors. These included sex-role attitudes, self-esteem, experiencing and witnessing violence in one's family of origin, the status of a dating relationship, past experiences in relationships, interpersonal communication, and so on. Although identifying factors was an important first step, these authors noted the lack of consistent findings, which they attributed, to some extent, to methodological differences among studies (Sugarman & Hotaling, 1989). In addition to such differences, it is now clear that inconsistent findings may have resulted from (1) not differentiating among types of violence, and (2) a lack of complex models and multivariate analyses to assess the *relative* role of each correlate of violence and the *process* by which various correlates relate to violence.

Social and behavioral scientists are making significant contributions to understanding the factors that are correlated with different types of violence. For instance, recent attempts to characterize batterers (e.g., Holtzworth-Munroe, Meehan, Herron, & Stuart, this volume; Dutton, this volume) are advancing our ability to discriminate among the types of individuals who engage in violent behaviors and to design appropriate treatments. Other research that examines the dynamics of marital interactions has revealed that couple violence may be rooted in specific communication problems (cf. Lloyd, this volume), which unfold most noticeably in the context of elevated levels of relationship distress (cf. Bradbury & Lawrence, this volume). In addition, social norms provide the broader context through which violent behaviors become sanctioned (Straus, this volume). Researchers are designing increasingly sophisticated models to identify the complex processes that precede violence, such as an analysis of distal versus proximal predictors of violence (cf. Holtzworth-Munroe et al., this volume; Leonard, this volume). Equally sophisticated models are being developed to assess mechanisms for coping with violence (e.g., Arias, this volume). Finally, researchers have begun to use the current accumulation of information on domestic violence to implement changes in the treatments offered by service providers (cf. Sharps & Campbell, this volume).

SUMMARY OF CHAPTERS IN THIS VOLUME

Each chapter in this volume contributes to advancing our understanding of violence in intimate relationships. Part I, on the nature of violence, establishes the "what" and the "who" of violence. Chapter 2 by Straus offers a conceptualization of violence that parallels and complements the one stated previously in this chapter. Straus further addresses the question of who is violent. His analysis of discrepant findings on the prevalence of violence among male and female intimate partners lays the foundation for a broader examination of the sociology of violence research. Consistent with Johnson's (1995) analysis, he asserts that discrepant findings can be reconciled by noting that violence resulting in injury tends to be perpetrated primarily by men, but less severe forms of abuse are equally perpetrated by men and women. By exploring the forces that have sustained controversy over female/male prevalence rates, he provides a useful clarification of the surrounding context and underlying assumptions of violence research.

Two chapters focus more specifically on who is violent. Chapter 3 by Holtzworth-Munroe and colleagues summarizes preliminary findings to test empirically her recent groundbreaking model of abusive men (Holtzworth-Munroe & Stuart, 1994). This chapter describes batterer subtypes (i.e., family only, dysphoric/borderline, generally violent/antisocial) that can be identified using three descriptive dimensions (severity of marital violence, generality of violence outside the marriage, and personality disorder/psychopathology). The authors propose a developmental model of husband violence and they suggest that the batterer subtypes differ on distal correlates of violence (i.e., genetic/prenatal factors, family of origin environment, and association with deviant peers), as well as proximal ones (i.e., attachment/dependency, impulsivity, social skills, and attitudes toward violence and toward women). The preliminary findings support hypotheses derived from the model and also extend the model in important ways. Chapter 4 by Dutton examines in more detail one of these batterer subtypes—ones displaying borderline personality organization and phasic behavioral patterns in which a build-up of anxiety over interactive intimacy leads to an episode of battering and then to a period of contrition. In this analysis, he emphasizes the limitations of adopting a strict social learning model to explain male aggression.

Part II of this volume, on correlates of violence, examines the interpersonal and situational context that may contribute to violent interaction—that is, it focuses on issues of "how" and "why" that underlie violent interactions. In Chapter 5, Lloyd approaches violence in intimate relationships from a communications perspective. She conceptualizes violence as a gendered, communicative act designed to exert control in a relationship. In this chapter, Lloyd reviews several sets of findings, including studies that underscore the social-skills and problem-solving deficits of violent men, research that examines conflict patterns and "everyday" interactions in abusive marriages, research on the negative affective styles of violent husbands, and studies on patterns of dominance and power dynamics. A central theme of this chapter is that each of these types of communication problems can create a context conducive to violent behavior.

In Chapter 6 Leonard demonstrates that an important situational factor contributing to violent interaction is alcohol use. He shows that men who engage in domestic violence are more likely to be heavy drinkers than men who do not engage in such violence, and importantly, violent men are also likely to have been drinking prior to violent outbursts. Leonard's well-supported model for understanding the association between drinking and domestic violence differentiates drinking patterns as a distal variable–an individual-difference variable and factor that contributes to marital discord–from drinking behavior as a proximal variable, occurring just prior to a violent event. He presents compelling results from a longitudinal study that compared the distal and proximal role of alcohol consumption in the occurrence of domestic violence among newlywed couples.

Part III, on the consequences of violence, provides an account of what happens to victims as a result of physical and psychological abuse, and how relationships change following violent interactions. Chapter 7 by Arias begins with a thorough review of the literature on adverse effects of violence on victims' physical and psychological well-being and the effects on their children. Arias summarizes results from two of her own studies, in which she examined effects of psychological abuse that occur independently from the effects of physical abuse. She also reports findings on women's responses to their victimization. Particularly noteworthy are results suggesting that whether women are sufficiently motivated and able to leave an abusive relationship depends largely on their styles of coping. Finally, Arias discusses the implications of her research for designing effective interventions.

In Chapter 8, Sharps and Campbell examine the effects of physical and sexual violence on the health and well-being of women. After discussing the high prevalence rate of intimate partner violence, they provide an extensive review of the literature which documents health consequences of violence for women and female teenagers. They also review studies on violence during pregnancy and its consequences for the mother and fetus. Chapter 8 provides important messages to health care providers, for it concludes with suggestions concerning health provider practice, intervention, and research that may begin to reduce women's risk for violence and its subsequent health consequences.

The final chapter by Bradbury and Lawrence provides an elegant analysis of the longitudinal course of violence in intimate relationships. In effect, it provides a method for "glimpsing into the future" of intimate relationships that are plagued by violence. The authors place primary emphasis on predicting whether violent relationships will persist over time. They examine the longitudinal course of aggressive and nonaggressive marriages, observing the fluctuations in interspousal aggression over time. A key idea in this chapter is that aggression is not a static, stable property of marriages but instead is best viewed as a dynamic, changing phenomenon. They discuss the implications of this view for models of marital dysfunction and for programs designed to prevent adverse marital outcomes.

EMERGING THEMES

Together, the chapters in this volume highlight a number of common themes. Across the contributions, shared points of emphasis can be identified on the nature and causes of violence; trends in the theories and methods used to study violence; and advances in the areas of prevention, intervention, and treatment.

Nature and Causes of Violence

First, several authors describe categorization schemes to characterize violent individuals and behaviors. For instance, Dutton (Chapter 4) suggests that the behaviors of male batterers typically warrant a diagnosis of borderline personality disorder. The typology advanced by Holtzworth-Munroe and her coauthors (Chapter 3) emphasizes the usefulness of categorizing male batterers in terms of personality characteristics, severity of violent behavior, and prevalence of violent behavior outside of the marriage. However, these authors acknowledge that some of these categories may not comprise independent groupings, and may instead incorporate continua of more/less psychopathology and higher/lower levels of violence. Arias (Chapter 7) and others (cf. Stets, 1990) have differentiated psychological and verbal abuse from physical abuse. However, they suggest that individuals within each of these categories vary in the degree to which they exemplify the characteristics comprising that category. The issue is not whether investigators prefer categories or find it easier to conceptualize categories; rather, it concerns the extent to which distinct, non-overlapping violence phenomena truly exist (cf. O'Leary, 1993). Ultimately, whether violent actions reflect distinct phenomena, or vary in terms of degree only, is an empirical question to be answered in future research and in careful re-analysis of existing data.

Some authors highlight the functions of violent behaviors. Dutton (Chapter 4) emphasizes the expressive nature of violence, noting that for many batterers, violent behaviors represent "outbursts." On the other hand, Lloyd (Chapter 5) asserts that violence may reflect an attempt to control the partner. She suggests that violence is as much an instrumental behavior aimed at control as it is an expressive action reflecting anger.

In conceptualizing the causes of violence, many of the authors share the view that there are multiple paths to violent interaction. Several individual-level characteristics have been shown to be associated with violence (Dutton, Chapter 4; Holtzworth-Munroe et al., Chapter 3; Lloyd, Chapter 5). Moreover, some batterers are violent in all contexts whereas others are violent only in their intimate relationships (Holtzworth-Munroe et al., Chapter 3). Indeed, there are a multitude of relationship dynamics that may contribute to violence. For instance, violence may occur as a result of an emotionally charged conflict or simply occur in the course of everyday interaction (Lloyd, Chapter 5). Multiple communication problems may emerge, any one of which, or the combination of which, may cause violence. Drinking behavior (Leonard, Chapter 6) and high levels of marital distress (Bradbury & Lawrence, Chapter 9) may exacerbate conflicted interactions. However, it seems that none of these factors (e.g., alcohol) create necessary or sufficient conditions for relationship violence to occur (Leonard, Chapter 6).

Trends in Theories and Methods For Studying Violence

The shared emphasis across chapters on the multiple pathways to violent relationships underscores the need to examine complex models of prediction. It also becomes necessary to consider more elaborate study designs and sophisticated analytic techniques. The contributions in this volume exemplify a trend in research on violence toward multilevel theoretical models, longitudinal designs, and relatively novel analytic strategies (e.g., survival analysis, cluster analysis, growth curve analysis).

Several authors have adopted theoretical models that can accommodate high levels of complexity. None of the chapters assume that there is a simple list of factors that explains violence (e.g., a main effects model), or that there is only one consequence of violence (Arias, Chapter 7; Sharps & Campbell, Chapter 8). Indeed, several authors have adopted process models of abuse, specifying how distal influences may create conditions under which proximal influences on violence exert effects (Holtzworth-Munroe et al., Chapter 3; Leonard, Chapter 6). Chapter 7 by Arias provides an example of this by advancing models that identify causal mechanisms (i.e., mediators) as well as factors that qualify key associations (i.e., moderators). For instance, it was only by adopting a more complex model that she was able to determine that a father's psychological abuse of the mother undermines her psychological adjustment, which in turn, adversely affects their child's levels of depression and self-esteem.

Attempts to refine theoretical accounts of violence have led some of the contributors to critically examine a number of commonly held assumptions. First, many scholars have assumed that, upon observing another person (e.g., a role model) who has behaved violently, an individual becomes more inclined to mimic this behavior—that is, many scholars have adopted a social learning theory (Bandura, 1979) account of violence. However, Dutton (Chapter 4) outlines the limitations of these assumptions, explaining why social learning theory cannot easily account for commonly observed characteristics among male batterers. Yet another set of commonly held assumptions concerns the association between physical and psychological abuse.

Although it is commonly assumed that physical abuse is more likely to lead an individual to leave a relationship than is psychological abuse, Arias' research (Chapter 7) shows that motivation to leave a relationship is better predicted by psychological abuse than by physical abuse.

Finally, it is commonly believed that males inflict violence and females sustain it, but several national surveys on family violence have repeatedly shown that women can be as violent as men (Straus, Chapter 2). Although these surveys may not be capturing the phenomenon of violence that involves extreme male battering (cf. Johnson, 1995), and although they show that violence by men is much more serious in its likelihood of causing injury than is violence by women, the fact that existing data do not support a commonly held assumption must be explained. This is precisely what Straus does in Chapter 2, in which he compares rates of assault by women outside versus within the family (see also Johnson, 1995, on the different forms of violence, which were briefly described above).

Increasingly sophisticated methodologies have been used to examine these increasingly complex theoretical models. Multiple methods have been used to study violence (see Lloyd, Chapter 5), including detailed analyses of interaction behaviors, observations of physiological changes during an inter-action, and large-scale national surveys describing the nature of violence. Arias notes that models of violence present unique measurement challenges because of the difficulty of assessing physical and psychological abuse. Measures of psychological abuse have been plagued by problems (cf. Arias, Chapter 7), and measures of physical abuse often tap an individual's cumu-lative history of abuse in a relationship, rather than the severity of the most recent abusive incident.

Indeed, it can be difficult to determine whether particular correlates of violence *precede* and closely *covary* with severe instances of violence. With that goal in mind, several contributors have conducted longitudinal studies (Bradbury & Lawrence, Chapter 9; Leonard, Chapter 6; Lloyd, Chapter 5) to assess the temporal order of violence correlates and to rule out alternative (i.e., spurious) causal explanations. For instance, Bradbury and Lawrence (Chapter 9) conducted a growth curve analysis that illustrates the temporal trajectory of violence. Unlike studies that focus on one or two measurement occasions, their multiwave data demonstrate that physical aggression can fluctuate over time, and that it can fluctuate in different ways for different individuals. These authors also conducted survival analyses to determine whether aggressive and nonaggressive couples differ in later levels of marital satisfaction and in rates of separation or divorce. Finally, Holtzworth-Munroe and colleagues (Chapter 3) used cluster analysis as a technique for developing profiles of batterers, and they stress that the ability to identify distinctive characteristics of different batterers is essential for treating the unique prob-lems exhibited by each type of batterer.

Advances in Prevention, Intervention, and Treatment

The authors in this volume highlight implications of their research for developing effective prevention, intervention, and treatment programs. For instance, Bradbury and Lawrence (Chapter 9) suggest that if aggression is a stable individual trait, interventions must focus on helping people select nonaggressive partners; if, instead, aggression is unstable and situation-specific, interventions should aim to identify temporal precursors of aggression–that is, they might focus on detecting situational "warning flags" signaling a risk for aggression.

Sharps and Campbell (Chapter 8) also provide suggestions for prevention efforts. According to these authors, several studies have shown that with abused women, compared to nonabused women, physicians tend to have poorer quality of communication and, more generally, health care providers tend to be less responsive. These authors outline several prevention and intervention efforts that could begin to address such problems.

Finally, as already noted, research on batterers' characteristics (Dutton, Chapter 4; Holtzworth-Munroe et al., Chapter 3) can help to develop unique and appropriate treatment plans. On the other hand, Straus (Chapter 2) warns that family conflict studies–which document more typical cases of violence– should not be used to develop policies and interventions for more extreme instances of male battering. Although the numbers of extreme cases may be relatively low, Straus asserts that these are "the cases that pose the most serious problems and which need to have priority in respect to interventions" (Chapter 2).

A related point about developing prevention and intervention efforts on the basis of research findings concerns the typical groups that are included in studies and targeted for interventions. Several chapters (e.g., Sharps & Campbell, Chapter 8) review findings of studies on severely battered women. Societal responses to aid this group may take the form of improved services in health care facilities (Sharps & Campbell, Chapter 8), an increase in the number and resources of shelters for women and transition homes (Sharps & Campbell, Chapter 8), and public support for giving this group first priority in intervention efforts.

Teenagers are a second target group that increasingly have gained attention in research (Sharps & Campbell, Chapter 8). Indeed, teenagers who initially establish healthy relationship patterns may be less likely to become involved in unhealthy adult relationships. Finally, two chapters (Bradbury & Lawrence, Chapter 9; Leonard, Chapter 6) emphasize the need to study newlywed couples. It is hoped that understanding marital dynamics in the early developmental stages of a relationship will lead to a greater understanding of long-term marital functioning and aid in the prevention of severe marital dysfunction and aggression.

DIRECTIONS FOR FUTURE RESEARCH

Although the contributions in this volume and many others comprise clear advances in understanding violence in intimate relationships, more research is needed on responses to violence and on the etiology of violent behaviors. Research could also develop further the methods available for studying violence.

Previous research has shown that there are numerous responses to violence. For instance, studies report that responses by victims include feeling angry, afraid, and surprised (Henton, Cate, Koval, & Lloyd, 1983) whereas responses by perpetrators often involve feelings of sorrow (Sugarman & Hotaling, 1989). As might be expected, victims also report general distress following a violent episode–distress that is exacerbated by perceiving little control over one's environment (Pape & Arias, 1995). Responses that constitute help-seeking are less common. Research has shown that only half of females and one quarter of males seek help following an incident of relationship abuse, and those that seek help typically talk with a friend rather than discuss their violent episode with a parent, counselor, physician, or criminal justice authority (Pirog-Good & Stets, 1989).

Leaving an abusive relationship can be difficult. As is the case in any committed relationship, a person may feel emotionally attached to a partner, despite the partner's abusive behavior (Stube & Barbour, 1983). Although dating partners have been shown to persist in abusive relationships (Hotaling & Sugarman, 1989)–probably mostly relationships involving less severe, more typical forms of violence–there are greater obstacles to leaving abusive marital relationships (cf. Strube, 1988). For instance, despite the hardships of sustaining violence, many wives experience guilt over leaving an abusive husband, thereby reducing the husband's contact with the children, given existing attachments between the father and children. Often battered women who lack feelings of closeness to their abusive husbands nonetheless depend economically on them (Rusbult & Martz, 1995; Strube & Barbour, 1983). Lacking a place to go, a steady income, or a stable means of transportation are just a few of the obstacles that severely abused women must overcome. Thus, changing the course of a violent relationship may require multiple types of responses, each of which mobilizes different types of resources (e.g., talking with a friend versus implementing a plan of escape).

Given the varied responses to violence and the low occurrence of help-seeking, it becomes increasingly important to understand coping responses to violence. Future research could compare the coping responses of people who experience common couple violence versus severe battery. It stands to reason that various stages of coping (e.g., denial, anger, acceptance) should differ for these two groups, and that different types of coping will be conducive to the behavioral responses that are differentially adaptive for each group (e.g., seeking couple therapy and changing interaction patterns versus seeking resources to establish economic independence). Particularly necessary are studies that examine how emotional reactions and coping styles influence inclinations to enact different behavioral responses. Research by Arias (Chapter 7) showing that styles of coping moderate the inclination to leave an abusive relationship, illustrates this needed direction for future research.

Another direction for future research is to examine further the etiology of violence. An important issue concerns how extreme violence emerges. For instance, were the male batterers who eventually severely assaulted their wives once husbands who engaged in less severe, common couple violence? Or, are these two different groups of men?–that is, do husbands who engage in common couple violence only rarely become severe batterers? Several lines of research provide indirect evidence supporting the two-group hypothesis. For instance, the research reported by Holtzworth-Munroe and colleagues (Chapter 3) establishes that there is more than one type of violent man. Further, as noted above, common couple violence tends to remain at mild or moderate levels and typically does not include psychological control tactics that characterize batterers' behaviors (Johnson, 1995). Indirect evidence notwithstanding, prospective and longitudinal studies are needed to examine the developmental path of severe batterers.

More also remains to be learned about the causal paths that lead to violent behavior. As illustrated by many of the chapters in this volume, research might work further to differentiate levels of causal factors (e.g., Leonard, Chapter 6), meaningful configurations of violence correlates (e.g., Holtzworth-Munroe et al., Chapter 3), and the temporal order of violence correlates (e.g., Bradbury & Lawrence, Chapter 9). Such efforts will continue to shed light on precisely which correlates are causes of violence, and whether particular correlates are more strongly associated with particular types of violence. However, greater emphasis might be placed on collecting experimental data that complement the current abundance of correlational data. Only by adopting a multi-method approach that includes experimental methods will it be possible to precisely assess causal relations. Research by Foshee and her colleagues (e.g., Foshee et al., 1998; Foshee, 1998) provides an excellent example of adopting experimental methodology to study the prevention of relationship violence among adolescents.

REFERENCES

Emery, R. E., & Laumann-Billings, L. (1998). An overview of the nature, causes, and consequences of abusive family relationships: Toward differentiating maltreatment and violence. *American Psychologist, 53,* 121-135.

Federal Bureau of Investigation. (1993). *Uniform Crime Reports.* Washington, DC: U.S. Department of Justice.

Foshee, V. A. (1998). Involving schools and communities in preventing adolescent dating abuse. In X. B. Arriaga & S. Oskamp (Eds.), *Addressing community problems* (pp. 104-129). Thousand Oaks, CA: Sage.

Foshee, V. A., Bauman, K. E., Arriaga, X. B., Helms, R. W., Koch, G. G., & Linder, G. F. (1998). An evaluation of Safe Dates, an adolescent dating violence prevention program. *American Journal of Public Health, 88,* 45-50.

Gibson, B. (Director). (1993). *What's love got to do with it?* [Film].

Henton, J., Cate, R., Koval, J., Lloyd, S., & Christopher, S. (1983). Romance and violence in dating relationships. *Journal of Family Issues, 4,* 467-482.

Holtzworth-Munroe, A., & Stuart, G. L. (1994). Typologies of male batterers: Three subtypes and the differences among them. *Psychological Bulletin, 116,* 476-497.

Johnson, M. P. (1995). Patriarchal terrorism and common couple violence: Two forms of violence against women. *Journal of Marriage and the Family, 57,* 283-294.

Loseke, D. R., & Gelles, R. J. (1993). Introduction: Examining and evaluating controversies on family violence. In R. J. Gelles & D. R. Loseke (Eds.), *Current controversies on family violence* (pp. ix-xvii). Newbury Park, CA: Sage.

O'Leary, K. D. (1993). Through a psychological lens: Personality traits, personality disorders, and levels of violence. In R. J. Gelles & D. R. Loseke (Eds.), *Current controversies on family violence* (pp. 7-30). Newbury Park, CA: Sage.

Pape, K. T., & Arias, I. (1995). Control, coping, and victimization in dating relationships. *Violence and Victims, 10,* 43-54.

Pirog-Good, M. A., & Stets, J. E. (1989). The help-seeking behavior of physically and sexually abused college students. In M. A. Pirog-Good & J. E. Stets (Eds.), *Violence in dating relationships: Emerging social issues* (pp. 108-125). Westport, CT: Praeger.

Rusbult, C. E., & Martz, J. M. (1995). Remaining in an abusive relationship: An investment model analysis of nonvoluntary dependence. *Personality and Social Psychology Bulletin, 21,* 558-571.

Stets, J. E. (1990). Verbal and physical aggression in marriage. *Journal of Marriage and the Family, 52,* 501-514.

Stets, J. E., & Pirog-Good, M. A. (1987). Violence in dating relationships. *Social Psychology Quarterly, 50,* 237-246.

Straus, M. A., & Gelles, R. J. (1990) (Eds.), *Physical violence in American families: Risk factors and adaptations to violence in 8,145 families.* New Brunswick: Transaction.

Straus, M. A., Gelles, R. J., & Steinmetz, S. K. (1980). *Behind closed doors.* New York: Anchor.

Strube, M. J. (1988). The decision to leave an abusive relationship: Empirical evidence and theoretical issues. *Psychological Bulletin, 104,* 236-250.

Strube, M. J., & Barbour, L. S. (1983). The decision to leave an abusive relationship: Economic dependence and psychological commitment. *Journal of Marriage and the Family, 45,* 785-793.

Sugarman, D. B., & Hotaling G. T. (1989). Dating violence: Prevalence, context, and risk markers. In M. A. Pirog-Good & J. E. Stets (Eds.), *Violence in dating relationships: Emerging social issues* (pp. 3-32). Westport, CT: Praeger.

Yllö, K. A. (1993). Through a feminist lens: Gender, power, and violence. In R. J. Gelles
& D. R. Loseke (Eds.), *Current controversies on family violence* (pp. 31-46).
Newbury Park, CA: Sage.

2

The Controversy Over Domestic Violence by Women

A Methodological, Theoretical, and Sociology of Science Analysis

Murray A. Straus

OVERVIEW

The methodological part of this chapter analyzes the discrepancy between the more than 100 "family conflict" studies of domestic physical assaults (those using the Conflict Tactic Scales and similar approaches), and what can be called "crime studies" (i.e., the National Crime Victimization Survey and studies using police call data). Family conflict studies, without exception, show about equal rates of assault by men and women. Crime studies, without exception, show much higher rates of assault by men, often 90% by men. Crime studies also find a prevalence rate (for both men and women) that is a small fraction of the rate

AUTHOR'S NOTE: An earlier version of this chapter was presented at the Claremont Symposium on Applied Social Psychology on Violence in Intimate Relationships, Claremont Graduate University, Claremont, CA 28 February, 1998. I would like to thank the 1997-98 Family Research Laboratory seminar, Patricia Tjaden, and Kersti Yllö for many comments, criticisms and suggestions which greatly aided in revising the chapter. Their assistance does not necessarily imply endorsement of the views expressed. The research was supported by National Institute of Mental Health grant T32MH15161 and the University of New Hampshire. This is a publication of the Family Violence Research Program of the Family Research Laboratory, University of New Hampshire. A program description and bibliography will be sent on request.

of assaults found by family conflict studies. The difference in prevalence rates and in gender differences between the two types of studies probably occur because crime studies deal with only the small part of all domestic assaults that the participants experience as a crime, such as assaults which result in an injury serious enough to need medical attention, or assaults by a former partner. These occur relatively rarely and tend to be assaults by men. The theoretical part of the chapter seeks to provide an explanation for the discrepancy between the low rates of assault by women outside the family and the very high rates of assault by women within the family. The sociology of science part of the chapter seeks to explain why the controversy over domestic assaults by women persists and is likely to continue. I argue that neither side can give up their position because it would be tantamount to giving up deeply held moral commitments and professional roles. I conclude that society needs both perspectives. Neither side should give up their perspective. Rather they should recognize the circum-stances to which each applies.

In the mid-1970s my colleagues and I made the disturbing discovery that women physically assaulted partners in marital, cohabiting, and dating rela-tionships as often as men assaulted their partners (Steinmetz, 1978; Straus, 1997; Straus, Gelles, & Steinmetz, 1980). This finding caused me and my former colleague, Suzanne Steinmetz, to be excommunicated as feminists. Neither of us has accepted that sentence, but it remains in force. So when Salman Rushdie was condemned to death for his heresy, we may have felt even more empathy than most people because we had also experienced many threats, including a bomb threat.

The vitriolic 20-year controversy (Straus, 1990c; Straus, 1992b; Straus, 1997) had largely subsided by 1997. There are a number of reasons the controversy subsided. One reason is the overwhelming accumulation of evidence from more than a hundred studies showing approximately equal assault rates. Another is the explosive growth of marital and family therapy from a family systems perspective which assumes mutual effects. In addition, research by clinical psychologists such as O'Leary (O'Leary et al., 1989) brought psychologists face to face with the assaults by both parties, as compared to studies of clients of shelters for battered women. In November 1997, however, the controversy was suddenly reignited by newspaper head-lines declaring "Partners Unequal in Abuse" (Peterson, 1997). These head-lines were based on findings from the "National Violence Against Women in America Survey" (called the NVAW survey from here on). The NVAW surveyed 8,000 women and 8,000 men representing 16,000 households. The study was sponsored by the National Institute of Justice and the Centers for Disease Control (Tjaden & Thoennes, 1997). The NVAW study found that men physically assaulted their female partners at three times the rate at which women engaged in such behavior.

Family Conflict Studies

The NVAW findings contradict findings from many studies of violence between dating, cohabiting, and married couples, including national household surveys in the U.S. and other countries. These studies, such as the National Family Violence Surveys (Straus & Gelles, 1990), the National Survey of Families and Households, and British and Canadian national surveys (Carrado, George, Loxam, Jones, & Templar, 1996; Grandin & Lupri, 1997) are presented to respondents as research on family problems. Following (Tjaden & Thoennes, 1997) I will refer to them as "family conflict" studies. I started to compile a table summarizing all the family conflict studies that reported assault rates for both men and women partners. But I stopped after tabulating 39 studies out of about 120 in my files because at that point I received a bibliography of 70 studies, all of which found that ". . . women are as physically aggressive, or more aggressive, than men in their relationships. . . . The aggregate sample size in the reviewed studies exceeds 58,000." (Fiebert, 1997, pp. 273).

I then tallied the 39 studies in my own table and found that more than two thirds reported somewhat *higher* rates for assaults by women. Moreover, every one of the remainder found very high rates for women, usually rates as high or almost as high as the male assault rate. Whenever the study provided separate figures for "severe" assaults such as kicking and punching (as compared to "minor" assaults such as slapping and throwing things at a partner) the pattern of similarly high rates was also reported for severe assaults. In addition there is the tabulation of 21 studies of dating couples by Sugarman and Hotaling (1989) which led them to conclude "A . . . surprising finding . . . is the *higher* proportion of females than males who self-report having expressed violence in a dating relationship."

Crime Studies

Despite the evidence from more than 100 of these family conflict and dating violence studies, the finding from the recent NVAW study of three assaults by men to one by women cannot be ignored because it is based on a well-conducted survey and the study was sponsored by respected agencies. Moreover, two other major sources of data show an even greater predominance by men. In fact they indicate that assaulting a partner is almost exclusively a crime committed by men. I will call these "crime studies." I grouped the following four studies or types of studies under this heading because they have in common that they are presented to respondents as studies of crime, crime victimization, personal safety, injury, or violence, rather than as studies of family problems and conflicts.

- National Crime Survey (NCS)

- National Crime Victimization Study (NCVS). This is a revision of the NCS

- Police statistics studies

- National Violence Against Women in America (NVAW) study. Because of the importance of the NVAW study a detailed analysis is available in a supplemental paper (Straus, 1998).

Chapter Objectives

Given the enormous discrepancies between over 100 family conflict studies and the fewer but excellent crime studies, the first objective of this chapter is to identify the source of these discrepancies. I will present evidence which suggests that the discrepancies reflect differences in the methodology of crime studies as compared to family conflict studies.

The second objective of the chapter is theoretical. If it is true that, in their domestic relationships, women are as assaultive as men, that needs to be explained because it is inconsistent with cultural norms and beliefs which hold that women are much less violent than men, and inconsistent with data showing that in nonfamily situations, the rate of assault by women is only a fraction of the male assault rate. In short, the theoretical issue is how to explain the high rate of domestic assaults by women.

The third objective of the chapter is to explain why the controversy has persisted despite the evidence, and in my opinion is likely to continue. The most fundamental reason is that the controversy is rooted in deep-seated differences in the underlying moral agenda and professional roles of the two sides.

WHAT IS VIOLENCE?

Much of the controversy over "violence" by women occurs because the participants in the debate use the same word for different phenomena. At one extreme are those who use violence as a synonym for any unjust or cruel state of affairs or maltreatment of another human being. Thus, marketing of baby formulas to mothers in underdeveloped countries is sometimes described as violence against children because of the harm it causes. At the other extreme, are those who restrict violence to physical assaults, i.e., to acts carried out with he intention of causing another person *physical* pain or injury (Gelles & Straus, 1979), regardless of whether an injury actually occurs. The concluding section of the chapter will explain why "violence" is used so differently.

My own research has been carried out from the perspective that defines violence exclusively as a physical assault. This perspective recognizes the importance of injury, and also that physical assaults are not necessarily the most damaging type of maltreatment. For example, one can hurt deeply—

even drive someone to suicide—without lifting a finger. Verbal aggression may be even more damaging than being the victim of physical attacks (Straus & Sweet, 1992; Vissing, Straus, Gelles, & Harrop, 1993). Those like me, who focus on the act of assault, also recognize that women, on average, suffer much more frequent and more severe injury (physical, economic, and psychological) than men (Stets & Straus, 1990; Straus, Gelles, & Steinmetz, 1980; Zlotnick, Kohn, Peterson, & Pearlstein, 1998). Consequently, it is necessary to explain the reasons for focusing exclusively on physical assaults. The immediate reason is that, with rare exception, the controversy has been about equal rates of physical assaults, not about whether women experience more injury. The more important reasons have to do with legal, social policy, and ethical considerations.

From a legal perspective, it is important to realize that injury is not required for the crime of assault. The National Crime Panel Report defines assault as "an unlawful physical attack by one person upon another" (U.S. Department of Justice, 1976). Neither this definition, nor the definition used for reporting assaults to the FBI requires injury or bodily contact (Federal Bureau of Investigation, 1995). Thus, if a person is chased by someone attempting to hit them with a stick or stab them and they escape, the attack is still a felony level crime—an "aggravated assault"—even though they were not touched. However, it is also true that police, prosecutors, and juries are strongly influenced by whether the assault did result in an injury and the seriousness of the injury.

From a social policy perspective, despite the much lower probability of physical injury resulting from attacks by women, one of the main reasons why "minor" assaults by women are such an important problem is that they put women in danger of much more severe retaliation by men (Feld & Straus, 1989). Assaults by women also help perpetuate the now implicit, but once explicit cultural norms that gave husbands the legal right to "physically chastise an errant wife" (Calvert, 1974). The legacy of that norm continues to make the marriage license a hitting license for both parties. To end "wife beating," it is essential for women to cease what may seem to be "harmless" slapping, kicking, or throwing things at a male partner who persists in some outrageous behavior or "won't listen to reason."

Assaults by women also need to be a focus of social policy because of the harm to children from growing up in a violent household. The link between partner violence and child behavior problems occurs not only when both partners are violent (about half of families with partner assaults), but also when the assaults are committed exclusively by the male partner (about a quarter of the cases), as well as when the assaults are committed exclusively by the female partner (Straus, 1992a).

The most fundamental reason for giving attention to assaults per se, regardless of whether an injury occurs, is the intrinsic moral wrong of assaulting a partner. Assaults by women are a crime and a serious social problem, just as it would be if men "only" slapped their wives or "only" slapped a fellow employee and produced no injury. Although this is a fundamental reason for morally condemning women who "only" slap their partners, it should not be allowed to obscure the fact that assaults by men are likely to be even more morally reprehensible because they result in injury so much more often than assaults by women. Nevertheless, an even greater wrong does not excuse the lesser wrong. A society in which dating, cohabiting, and married partners never hit each other is not a more unrealistic goal than a society in which coworkers never hit each other, and is certainly no less a hallmark of a humane society.

METHODOLOGICAL EXPLANATIONS
FOR THE DISCREPANT FINDINGS OF
FAMILY CONFLICT AND CRIME STUDIES

Explaining Discrepancies in the Rate of Partner Assault

Before examining the differences between family conflict and crime studies that could explain the discrepancies in their findings on assaults by men and women, it is necessary to examine and explain the much lower rate of assault by *both* men and women found by crime studies. This is necessary because the same processes result in both the low prevalence rate for both men and women and the high ratio of male to female offenders.

The first row of Table 2.1 summarizes findings from many studies showing that, relative to family conflict studies, crime studies uncover a much lower number of domestic assaults. The rates from crime studies range from a low of 0.02% to 1.1%, whereas the rates from family conflict studies tend to be about 16%. The second row of Table 2.1 shows that disclosure of domestic assaults in crime studies is only a small fraction of the rate obtained by family conflict studies. Even with the improvement in the National Crime Survey to deal with the extremely low prevalence, the rate obtained by the revision is still only one eighteenth of the rate obtained by family conflict surveys (Bachman & Saltzman, 1995). Similarly, the recent NVAW study found only one fifteenth of the number of assaults that have been found by family conflict studies.

The low rate of assaults by both husbands and wives found by crime studies, and especially the NCS probably results from a number of situational and unintended "demand characteristics" (Orne, 1962) of the study. These surveys were presented as a study of crime, or in the case of the NVAW study, "personal safety," injury, and "violence." Unfortunately, when a survey of crime, violence, or injury is the context for estimating rates of domestic assault, the contextual message can take precedence over specific instructions to include all assaults, regardless of the perpetrator and regardless of whether injury resulted. The contextual message can lead some respondents to mis-

TABLE 2.1. Variations in Domestic Assault Statistics

	Family Conflict Studies	National Crime Survey	National Crime Victim Survey	Police Call Data	NVAW Study[1]
Annual Assault Rate	16% (10-35%)[2]	0.2%	0.9%	0.2%[3]	1.1%
Fraction of Family Conflict Rate	=======>	1/80th	1/18th	1/80th	1/15th
Injury Rate	1-3%	75%	52%	unknown	76%
Male Rate (top) & Female Rate	12.2%	0.4%	0.76%	90% male[5]	1.3
	12.4%[4]	0.03%	0.11%		0.9
Male to Female Ratio	1:1	13:1	7:1	9:1	1.4:1

1. National Violence Against Women Survey (Tjaden & Thoennes, 1998).
2. The lower end of this range is for married couples. The upper end reflects the large number of studies which show that rate for dating couples of 25% to 40% (Sugarman & Hotaling, 1989). Stets and Straus (1990) attribute the high rate to the youthfulness of dating couples. They found that, for young married couples, the rates were even higher than for dating couples of that age.
3. Based on *all* aggravated assaults known to the police in 1994 (Federal Bureau of Investigation, 1995) because Uniform Crime Reports (UCR) do not distinguish between domestic assaults and other assaults. In 1994 the UCR rate of assaults 430 per hundred *thousand* population (0.4%). An unknown fraction of these were domestic assaults. To be on the safe side, I used half of that as domestic assaults.
4. To avoid bias due to possible under-reporting by men of their own assaults, these rates were computed from information provided by the 2,994 women in the 1985 National Family Violence Survey. The rates given are for any assault. The ratio was essentially the same for minor and severe assaults. See Straus, 1994.
5. The rates for men and women cannot be given because police call data are only reported as the percent of cases with a male offender, not as rates per 100 or 1,000 men and women.

perceive the study as being concerned only with assaults that are experienced as a crime or as violence, or assaults that resulted in or are likely to result in injury . However, only a small percentage of domestic assaults are experienced as a crime or as a threat to personal safety or violence. For example, while being slapped or kicked by a partner may be experienced as horrendous or despicable, it takes relatively rare circumstances to perceive it as a "crime" (Ferraro, 1989; Ferraro & Johnson, 1983; Langan & Innes, 1986). One such circumstance is an injury. Injury serious enough to need medical attention occurs in only 1% to 3% of domestic assaults on women and 0.5% of domestic assaults on men (Stets & Straus, 1990; Zlotnick, Kohn, Peterson, & Pearlstein, 1998). To the extent that it takes injury for a respondent in a crime survey to perceive there is something to report, the low injury rate is part of the explanation for the extremely low rate of partner assaults found by the crime studies. This does not mean that all respondents misperceived what was expected in this way. Indeed, 49% of NCVS domestic assault victims reported no injury, but this is still much less than the 97% to 99% reporting no injury in family conflict studies (see next paragraph).

The middle row of Table 2.1 gives the injury rates from family conflict and crime studies. It shows rates of 3% or less for family conflict studies, and rates of 75%, 52%, and 76% for the NCS, the NCVS, and the NVAW study. The implausibly high injury rates from the latter three studies are probably the result of the crime and threat to safety focus of those studies, i.e., partner assaults tend to not be reported unless there is something, such as injury, that moves them from the category of a "family fight" to a "crime" or a threat to safety. So assaults resulting in injury make up an extremely large proportion of the cases that are reported.

Another similar process probably accounts for the extremely high rate of assaults by *former* partners in crime studies. That is, one of the circumstance leading a respondent in crime studies to report an assault by a partner is if the attack is by a former spouse. That makes it a "real crime" because a former spouse "has no right to do that." Even with the revisions intended to avoid this problem, the NCVS found 25 times more assaults by former partners in the previous 12-month period than by current partners (Bachman & Saltzman, 1995). Given the vastly greater time exposure to current spouses during the 12-month referent period, that ratio does not seem plausible.

In summary, assaults by a partner are most likely to be experienced as a crime if the attacks result in injury or if it is an attack by a former partner. To the extent that this is correct, it helps explain the drastically lower prevalence rate for intimate partner assaults in crime studies because those circumstances are relatively rare.

Explaining Discrepancies in the
Ratio of Male to Female Offenders

The last two rows of Table 2.1 show the contrast between the roughly equal rates for family conflict studies and the predominance of men in the crime studies and the NVAW study. Although a number of factors are likely to be involved, the methodological differences described in the preceding section are an important part of the explanation. Specifically, the same demand characteristics of a crime study that produced the extremely low rates for both men and women, also produce the high ratio of male to female offenders. If one of the circumstances that leads a respondent to experience being hit by a partner as a crime, or one of the circumstances that leads a police officer to make an arrest, is an injury that needs medical attention, and if assaults resulting in injury are much more likely to occur when a man is the offender, it follows that men predominate in statistics based on crime surveys or crime reports. The following sections examine each of the sources of data from that perspective.

National Crime Survey and
National Crime Victimization Survey

In 1992, after 10 years of considering revisions to reduce demand characteristics such as those just discussed, the National Crime Survey (NCS) was revised to secure more complete reporting of crimes in which the offender is often an intimate, such as rape and assault, and renamed as the National Crime Victimization Survey (NCVS). The result of these changes, as predicted, was to quadruple the overall prevalence rate for domestic assaults from 2.2 to 8.7 per thousand, i.e., from 0.2% to 0.9% (Bachman & Saltzman, 1995, Table 5). A change that was not predicted by the NCVS sponsors, but which follows from the demand characteristics explanation for the low prevalence rate in crime studies, was to decrease the ratio of male to female assaults on partners from 13:1 to 7:1. The injury rate also decreased (as predicted on the basis of the demand characteristics explanation) from 75% to 52%. Thus the redesign helped to reduce the demand characteristics that probably account for the extremely low prevalence rate, the implausibly high injury rate, and the high ratio of male to female assaults. Nevertheless, the statistics just presented suggests that the demand characteristic problem persists to a significant degree.

Another consideration that may lead to under reporting of assaults on partners by women as a crime or a threat to safety is that such attacks are often discounted as a joke because, for men, the risk of injury and therefore fear of injury, is relatively low. In one of my early interviews on domestic assaults, I asked the husband if his wife had ever hit him. He stood up and shoved his shoulder toward me as if I were his wife. He said "Yeah, I told her, go ahead and hit me." For still another group, the idea of being assaulted by one's wife may be so threatening to their masculine identity that they would be ashamed to report it to the NCVS interviewer.

Police Statistics

Statistics based on analysis of police calls for domestic disturbances result in a rate of assaults by men that is hugely greater than the rate of assaults by women. Dobash and Dobash (1979), for example, found that 99% of intrafamily assault cases in two Scottish cities were assaults by men. Since then, a number of studies of statistics based on police calls show that men are eight or nine times more often the assailants than women. However, the proportion of men may be declining slightly. To take one recent example, Brookhoff (1997) found that 78% of assailants in police calls were men. This is less than 90 or 99%, but it is still extremely high.

The proportion of incidents of partner assault known to the police, like the proportion in the NCVS, is only a small faction of the number of such incidents estimated on the basis of family conflict studies. Kaufman Kantor and Straus (1990) for example, examined a nationally representative sample of domestic assaults and found that 93% were not reported to the police. Given the absence of such a large proportion of cases from police statistics, an understanding of what might be filtering out most of the cases can provide a clue to gender differences in police statistics on partner assault.

The high percentage of male offenders in police statistics reflects the circumstances that lead to a police call. An obvious circumstance is that a call to the police for help is much more likely if there is injury or imminent danger of injury. Because injury is more likely if the assailant is a male, assaults by men are much more likely than assaults by women to occasion a police call. If the injury rate for assaults by men is about seven times greater than the injury rate for assaults by women (Stets & Straus, 1990), and if injury is a virtually a requirement for the police to be called in, that alone would contribute importantly to producing a 7:1 ratio. It is also one of the main reasons why I have always insisted that ". . . although women may assault their partners at approximately the same rate as men, because of the greater physical, financial, and emotional injury suffered by women, they are the predominant victims. Consequently, first priority in services for victims and in prevention and control must continue to be directed toward assaults by husbands" (Straus, 1997).

Other reasons assaults by women are rare in police statistics probably include the reluctance of men to admit that they cannot "handle their wives." In addition, although police in some jurisdictions are now arresting female offenders more than previously, analogous to their former reluctance to make arrests of husbands, they remain reluctant to make arrests in such cases (Cook, 1997). Still another factor that probably influences the probability of police involvement is drunken, loud, and destructive behavior, and those are more often male than female accompaniments of partner assault. This is especially likely to be the case among the low-income and low-education families where partner assaults and police calls for partner assaults are most common.

NVAW Study

I classified the National Violence Against Women (NVAW) study as a crime study because it was presented to respondents as a study of "personal safety" and that term is used repeatedly. In addition, the second question in the survey was "Do you think violent crime is more or less of a problem for men today than previously." This question, at the very start of this study, can signal to respondents that the study is about crime. The tone of the NVAW keeps threats, injuries, violence, and safety constantly before the respondent. In this context, reporting that one's partner has done any of the things asked about is the same as saying that the partner is a criminal or is about to injure them.

These and other aspects of the wording and questions, which are detailed in a supplemental paper (Straus, 1998), may have created a set of demand characteristics that led many respondents to perceive the NVAW as a study of injury and crime, and therefore to restrict their reports to assaults that have resulted in injury or are experienced as a threat to safety or as a "crimes." To the extent that this occurred, it would exclude most instances of assault by a partner, and especially the culturally acceptable "harmless" assaults by women, and result in the 3:1 ratio of male to female offenders featured in the press release on the NVAW study. If this explanation is correct, the NVAW study does not contradict the large number of family conflict studies which show that women initiate and carry out assaults on male partners at about the same rate as men attack female partners.

A puzzling aspect of the NVAW study needs to be explained. The 3:1 ratio featured in the press release is based on lifetime prevalence rates (assaults by any partner, past or present). However, to be comparable to other studies, the published report (Tjaden and Thoennes, 1998) also had to present annual prevalence rates (assaults in the past year). These rates are given in the last column of Table 2.1 in this chapter. They show a 1.4:1 ratio of male to female offenders, which is much closer to the 1:1 ratio of family conflict studies. One possible explanation for the 3:1 lifetime rate goes back to the threat to safety context of the NVAW study. If one assumes that events experienced as a threat to safety are more likely to be remembered over a long time period, and that women are more likely to experience a slap or a kick by their partner as a threat to safety, it follows that women will remember and be able to report a larger percent of the assaults that occurred years back than men will be able to remember.

Family Conflict Studies

The near equal rates of assault found by family conflict studies have been attributed to a different set of methodological problems. These include purported defects in the Conflict Tactics Scales or CTS (Straus, 1979; Straus, 1990a; Straus, Hamby, Boney-McCoy, & Sugarman, 1996), under reporting of assaults by male respondents, and failure to take into account self-defensive violence by women and injury.

Under Reporting by Men

Family conflict studies often interview one partner to find out about the relationship, i.e., what the respondent has done and also what the partner has done. When men are the respondents, they may minimize their own violence and exaggerate violence by their partner. However, that cannot be the explanation for the equal rates because, regardless of whether the information comes from a male or female respondent, family conflict studies have found about equal rates of assault by the male and female partner (Straus, 1997).

The Conflict Tactics Scales

Most of the family conflict studies used the Conflict Tactics Scales or CTS, and the near equality in rates of assault by men and women has been attributed to purported biases in the CTS (Straus, 1990a; Straus, 1997, for a discussion of the purported biases). Consequently, it is important to examine studies that used other methods. An early study by Scanzoni (1978), asked a sample of 321 women what they did in cases of persistent conflict with their husband. Sixteen percent reported trying to hit the husband. Sorenson and Telles's (1991) analysis of 2,392 households in the Los Angeles Epidemiological Catchment Area Study found that "women reported higher rates . . .(than men)." The National Survey of Families and Households asked "During the past year, how many fights with your partner resulted in (you/him/her) hitting, shoving, or throwing things at (you/him/her)." Zlotnick (1998), analyzed this data for the 5,474 couples in the sample and found very similar rates for assaults by men and women (5% rate of assaults by men and 4% of assaults by women).

Self Defense and Injury

In my early research on domestic assaults, it seemed so obvious that women were injured more often and more seriously than men, and that domestic assaults by women were primarily in self defense, that I did not collect data on injury and self defense. I simply asserted it as a self-evident fact (Straus, Gelles, & Steinmetz, 1980). So, when, in the 1985 National Family Violence Survey, I did ask who was the first to hit, I was surprised to find that half of the women respondents reported they had hit first (Stets & Straus, 1990). Several other studies (Bland & Orn, 1986; Carrado, George, Loxam, Jones, & Templar, 1996; Demaris, 1992; Gryl, Stith, & Bird, 1991; Sorenson & Telles, 1991) also found about equal rates of *initiation* by men and women.

Family conflict studies rarely measure who is injured. The original CTS did not obtain data on injury. The CTS2 (Straus, Hamby, Boney-McCoy, & Sugarman, 1996) includes a supplemental scale to measure injury, but retains the system of measuring assaults regardless of injury. However, when injury data has been obtained along with the CTS and this is used as a criterion for estimating "violence," the rate drops to a one that is similar to the extremely low rate found in crime studies, and the percentage of assaults by men also increases to approximately the ratio found in crime studies (Straus, 1991; Straus, 1997). These findings further support the idea that one of the main reasons crime studies find that domestic assaults are overwhelmingly committed by men is because they tend to omit so many of the assaults that do not result in injury.

APPROPRIATE USES OF FAMILY CONFLICT AND CRIMINAL JUSTICE OR INJURY DATA

The explanations just offered for the discrepancies between family conflict studies and crime studies or injury studies suggests that the findings from the two types of studies apply to different groups of people and reflect different aspects of domestic assault. Most of the violence that is revealed by surveys of family problems is relatively minor and relatively infrequent, whereas a large portion of the violence in crime studies and clinical studies is chronic and severe and often involves injuries that need medical attention. These two types of violence probably have a different etiology and probably require a different type of intervention (see Johnson, 1995). If this is correct, it is important to avoid using findings based on cases known to police or shelters for battered women as the basis for understanding and dealing with the relatively minor and less chronic violence found in the population in general. That type of unwarranted generalization is often made and it is known as the "clinical fallacy."

Family conflict studies pose the opposite problem. It can be called the "representative sample fallacy" (Straus, 1990b). Family conflict studies contain very few cases involving weekly or daily assaults and injury. Consequently, family conflict studies may provide an erroneous basis for policies and interventions focused on these relatively few but extreme cases. This is a serious shortcoming because although the numbers may be relatively low, they are the cases that pose the most serious problems and which need to have priority in respect to interventions.

Much of the controversy over assaults by women stems from assuming that data from family conflict studies on assaults by women apply to cases known to the police and shelters, and the similar unwarranted assumption that the predominance of assaults by men in data from crime studies and battered women shelters applies to the population at large.

Both family conflict study data and also data from crime and battered women shelter samples are needed. Findings based on crime studies are needed to provide information on the more serious types of domestic assaults and therefore to provide a realistic basis for programs designed to aid the victims and to end this type of domestic violence. At the same time, to understand assaults on partners in the general population, which seldom involve injury, and for informing "primary prevention" efforts (Cowen, 1978), it is crucial to have family conflict data, including data on the most minor and "harmless" slap. In fact, understanding assaults that respondents do *not* think of as "a crime" may be the most important information for purposes of primary prevention because that is where more serious assaults start.

A SOCIOLOGICAL PERSPECTIVE ON ASSAULTS BY WOMEN WITHIN AND OUTSIDE THE FAMILY

One reason the repeated findings on equal rates of partner assault by men and women have been suspect is the absence of a theory to explain those findings. A similar doubt and incredulity existed when the extremely high rate of partner assaults by men was first brought to public and scientific attention by feminists. This was soon followed by a rich theoretical analysis from both a feminist and other perspectives (Gelles & Straus, 1979; Straus, 1976).

Although that sort of theoretical development has not yet happened for domestic assaults by women, some of the principles explaining domestic assaults by men also apply to women; for example, the proposition from criminology and exchange theory that the prevalence of crime is partly a function of what one can get away with. Since domestic assaults usually occur in private, both men and women can get away with it and this contributes to the high rate of domestic assault for both genders. However, the unique circumstances explaining assaults by women have not been analyzed theoretically. Table 2.2 makes a start in developing such a theory. It identifies variables that are hypothesized to inhibit physical assaults by women outside the family and variables that are hypothesized to facilitate physical assaults within the family by women. I label it a sociological perspective because, not surprisingly, as a sociologist, most of the processes I identify refer to social norms, social relationships, and social control processes. It is also important to keep in mind that many of the starting propositions are in the form of assumptions rather than empirically demonstrated propositions. So what follows is intended as a basis for further theoretical development and empirical research.

Different Cultural Norms For Women and Men

Violence Is Rule Following Behavior

Row A of Table 2.2 is based on the assumption that most human behavior, including acts of violence, is influenced by cultural norms. Typically, the actors are unaware they are following cultural prescriptions. I have often asked students in my introductory sociology class to do small experiments based on the work of Garfinkel (1964), to demonstrate behavior guided by unperceived cultural rules. For example, I asked them, the next time they go home, to be very polite and always say please and thank you. Their notes on what happened almost invariably reveal expressions of concern such as "Are you OK. Are you sure everything is OK?" This exercise brings to light an implicit cultural rule which allows and expects a relaxation within the family of the usual standards of civil social interaction.

Interpersonal violence, both within the family and outside the family also tends to follow unperceived rules and cultural scripts (Black, 1983; Kennedy

TABLE 2.2. What Explains Equal Assault Rates By Women in the Family, But Much Lower Rates Elsewhere?

Inhibitors of Assault By Women Outside the Family	Facilitators of Assault By Women Within the Family
A. *Cultural Norms:* "Unfeminine" for women to hit, but "manly" for men.	A. *Cultural Norms:* An indignant woman slapping a man's face epitomizes femininity to many • "if he gets fresh, slap him" • survey data "ok for a wife to slap" • examples in media
B. *Lesser Size and Strength:* Makes women fearful of retaliation and injury by someone who is not committed to them.	B. *Lesser Size and Strength:* "I knew I wouldn't hurt him."
C. *Self Defense or Retaliation:* Low because women assaulted less often (except for rape).	C. *Self Defense or Retaliation:* High because women assaulted frequently by partners.
D. *Gender Norms for Conflict:* Outside the family, women interact more with women and men more with men and male culture is more pro violence as a means of conflict resolution.	D. *Gender Norms for Conflict:* In couple relations, male partners may be less reachable with non-violent problem solving that works in woman-to-woman relationships. This increases probability of violence to force attention to the problem.
E. *Source of Identity:* Women's identity is not as strongly based on extra-family interests. Therefore less need to defend interests and reputation by violence.	E. *Source of Identity:* Women's identity is as strongly or more strongly based on family than men's. Therefore equal need o defend interests and reputation.
F. *Violence Level of Setting:* Women are less often in high violence occupations: those requiring violence (police, military, some sports) and jobs with high violence rates such as heavy physical labor jobs.	F. *Violence Level of Setting:* Women spend more time at home, and 90% hit toddlers. Mothers get 5 to 14 years of practice in hitting as morally correct through corporal punishment of their own children.
G. *Criminal Justice System Involvement:* Police involvement not greatly different for men & women.	G. *Criminal Justice System Involvement:* • Men not likely to call the police. • Police are not likely to arrest women, so women can get away with it even more than men.

& Sacco, 1998; Luckenbill, 1977; Zimring & Hawkins, 1997). For example, lashing out physically when infidelity is discovered, is typically experienced as something that happens when a person "loses control." However, a large percentage of the population finds hitting an unfaithful partner to be "understandable." This indicates an implicit cultural norm that permits one to "lose it" when a partner is unfaithful, and even more so when the partner is flagrantly unfaithful. Thus, "losing control" under those circumstances is culturally expected (Ptacek, 1988).

An implicit norm that helps explain the high rate of domestic assaults by women makes the marriage licence a hitting licence (Straus & Hotaling, 1980). That implicit norm is a carry over from a previous explicit legal norm that held sway until the 1870s when the courts ceased to recognize the common law right of husbands to "physically chastise an erring wife," i.e., the right to use corporal punishment (Calvert, 1974). Other norms permitting violence include the legal right of parents to hit children for purposes of correction and control.

Gender Differences in Rules for Violence

There are also norms about violence that are different for men and women, and different for behavior inside and outside the family. These are illustrated in Row A of Table 2.2 As indicated in this row, physical assaults by women, if outside the family, are considered "unfeminine" but in the family and other intimate partner relationships, physical attacks by women are expected and lauded under certain circumstances. For example, in my generation, probably millions of young women were told by their mother, "If he gets fresh, slap him" rather than "If he gets fresh, leave immediately." Then as now, slapping a man who does or says something outrageous is often seen as quintessentially feminine. Kathleen Willie, who charged President Clinton with unwanted sexual touching, said that she should have slapped his face ". . . but I don't think you can slap the president of the United States." In short, because of his position of power, she failed to follow the culturally prescribed script. Other examples can be seen every day on television or in films.

Perhaps the most direct evidence of the norm permitting assault by women against male partners comes from the survey done for the National Commission on the Causes and Prevention of Violence, appointed in the wake of the upsurge of violence in the 1960s (National Commission on the Causes and Prevention of Violence, 1969). My colleagues and I replicated that study in 1985, 1992, and 1995 (Straus, Kaufman Kantor, & Moore, 1997). In 1968, more than one out of five American adults (22%) believed there are circumstances when it is permissible for a wife to slap her husband's face. That percentage has remained essentially the same up through our latest survey in 1995. The percentage approving a *husband* slapping his wife was slightly lower in 1968 (20%), but it declined to half that by 1995. So society is becoming less tolerant of assaults by husbands, but continues to find such assaults acceptable if done by a wife.

Size and Strength Differences

Row B of Table 2.2 suggests that the smaller average size and muscle development of women contributes to both the lower rate of assaults outside the family and the equal rate within the family. Outside the family this physical disadvantage tends to make women fearful of retaliation and injury by someone who is not committed to them, and hence to avoid physical confrontation. But inside the family, a combination of belief that the partner will not really hurt them, and the belief that hitting is okay because, as many women told me, "I knew I wouldn't hurt him" (in the sense of no physical injury as compared to causing pain) reduces inhibitions about hitting the partner and limits fear of retaliation. Statistical evidence consistent with this interpretation comes from a study by Fiebert and Gonzalez (1997). They found that 29% of their sample of 978 women college students reported having hit a male partner. Of the women who had hit, two thirds (62%) checked as one of the reasons "I do not believe my actions would hurt my partner" or "I believe that men can readily protect themselves so I don't worry when I become physically aggressive." The lower probability of injury for assaults by women is probably also one of the reasons why the cultural norms are more tolerant of assaults by women on their partners.

Self Defense or Retaliation

Row C of Table 2.2 is based on the fact that the risk of a woman being assaulted by a stranger (even after including the risk of being raped) is less than half of the risk to which men are exposed (Craven, 1996). But within the family, the risk of a woman being assaulted by a partner is very high. The implications of this difference stem from the fact that almost all assaults are attempts to correct what the assailant perceives as the misbehavior of the victim, such as "making a pass at my wife" or not paying back a loan, or an insulting remark. The probability of a woman getting into a physical fight with a man other than her partner who has attacked her to correct some perceived misbehavior is low. Hence the probability of a nonfamily assault is also low. On the other hand, the probability of being attacked by a male partner for some perceived misbehavior is high. Given the norms of American society which favor retaliation (as illustrated by a parent advising a child "If hit, hit back") the probability of a woman physically retaliating against her partner is therefore also high.

Gender Norms for Conflict

Row D of Table 2.2 is based on the assumption that women are more inclined to discuss disagreements and men are more inclined to use an avoidance strategy. Conversely, physical attacks are more acceptable as a means of conflict resolution among men than women. Consequently, the fact that, outside the family, women interact more with other women than with men means that they interact more with a less violence-prone part of the population, and this reduces the chances of a nonfamily conflict escalating into violence relative to the same conflict between two men. In couple relations, on the other hand, women interact with male partners who may be less reachable through discussion than in woman-to-woman relationships. When faced with a man who withdraws and refuses to talk about a problem, and the problem persists, as it often does in the family, many women resort to slapping, kicking, and throwing things in an attempt to coerce the partner to attend to the issue. Fiebert and Gonzales's (1997) data on 285 college women who had assaulted a partner are consistent with this line of reasoning. When asked about reasons for hitting the partner, 38% checked "I wished to gain my partner's attention" and 43% checked "My partner was not listening to me." Because there was likely to be some overlap of the two responses, these data can only indicate that somewhere between 43% (complete overlap) and 81% (no overlap) indicated violence to physically coerce the partner's attention.

Source of Identity

Row E in Table 2.2 is based on research (discussed earlier) indicating that most violent acts are intended to correct the misbehavior (as the assailant sees it) of the victim. One of the most important categories of misbehavior consists of slighting or denigrating personal identity. Assuming that the identity of women is less closely linked to the public world outside the family than is the identity of men; women, on average, have fewer occasions and less motivation for defending nonfamily interests and reputation by violence. On the other hand, interpersonal relationships are more important in the lives of women than men (Gilligan, 1982). The identity of women is as strongly or more strongly based on what occurs within the family than is the case for men. Consequently, the need for women to defend their interests and identity in family roles is at least as great as for men. Moreover, the probability of needing to do so is increased because of cultural norms which presume that the husband is the head of the household. This creates a situation in which male partners feel privileged to direct and evaluate the behavior of their partners in the very spheres of life that are so crucial for a woman's identity. Far more women than men, for example, are likely to be deeply offended and hurt by negative comments on their cooking, tastes in household furnishing, or methods of child care.

Violence Level of Setting

The left column of Row F in Table 2.2 is based on the sex segregation of the labor market. The large differences in type of employment that are typical of men and women locate many men, but few women, in job settings where the assault rate is high. This includes occupations directly involving violence such as the and the military, and some sports. It also includes occupations requiring heavy physical labor, which perhaps because they are male occupations, tend to have higher rates of violence than do white collar occupations. Thus, women are not involved in the violence associated with many male occupational settings and this keeps their nonfamily assault rate down. The same principle applies to the lower involvement of women in many violence prone recreational settings, such as visiting bars (Felson, 1997).

The right column of row F refers to the domestic setting. Ironically, the domestic setting tends to be high in violence, even in the households of college educated couples (Gelles & Straus, 1988; Straus, Gelles, & Steinmetz, 1980). The violence in domestic settings that has come to public attention in recent decades (but has always been present) is assaults on spouses. But in addition, households are the locus of the most violent relationship in American families — the relation between parents and children. Over 90% of parents hit toddlers (Straus, 1994; Straus & Stewart, 1999) and over a third are still doing it when the children are in their early teens. Because mothers are the primary caretakers, more of this is done by women.

The violent child rearing that American children experience under such euphemisms as "physical punishment," "spanking," "a good swat on the behind," and "a good slap on the face for mouthing off," has many profound negative consequences which are only now starting to be recognized (Straus, 1994; Straus & Paschall, 1998; Straus, Sugarman, & Giles-Sims, 1997). One of these is that having been hit repeatedly by parents as a child (the typical experience of American children) and hitting one's own children provide role practice in violence to correct misbehavior, and this tends to spill over to correcting the misbehavior of the mother's partner (Straus, 1994; Straus & Yodanis, 1996, Chart 7-3), thus constituting one more factor contributing to the high rate of partner assault by women.

Criminal Justice System Involvement

Traditionally, police and prosecutors have been reluctant to become involved in the crime of assault, regardless of whether it occurs outside the family or inside (Buzawa & Buzawa, 1996). One of the reasons is that arrests and prosecutions for assault do not receive the public recognition of arresting, for example, a robber. Moreover, assaults are typically in the form of "fights" involving both parties and, legally, both parties should be prosecuted regardless of who started it. Under those circumstances, the probability of a case actually being tried, much less resulting in a conviction, are low relative to arrests for other crimes. Such cases are regarded as "trouble." Police and prosecutors do not get much recognition, and may even be faulted, if there are very many such cases in their record. Outside the family, those principles apply to both men and women and the risk of police involvement is not greatly different for men and women.

As a result of the women's movement, the traditional reluctance of the police to become involved in "domestics" (Kaufman Kantor & Straus, 1990; Straus, 1977) has changed. In most jurisdictions in the United States, state laws or police regulations now require or recommend arrest. However, consistent with the greater injury rate for women, these laws and regulations may state or imply a male offender. Although on average, when there is an injury, this is correct, it denies male victims equal protection under the law. In fact, there are a growing number of complaints that attempts by men to obtain police protection may result in the man being arrested (Cook, 1997). That ironic situation is an additional reason that men are reluctant to call for police protection. The main reason is one already discussed in explaining gender differences in police statistics: The injury rate is much lower when the offender is a woman and there is therefore less perceived need to call for protection. The fact that assault is a legal and moral crime, regardless of whether there is injury, is lost from view.

Men are also less likely to call the police, even when there is injury, because, like women, they feel shame about disclosing family violence. But for many men, the shame is compounded by the shame of not being able to keep their wives under control. Among this group, a "real man" would be able to keep her under control. Moreover, many police share these same traditional gender role expectations. This adds to the legal and regulatory presumption that the offender is a man. As a result, the police are reluctant to arrest women for domestic assault. Women know this. That is, they know they are likely to be able to get away with it. As in the case of other crimes, the probability of a woman assaulting her partner is strongly influenced by what she thinks she can get away with (Gelles & Straus, 1988).

The Theoretical Agenda

To convert the above discussion of factors that inhibit and facilitate assaults by women in different settings into a theory requires expanding the number of etiological factors considered and less exclusive reliance on social factors. It requires tracing out the links and interactions among the factors. Although developing such a theory is a large task, even the limited discussion in this chapter may help advance research on gender differences in partner assaults. Such a theoretical development is needed because one of the paradoxical aspects of science is that although empirical data are the ultimate determinants of what is "scientific knowledge," empirical facts by themselves are suspect until there is a plausible theory to explain them. My hope is that by providing at least part of the needed theoretical understanding, this chapter may contribute to transforming the question of gender differences in partner assault from the realm of polemics and recrimination to the realm of theoretically based empirical research.

A SOCIOLOGY OF SCIENCE ANALYSIS
OF THE CONTROVERSY

The previous paragraph assumes that the parties involved would like to see the controversy over domestic assaults by women transformed from the realm of polemics to the realm of theoretically based empirical research. But that is not necessarily the case. In order to understand why it may not be the case, it is helpful to return to the question how violence is defined. This is because much of the controversy over violence by women occurs as a result of each side using "violence" to refer to something different. I will call these two approaches broad and narrow definitions. The focus on broad versus narrow conceptions of violence is a huresitc device to help identify some of the underlying issues. Moreover, some of the differences are artificial in the sense that they are not mutually exclusive. Finally, not every basis for this controversy is linked to the issue of broad versus narrow definitions.

As shown in the first two rows of Table 2.3, the narrow definition restricts violence to the act of assault, regardless of injury, whereas the broad definition defines violence to include multiple modes of maltreatment and the resulting injury. One reason each of these definitions is unacceptable to those who adhere to the other is that more than scientific issues are at stake. Each definition also reflects an underlying moral agenda and professional role as indicated in row F. Consequently, to abandon one or the other definition is tantamount to abandoning that agenda and professional role.

As indicated in Row C of Table 2.3 those using a broad definition tend to be service providers and feminist activists and those using a narrow definition tend to be researchers, but there are many researchers who use a broad definition. A broad definition is essential for service providers. It would be ridiculous and unethical if service providers such, as shelters, batterer treatment programs, or marital therapists, restricted their focus to physical assaults and ignored psychological assaults, sexual coercion, subjugation, and other forms of degradation. On the other hand, researchers tend to focus on investigating one specific type of maltreatment, such as physical assaults, because each type is complex and difficult to investigate. Much can only be learned by a concentrated research focus. I believe that most of those who focus on just one form of maltreatment also recognize the need to take into consideration multiple modes of maltreatment, even though they themselves do not conduct that type of research.

The difference in emphasis on injury reflects the different needs of service providers and researchers. For a service provider, it is essential to

TABLE 2.3. Variables Underlying Broad Versus Narrow Definitions of Violence.

	Broad Definition	*Narrow Definition*
A. **Coverage**	All types of maltreatment	Only physical assault
B. **Role of Injury in Concept of Violence**	An inherent part of the concept	One of many *possible* consequences to be investigated
C. **Occupation/Role**	Service providers/Feminist activists	Academics/Researchers
D. **Statistics Favored to Describe Nature of the Problem**	police and crime survey because they show more women victims and suggest cause is patriarchy	Family conflict data because they show ubiquity of the problem and suggest multiple causes
E. **Statistics Favored to Mobilize Resources**	Family conflict because rates are many times greater	Family conflict because rates are many times greater
F. **Primary (But Not Exclusive) Moral Concern**	End oppression of women, regardless of the type of oppression	End physical assaults, regardless of the gender of perpetrator or victim
G. **Primary Use of Research Using the Definition**	Cessation of assaults on women, especially assaults experienced as a "real crime"	"Primary prevention" of physical violence of all types, from spanking to murder

know if the assault resulted in injury because different steps are needed to deal with cases involving injury. For a researcher who is investigating such things as the type of family or type of society in which partner assaults are most likely to occur, injury may not be a crucial issue because it can be assumed that injury occurs in a certain proportion of cases. Moreover, for some purposes it is necessary to exclude injury as a criterion. One of these is research that seeks to estimate the prevalence of domestic assaults. If injury is one of the criteria, it restricts the data to more serious assaults and, as we have seen, the overall prevalence rate is vastly underestimated. Thus, the widely cited figure from the National Family Violence Survey of 1.8 million women severely assaulted each year becomes only 188,000 when the criteria for a severe assault includes injury (Straus, 1990b; Straus, 1991; Straus, 1997). Of course, this is a false dichotomy. As indicated in a previous section, both figures are needed. Feminist activists, for example use both figures (see rows D and E of Table 2.3). They have made extensive use of the 1.8 million figure (often presented as a woman is battered every 15 seconds) to mobilize resources. At the same time they also use police, crime survey, and emergency room statistics to show that there are many more women victims (in the sense of injured or fearing injury) than male victims.

Row F of Table 2.3 was included to suggest that, underlying the differences just discussed is a deep seated difference in moral agenda. Those who use a broad definition tend to be primarily concerned with the well being of women. They are, of course, also concerned with physical assaults regardless of who is the victim, but their primary concern is ending maltreatment of women. Moreover, as is to be expected, they are hostile to research that might be used by critics of feminism, and this includes research on assaults by women. On the other hand, those defining violence as a physical assault, tend to place ending physical violence at the top of their agenda, regardless of whether the offender is a man, woman, or child. Of the two evils, physical violence and the oppression of women, physical violence tends to take priority, even though (as in my case) they are also concerned with ending all types of gender inequality and maltreatment.

The last row of Table 2.3 brings us back to the idea that research using a broad definition and emphasizing injury may be most useful for informing programs designed to treat offenders or help victims of repeated severe assault. By contrast, research focusing on the act of assault, most of which does not involve injury but does involve millions of couples, may be most useful for informing programs of "primary prevention," i.e., steps that will prevent physical assaults from ever happening.

It is also important to realize that some of the participants in this controversy do not realize (or deny) that moral agendas and professional roles are involved. For example, Patricia Tjaden (personal communication, March 11, 1998.) wrote, "I certainly hope that you are not suggesting that I or my colleagues are motivated by any type of moral agenda when we developed and implemented the NVAW Survey." In fact, a moral agenda is evident from the title of her study, the "National Violence Against Women Survey" and from the fact that the original plan was to interview only women and to ask only about their victimization, omitting violence perpetrated by women. Perhaps Tjaden meant that this moral agenda was specified by the sponsoring agencies. I hope she did not mean that because research to provide a deeper understanding of violence against women is a worthy moral goal, it is necessarily unscientific. My own insistence that we also study assaults by women is driven by a different, but I think also worthy, moral agenda—that of ending violence, regardless of who is the perpetrator.

WILL THE CONTROVERSY END?

The analysis in the preceding section suggests that neither side is motivated to understand the other. Rather, each seeks to impose its perspective because they believe the preferred definition is vital to advancing their moral agenda and professional objectives. In my opinion, that will continue. Moreover, society would lose if either side gives up their perspective because society benefits from the moral agenda and professional contribution of both sides. I for one do not intend to give up attempting to advance the "no violence *by anyone*" moral agenda that has informed my research on domestic assaults and spanking children for 30 years (Straus, 1994).

I believe humanity needs research inspired by the moral agenda and perspective of those who focus on the *oppression of women,* regardless of whether the oppression is physical, sexual, psychological or economic; and also research inspired by the moral agenda of those who focus on *physical assault,* regardless of whether the assault is by a man, woman or child. I even dare to hope that the controversy will be resolved by recognizing the need for both perspectives, and that this will bring an end to attempts to discredit those whose agenda and professional contribution requires a different approach and different perspective.

REFERENCES

Bachman, R., & Saltzman, L. E. (1995). *Violence against women: Estimates from the redesigned survey* (BJS Publication No. 154-348). Washington, DC: U.S. Department of Justice, Bureau of Justice Statistics.

Black, D. (1983). Crime as social control. *American Sociological Review, 48,* 34-45.

Bland, R., & Orn, H. (1986). Family violence and psychiatric disorder. *Canadian Journal of Psychiatry, 31*(2), 129-137.

Brookoff, D. (1997). *Drugs, alcohol, and domestic violence in Memphis* (National Institute of Justice Research Preview No.). Washington, DC: U.S. Department of Justice.

Buzawa, E. S., & Buzawa, C. G. (Eds.). (1996). *Do arrests and restraining orders work?* Thousand Oaks, CA: Sage.

Calvert, R. (1974). Criminal and civil liability in husband-wife assaults. In S. K. Steinmetz & M. A. Straus (Eds.), *Violence in the Family* (chap. 9). New York: Harper and Row.

Carrado, M., George, M. J., Loxam, E., Jones, L., & Templar, D. (1996). Aggression in British heterosexual relationships: A descriptive analysis. *Aggressive Behavior, 22,* 401-415.

Cook, P. W. (1997). *Abused men: The hidden side of domestic violence.* Westport, CT: Praeger.

Cowen, E. (1978). Demystifying primary prevention. In D. G. Forgays (Ed.), *Primary prevention of psychopathology* (chap. 2). Hanover, NH: University of New England Press.

Craven, D. (1996). *Female Victims of Violent Crime* (Bureau of Justice Statistics Selected Findings No. NCJ-162602). Washington, DC: U.S. Department of Justice, Office of Justice Programs.

Demaris, A. (1992). Male versus female initiation of aggression: The case of courtship violence. In E. C. Viano (Ed.), *Intimate violence: Interdisciplinary perspectives* (pp. 111-120). Bristol, PA: Taylor & Francis.

Dobash, R. E., & Dobash, R. P. (1979). *Violence against wives: A case against the patriarch.* New York: Free Press.

Federal Bureau of Investigation (1995). *Crime in the United States, 1993: Uniform crime reports.* Washington, DC: U.S. Department of Justice.

Feld, S. L., & Straus, M. A. (1989). Escalation and desistance of wife assault in marriage. *Criminology, 27*(1), 141-161.

Felson, R. B. (1997). Routine activities and involvement in violence as actor, witness, or target. *Violence and Victims, 12*(3), 209-221.

Ferraro, K. J. (1989). Policing woman battering. *Social Problems, 36*(1), 61-74.

Ferraro, K. J., & Johnson, J. M. (1983). How women experience battering: The process of victimization. *Social Problems, 30*(3), 325-339.

Fiebert, M. S. (1997). Annotated bibliography: References examining assaults by women on their spouses/partners. In B. M. Dank & R. Refinette (Eds.), *Sexual harassment & sexual consent* (Vol. 1, pp. 273-286). New Brunswick: Transaction Publishers.

Fiebert, M. S., & Gonzalez, D. M. (1997). College women who initiate assaults on their male partners and the reasons offered for such behavior. *Psychological Reports, 80,* 583-590.

Garfinkel, H. (1964). Studies of the routine grounds of everyday activities. *Social Problems, 11*(Winter), 225-250.

Gelles, R. J., & Straus, M. A. (1979). Determinants of violence in the family: Towards a theoretical integration. In W. R. Burr, R. Hill, F. I. Nye, & I. L. Reiss (Eds.), *Contemporary theories about the family* (Vol. 1, chap. 21). New York: Free Press.

Gelles, R. J., & Straus, M. A. (1988). *Intimate violence.* New York: Simon & Schuster.

Gilligan, C. (1982). *In a different voice: Psychological theory and women's development.* Cambridge, MA: Harvard University Press.

Grandin, E., & Lupri, E. (1997). Intimate violence in Canada and the United States: A cross-national comparison. *Journal of Family Violence, 12*(4), 417-443.

Gryl, F. E., Stith, S. M., & Bird, G. W. (1991). Close dating relationships among college students: Differences by use of violence and by gender. *Journal of Social and Personal Relationships, 8,* 243-264.

Johnson, M. P. (1995). Patriarchal terrorism and common couple violence: Two forms of violence against women. *Journal of Marriage and the Family, 57*(May), 283-294.

Kaufman Kantor, G., & Straus, M. A. (1990). Response of victims and the police to assaults on wives. In M. A. Straus & R. J. Gelles (Eds.), *Physical violence in American families: Risk factors and adaptations to violence in 8,145 families* (pp. 473-487). New Brunswick: Transaction Publishers.

Kennedy, L. W., & Sacco, V. F. (1998). *Crime victims in context.* Los Angeles, CA: Roxbury Publishing.

Langan, P. A., & Innes, C. A. (1986). *Preventing domestic violence against women* (Special Report No. NCJ 102037). Washington, DC: U.S. Department of Justice, Bureau of Justice Statistics.

Luckenbill, D. F. (1977). Criminal homicide as a situated transaction. *Social Problems, 25*(2), 176-186.

National Commission on the Causes and Prevention of Violence. (1969). *Report of the Media Task Force.* Washington, DC: Government Printing Office.

O'Leary, K. D., Barling, J., Arias, I., Rosenbaum, A., Malone, J., & Tyree, A. (1989). Prevalence and stability of physical aggression. *Journal of Consulting and Clinical Psychology, 57*(2), 263-268.

Orne, M. (1962). Amount of experience in experiments as a determinant of performance in later experiments. *Journal of Personality and Social Psychology, 17,* 776-783.

Peterson, K. S. (1997, Nov. 18). Partners unequal in abuse: Study, women's risk is greater. *USA Today.*

Ptacek, J. (1988). Why do men batter their wives? In K. Yllo & M. Bograd (Eds.), *Feminist perspectives on wife abuse* (pp. 133-157). Newbury Park, CA: Sage.

Scanzoni, J. (1978). *Sex roles, women's work, and marital conflict.* Lexington, MA: Lexington.

Sorenson, S. B., & Telles, C. A. (1991). Self-reports of spousal violence in a Mexican-American and non-Hispanic white population. *Violence and Victims, 6*(1), 3-15.

Steinmetz, S. K. (1978). The battered husband syndrome. *Victimology, 2,* 499-509.

Stets, J. E., & Straus, M. A. (1990). Gender differences in reporting of marital violence and its medical and psychological consequences. In M. A. Straus & R. J. Gelles (Eds.), *Physical violence in American families: Risk factors and adaptations to violence in 8,145 families* (pp. 151-165). New Brunswick, NJ: Transaction.

Straus, M. A. (1976). Sexual inequality, cultural norms, and wife-beating. In E. C. Viano (Ed.), *Victims and society* (pp. 543-559). Washington, DC: Visage Press.

Straus, M. A. (1977). A sociological perspective on the prevention and treatment of wifebeating. In M. Roy (Ed.), *Battered women.* New York: Van Nostrand Reinhold.

Straus, M. A. (1979). Measuring intrafamily conflict and violence: The Conflict Tactics (CTS) Scales. *Journal of Marriage and the Family, 41*(1), 75-88.

Straus, M. A. (1990a). The Conflict Tactics Scales and its critics: An evaluation and new data on validity and reliability. In M. A. Straus & R. J. Gelles (Eds.), *Physical violence in American families: Risk factors and adaptations to violence in 8,145 families* (pp. 49-73). New Brunswick, NJ: Transaction Publications.

Straus, M. A. (1990b). Injury, frequency, and the representative sample fallacy in measuring wife beating and child abuse. In M. A. Straus & R. J. Gelles (Eds.), *Physical violence in American families: Risk factors and adaptations to violence in 8,145 families* (pp. 75-89). New Brunswick, NJ: Transaction Publications.

Straus, M. A. (1990c). The national family violence surveys. In M. A. Straus & R. J. Gelles (Eds.), *Physical violence in American families: Risk factors and adaptions to violence in 8,145 families* (pp. 3-16). New Brunswick: Transaction Publications.

Straus, M. A. (1991). Conceptualizaton and measurement of battering: Implications for public policy. In M. Steinman (Ed.), *Woman battering: Policy responses* (pp. 19-47). Cincinnati: Anderson Publishing.

Straus, M. A. (1992a). *Children as witnesses to marital violence: A risk factor for lifelong problems among a nationally representative sample of American men and women.* Paper presented at the 23rd Ross roundtable on critical approaches to common pediatric problems. Ohio: Ross Laboratories.

Straus, M. A. (1992b). Sociological research and social policy: The case of family violence. *Sociological Forum, 7*(2), 211-237.

Straus, M. A. (1994). *Beating the devil out of them: Corporal punishment in American families.* San Francisco: Jossey-Bass/Lexington Books.

Straus, M. A. (1997). Physical assaults by women partners: A major social problem. In M. R. Walsh (Ed.), *Women, men and gender: Ongoing debates* (pp. 210-221). New Haven, CT: Yale University Press.

Straus, M. A. (1998). *Characteristics of the National Violence Against Women Study that might explain the low assault rate for both sexes and the even lower rate for women.* Durham, NH: Family Research Laboratory, University of New Hampshire.

Straus, M. A., & Gelles, R. J. (1990). *Physical violence in American families: Risk factors and adaptations to violence in 8,145 families.* New Brunswick, NJ: Transaction.

Straus, M. A., Gelles, R. J., & Steinmetz, S. (1980). *Behind closed doors: Violence in the American family.* New York: Doubleday.

Straus, M. A., Hamby, S. L., Boney-McCoy, S., & Sugarman, D. B. (1996). The revised Conflict Tactics Scales (CTS2): Development and preliminary psychometric data. *Journal of Family Issues, 17*(3), 283-316.

Straus, M. A., & Hotaling, G. T. (Eds.). (1980). *The social causes of husband-wife violence.* Minneapolis, MN: University of Minnesota Press.

Straus, M. A., Kaufman Kantor, G., & Moore, D. W. (1997). Change in cultural norms approving marital violence: From 1968 to 1994. In G. Kaufman Kantor & J. L. Jasinski (Eds.), *Out of the darkness: Contemporary perspectives on family violence.* Thousand Oaks, CA: Sage.

Straus, M. A., & Paschall, M. J. (1998). *Corporal punishment by mothers and child's cognitive development: A longitudinal study.* Paper presented at the 14th World Congress of Sociology, Montreal, Quebec, Canada. Durham, NH: Family Research Laboratory, University of New Hampshire.

Straus, M. A., & Stewart, J. H. (in press). Corporal punishment by American parents: National data on prevalence, chronicity, severity, and duration, in relation to child, and family characteristics. *Clinical Child and Family Review, 2.*

Straus, M. A., Sugarman, D. B., & Giles-Sims, J. (1997). Spanking by parents and subsequent antisocial behavior of children. *Archives of Pediatric and Adolescent Medicine, 151*(August), 761-767.

Straus, M. A., & Sweet, S. (1992). Verbal/symbolic aggression in couples: Incidence rates and relationships to personal characteristics. *Journal of Marriage and the Family, 54*, 346-357.

Straus, M. A., & Yodanis, C. L. (1996). Corporal punishment in adolescence and physical assaults on spouses later in life: What accounts for the link? *Journal of Marriage and the Family, 58*(4), 825-841.

Sugarman, D. B., & Hotaling, G. T. (1989). Dating violence: Prevalence, context, and risk markers. In A. A. Pirog-Good & J. E. Stets (Eds.), *Violence in dating relationships: Emerging social issues* (pp. 3-31). New York: Praeger.

Tjaden, P. G., & Thoennes, N. (1997). *The prevalence and consequences of intimate partner violence: Findings from the National Violence Against Women Survey.* Paper presented at the American Society of Criminology 49th Annual Meeting, San Diego, CA.

U.S. Department of Justice (1976). *Dictionary of criminal justice data terminology.* Washington, DC: National Criminal Justice Information Service.

Vissing, Y. M., Straus, M. A., Gelles, R. J., & Harrop, J. W. (1993). Verbal aggression by parents and psychosocial problems of children. *Child Abuse and Neglect, 15,* 223-238.

Zimring, F. E., & Hawkins, G. (1997). *Crime is not the problem: Lethal violence in America.* New York: Oxford University Press.

Zlotnick, C., Kohn, R., Peterson, J., & Pearlstein, T. (1998). Partner physical victimization in a national sample of American families: Relationship to psychological functioning, psychosocial factors, and gender. *Journal of Interpersonal Violence, 13*(1), 156-166.

3

A Typology of Male Batterers
An Initial Examination

Amy Holtzworth-Munroe
Jeffrey C. Meehan
Katherine Herron
Gregory L. Stuart

Husband to wife violence is a serious problem in this country. Data from nationally representative surveys suggest that each year 1 out of every 8 married men will be physically aggressive toward his wife and nearly 2 million women will be severely assaulted by their male partners (Straus & Gelles, 1990). Husband violence has been demonstrated to have a variety of serious negative consequences, including both physical injury and psychological harm (see review in Holtzworth-Munroe, Smutzler, & Sandin, 1997), making it a major health problem.

In attempting to understand the correlates and potential causes of husband to wife violence, it is imperative to examine how men who engage in marital violence differ from men who do not. Indeed, there are many studies in which researchers compared "violent" to "nonviolent" samples of men. However, recent research has made it clear that samples of maritally violent men are actually heterogeneous, varying along many theoretically important dimensions (Holtzworth-Munroe & Stuart, 1994).

AUTHORS' NOTE: This project was supported by a NIH grant, #PHS R01-MH51935, awarded to the first author. Requests for reprints should be sent to Amy Holtzworth-Munroe, Department of Psychology, Indiana University, Bloomington, IN 47405. We would like to thank Kristy Dreher, Joelene Bergonzi, Scott Carlson, and Brian Gmutza for their help in recruiting and assessing subjects and with data management.

We believe that our understanding of marital violence is more likely to be advanced by attention to these differences than by continuing to treat all violent husbands as one homogeneous group. Comparing various subtypes to each other, and pinpointing how each type differs from nonviolent relationships, may increase our understanding of husband violence and help us to identify different underlying processes resulting in violence. Moreover, the identification of batterer subtypes opens the possibility of matching patients to treatments which would be hoped to lead to increases in intervention effectiveness. In the present chapter, we briefly review our proposed batterer typology and present preliminary findings from a study designed to examine the validity of this typology.

PROPOSED TYPOLOGIES OF BATTERERS

Holtzworth-Munroe and Stuart (1994) proposed a comprehensive review of previous batterer typologies, including 9 studies using deductive approaches (e.g., splitting batterers into groups on the basis of clinical observations or *a priori* theorizing) and 6 studies using inductive approaches (e.g., factor or cluster analysis of subjects' scores on measures). In a recent update of this paper, we added one more recent typology (i.e., Gottman, Jacobson, Rushe, Shortt, Babcock, La Taillade, & Waltz, 1995) and further elaborated upon the clinical implications of male batterer typologies (Stuart & Holtzworth-Munroe, 1995).

Holtzworth-Munroe and Stuart (1994) observed that the batterer subtypes identified in previous typologies could be classified along three descriptive dimensions. These are: (1) the *severity* of marital physical violence and related abuse, such as psychological and sexual abuse; (2) the *generality* of violence (i.e., family only or extra-familial violence) and related variables, such as criminal behavior and legal involvement; and (3) the batterer's *psychopathology or personality disorders*. We proposed that three subtypes of batterers would be identified using these descriptive dimensions.

First, *family only* batterers would engage in the least severe marital violence and be the least likely to engage in psychological and sexual abuse. The violence of this group would be generally restricted to within their family; this group would be the least likely to engage in violence outside the home or to have related legal problems. This group would consist of men who evidence little psychopathology and either no personality disorder or, perhaps, a passive-dependent personality disorder.

Second, *dysphoric/borderline* batterers would engage in moderate to severe wife abuse, including psychological and sexual abuse. This group's violence would be primarily confined to the wife, although some extra-familial violence and criminal behavior might be evident. This group would be the most dysphoric, psychologically distressed, and emotionally volatile. Men in this group would evidence borderline personality characteristics and might have problems with alcohol and drug abuse; they would have difficulty controlling their explosive anger, particularly anger at their wives.

Third, the *generally violent/antisocial* batterer would engage in moderate to severe marital violence, including psychological and sexual abuse. These men would engage in the most extra-familial aggression and have the most extensive history of related criminal behavior and legal involvement. They would be likely to have problems with alcohol and drug abuse. These batterers would be the most likely to have an antisocial personality disorder and psychopathy.

Holtzworth-Munroe and Stuart (1994) then presented a developmental model of husband violence, highlighting the potential importance of both distal/historical and proximal correlates of male violence as potential risk factors for the development of differing batterer subtypes. They hypothesized that the three proposed batterer subgroups would differ on the variables in this model, including distal/historical (i.e., genetic/prenatal factors, family of origin home environment and violence, and association with deviant peers) and proximal (i.e., attachment/dependency, impulsivity, social skills—in both marital and nonmarital relationships—and attitudes—both hostile attitudes toward women and attitudes supportive of violence) correlates of husband violence.

Family only batterers would evidence the lowest levels of both distal and proximal risk factors; indeed, it might be difficult to distinguish men in this group from men who experience relationship distress and dysfunction but who do not engage in marital violence. family only batterers would have low genetic risk for antisocial/aggressive behavior, would report only low to moderate levels of aggression in their family of origin, and would not have extensive associations with deviant peers. They would have generally normal attachments to others, although they might experience some dependency on an intimate partner. Relative to the other subtypes of batterers, they would be the least impulsive. Given their lack of general violence, their social skills outside of relationships were expected to be adequate but, given their engagement in marital violence, they were likely to evidence some deficits in relationship skills. They would not hold positive attitudes toward violence or hostile attitudes toward women. Their violence was proposed to result from a combination of stress and marital stress such that, on some occasions, their anger and lack of relationship skills would lead them to engage in physical aggression during escalating marital conflicts. However, their lack of psychopathology, their positive attitudes toward women, and their negative attitudes about violence would keep their aggression from escalating.

Dysphoric/borderline batterers were assumed to come from a traumatic background, which may have involved child abuse and parental rejection. As a result, these men would be expected to have difficulty forming a stable and trusting attachment with an intimate partner. Instead, they would be highly dependent upon, yet fearful of losing, their wives. They would be very jealous and fear wife abandonment, consistent with their borderline personality characteristics. They also would lack relationship skills, have hostile attitudes toward women, and have attitudes that were moderately supportive of violence. This group is similar to the batterers studied by Dutton (1995; see Chapter 4 by Dutton in this volume); he has suggested that their past traumatic experiences (e.g., abuse in the family of origin) leads to a borderline personality organization and related anger and insecure attachment which, when combined with frustration, results in violence against the attachment figure (i.e., the wife).

The *generally violent/antisocial* batterer was predicted to resemble other antisocial, aggressive, criminal groups on the model variables. Relative to the other batterer subtypes, they would be the most likely to have a genetic/prenatal risk for antisocial and aggressive behavior, to have been exposed to the highest levels of family-of-origin violence, and to have associated with deviant peers as youths. They would not be expected to feel dependent upon or empathetic toward their partners. They would be the most impulsive and would lack skills in both marital and nonmarital situations. They would have hostile attitudes toward women and would view violence as acceptable. Their marital violence was conceptualized as a part of their general use of violence and engagement in antisocial, criminal behavior.

The present study was conducted to examine the validity of the batterer typology proposed by Holtzworth-Munroe and Stuart (1994). The overall study plan involved assessing 100 or more maritally violent men and their wives, using the three descriptive dimensions (i.e., severity of marital violence, generality of violence, psychopathology/personality disorders) to form subtypes of batterers, and then comparing the subtypes on the distal and proximal correlates of violence outlined in the Holtzworth-Munroe and Stuart (1994) developmental model. In addition, we are assessing two nonviolent comparison samples (i.e., maritally distressed and nondistressed men) to compare these groups to the three batterer subtypes. Finally, we are conducting 18-month follow-up assessments with the husband-violent couples to examine the stability of the typology over time. While the study is not yet complete, this chapter reports the typology findings from the first 63 maritally violent men included in the study.

PARTICIPANTS AND PROCEDURES

All participants were recruited from Indianapolis and surrounding communities, with newspaper ads and flyers placed around town. We also sent flyers to professionals who work with couples experiencing marital problems and/or men engaging in violence (e.g., staff members of domestic violence treatment programs; attorneys specializing in divorce and/or criminal law). Throughout the course of the study, a variety of ads and flyers were used. All stated that "married couples" were wanted for a research study of husbands. Some stated that we were looking for a wide variety of couples; others targeted couples having problematic or happy relationships.

Interested participants called our laboratory and the study was explained to them. Those who expressed continued interest then participated in a phone screening interview; husbands and wives were interviewed separately and asked to complete the interview only if they had privacy from their partner. The phone screening interview included: (1) a demographics questionnaire; (2) the Short Marital Adjustment Test (SMAT; Locke & Wallace, 1959), a widely used, reliable, and valid measure of marital adjustment and satisfaction; and (3) the Conflict Tactics Scale (CTS; Straus, 1979), the most widely used research measure of marital violence. To be eligible for the study, couples had to be married or "living together as if married," comfortable with English, and both partners had to be willing to participate.

Based on their responses to this phone screening interview, couples were either excluded from the study or assigned to one of the following groups:

Husband Violent Group. To be included in this group, either the husband or wife had to report, on the CTS, that the husband had engaged in at least one physically aggressive action toward the wife (defined as endorsement of CTS item #12, "pushed/grabbed/shoved" or the later items which represent increasingly severe violence) in the past year. At the time of writing this chapter, a total of 63 couples have been recruited for this group, and this chapter reports analyses involving these 63 men.

Nonviolent Husband Comparison Groups. We recruited two comparison samples of couples in which the husband was not violent. To be included in these groups, both the husband and wife had to agree that the husband had not engaged in any physical aggression in the past 5 years. Couples were classified as either *maritally distressed* or *nondistressed,* based on their SMAT scores. Nonviolent couples are not included in the present analyses.

Couples who qualified for the study were invited into the laboratory for a series of assessment meetings. Both spouses attended the first session, which could last up to 4 hours (3 hours for most couples). Husbands attended the second session alone; this session could last up to 4 hours (3.5 hours for most men). Finally, husbands and wives both attended the third session; this session usually lasted 1 hour for wives and 2 hours for husbands. Husbands and wives completed all measures in separate rooms. Across sessions, measures were administered such that husbands and wives completed the same measures in the same sessions, to prevent participants from discussing their responses to a measure with their partner before their partner had completed the same measure.

Participants were paid part of their compensation at the end of each session. However, to encourage participation in the full study, at the completion of the third session, they also received a bonus for completing the study. Initially, couples who completed the study were paid a total of $190 for their participation. Part way through the study, to increase our recruitment of subjects, we changed our compensation for couples, so that each couple received $250 for completing the study (husbands received $165; wives received $85). The majority of subjects received this higher payment.

THREE DESCRIPTIVE DIMENSION MEASURES

In the first lab session, subjects completed measures of the three descriptive dimensions: (1) severity of marital violence; (2) generality of violence; and (3) personality disorder. Scores derived from these measures were entered into the cluster analyses to identify subtypes of maritally violent men.

Severity/Frequency of Marital Violence

The severity/frequency of the man's marital violence was measured using the spouses' report on an expanded version of the *Revised Conflict Tactics Scale* (CTS2; Straus, Hamby, Boney-McCoy, & Sugarman, 1996). This measure was independently completed by both husbands and wives. The CTS2 was designed to improve upon the CTS. It includes more violent items (i.e., 5 minor and 7 severe); we added 4 additional physical violence items. The CTS2 lists each behavior twice—asking once what the participant has done to his/her partner and once what the partner has done to the participant. For each behavior listed, a participant indicates whether the behavior has ever occurred, has occurred in the past but not the past year, or, if it has occurred in the past year, how often is has occurred; for each behavior, participants provide the frequency of occurrence in the past year on a scale from 1 to more than 20 times.

To derive a score representing each man's level of violence in the past year, for the cluster analysis, we used the highest report of husband violence given by either the husband or wife. Based on scoring guidelines for the original CTS, we assigned each CTS2 violence item a severity-weighted score (reflecting likelihood of injury) and then multiplied that weight by the frequency of occurrence of the behavior to yield an item severity-weighted score. The total score was derived by adding these severity-weighted item scores for husband violent behaviors occurring in the past year. Given the commonly found skewed distribution of husband physical aggression scores (i.e., most men had engaged in low levels of violence), we log-transformed these scores. We then computed z-scores, to standardize the measures entered into the cluster analysis.

Generality of Violence

Unfortunately, in marital violence research, no standardized measure of a man's use of violence outside of his marriage exists. Thus, we designed the *Generality of Violence Questionnaire* (GVQ) for this study. Men completed the GVQ, reporting on their own use of violence. (Pilot data indicated that wives did not have enough information about their husbands' use of violence outside the relationship to provide useful data.)

On Part I of the GVQ, participants indicated whether they had ever engaged in any physical aggression toward 10 categories of people and situations: behaviors as part of a gang or group, family members, male friends, female friends (not girlfriends), people at work, acquaintances, strangers, ex-wives and ex-girlfriends, as part of a job requirement, and other. For each category, physically aggressive behaviors were listed; the participant read the list and indicated if he had ever done any of these things to any person in the category being assessed. If so, he listed the first name and/or his relationship to each person. For any individual identified as an object of the participant's violence on Part I, the participant then completed Part II. On Part II, the participant was given a sheet for each person toward whom he had been violent; the sheet listed the victim and 15 violent behaviors from the CTS2. For each violent behavior listed, the participant reported how many times he engaged in that behavior toward that person in the past year (using the CTS2 range of 0 to 20). We assigned CTS severity weights to each item.

For the cluster analyses, to derive a score reflecting violence outside the participant's intimate relationship in the past year, we derived a composite score of violence across all victims in eight of the categories of people and situations (i.e., we excluded violence reported to be part of a job requirement and violence against ex-wives and ex-girlfriends). We computed a severity-weighted summary score, multiplying the frequency of each violent action by the severity weight for the violent behavior and summing these. Thus, our total score summarized all the violence each man had perpetrated, in the past year, which was not carried out as part of a job requirement and which was not directed against a current or past intimate partner. Given the skewed distribution of generality of violence scores (i.e., most men had engaged in no or little violence), we first log-transformed these scores. We then computed z-scores to standardize the measures.

Psychopathology/Personality Disorder

The third descriptive dimensions in our typology, psychopathology/personality disorder, was measured with the newest version of the *Millon Clinical Multiaxial Inventory-III (MCMI-III; Millon, 1983).* We chose the MCMI, in part, because it is a continuous measure and, in part, to make our typology comparable to those of others, as it is the most commonly used personality disorder measure in previous typologies (e.g., Hamberger et al., 1996; Gottman et al., 1995). The MCMI was administered to male participants only.

Given our typology, we were particularly interested in personality disorder. Thus, for the present analyses, we focused on the 14 personality disorder scales: 3 scales measure severe personality pathology (i.e., schizo-typal, borderline, paranoid) and 11 scales measure clinical personality patterns (i.e., schizoid, avoidant, depressive, dependent, histrionic, narcissistic, anti-social, aggressive/sadistic, compulsive, passive aggressive, and self-defeating).

We needed to reduce the 14 MCMI personality disorder scales to a minimum number of variables for the cluster analysis. To do so, we conducted a generalized least squares factor analysis, with varimax rotation, and exam-ined the rotated factors. Two of the three factors that emerged were consistent with our theory. On the first factor, the two highest and uniquely loading personality disorder scales were antisocial personality disorder (loading of .90) and aggressive/sadistic personality disorder (loading of .89). Thus, we created one *antisocial summary score* by summing a man's scaled scores on these two scales. High scores on this scale reflect that the man self-reported a pattern of disregard for, and violation of, the rights of others (e.g., does not feel remorse, has engaged in aggression and/or criminal behavior). On the second factor, a series of scales loaded most highly and uniquely and above the .60 level; these included the scales of depressive personality (loading of .67), dependent personality (loading of .67), self-defeating personality (load-ing of .63), avoidant personality (loading of .69), and narcissistic personality (loading of – .67). Thus, we created one *dysphoric personality summary score* by summing a man's scaled scores on these scales (with the narcissistic scale reverse-scored). High scores on this scale reflected a man's self-report that he tends to be depressed, feels an excessive need to be taken care of, feels inadequate and sensitive to negative evaluations from others, etc. On the third factor, two scales loaded highly and uniquely-schizoid (loading of .97) and schizotypal personality (loading of .60). Thus, we summed these scales to create a *schizoid scale*. High scores on this scale indicate that a man self-reported detached social relationships, discomfort in close relationships, or perceptual/cognitive distortions and eccentric behavior.

It should be noted that, despite our prediction, the borderline personality disorder scale loaded highly on both of the first two factors and thus was not included in any of the summary scores. The correlations between these three summary scores were as follows: antisocial/dysphoric $r = .29$; antisocial/schizoid $r = .43$; dysphoric/schizoid $r = .61$. Thus, the three summary scores were measuring overlapping yet distinct clusters of personality disorder. Given the distributions of these summary scores, we did not log-transform these variables. However, we did compute z-scores to standardize the mea-sures across variables.

MEASURES OF DISTAL AND PROXIMAL CORRELATES IN THE DEVELOPMENTAL MODEL

In addition, the couples completed measures of theoretically relevant variables (i.e., distal and proximal correlates of violence) outlined previously (e.g., family of origin violence, association with deviant peers, dependency, impulsivity, skills, attitudes). Some of these measures are presented below, under each relevant section of results.

RESULTS

Cluster Analyses

Cluster analysis includes a variety of multivariate statistical procedures used to classify individuals into relative homogeneous groups or "clusters." In the present study, for our cluster analyses, we entered data on the three descriptive dimensions (i.e., CTS2 marital violence in past year; GVQ general violence in past year; 3 MCMI personality disorder summary scores) for the 63 maritally violent men assessed thus far. We conducted a series of cluster analyses, and generally consistent findings emerged across these methods. Thus, we chose to examine further the most representative cluster solution.

This solution emerged from a hierarchical cluster analysis using Ward's linkage (Ward, 1963). This method is one of the most widely used in the social sciences. It is agglomerative; in other words, at the first step of the process, each case is its own cluster, but at each following step, cases (and, later, groups) are joined together to create larger clusters. Cases are joined based on their similarity, with Ward's method designed to optimize the minimum variance within clusters by joining groups or cases that result in the minimum increase in the error sum of squares. Determination of the number of clusters to interpret is basically heuristic but, in this study, was guided both by our theory and an examination of a plot of the agglomeration coefficients (e.g., analogous to the scree test used in factor analysis). (See Aldenderfer & Blashfield, 1984, for a general introduction to cluster analysis procedures).

In the hierarchical cluster analysis using Ward's linkage, the changes in the agglomeration figures suggested that the 3, 4, or 5 cluster solutions would be interpretable. However, the 5 cluster solution was unacceptable as it split a group of five men into two clusters, with two and three men in each. In addition, the 3 cluster solution was unacceptable as one cluster was too large (i.e., composed of 43 of the 63 men) and, in the 4 cluster solution, this cluster split into 2 smaller clusters (i.e., labeled below as the dysphoric and low-level antisocial clusters), with significant differences emerging between these clusters. Thus, we present the 4 cluster solution.

Cluster Differences on the
Three Descriptive Dimensions

We initially examined how the groups differed on the three descriptive dimensions used in the cluster analysis (see Table 3.1).

TABLE 3.1 Three Descriptive Dimensions

Clusters:	Family Only	Dysphoric	Low-Level Antisocial	Generally Violent/ Antisocial	F
Sample Size (N)	15	26	17	5	
MCMI					
Antisocial:	31.0_a	64.9_b	80.6_b	64.7_b	p < .01
Dysphoric:	29.5_a	66.2_b	31.2_a	47.1_a	p < .01
Schizoid:	20.2_a	63.2_b	61.0_b	49.6_b	p < .01
GVQ					
General					
Violence					
past year:	$.01_a$	$.20_a$	$.29_a$	3.4_b	p < .01
CTS2					
Marital Violence,					
past year:	2.0_a	2.9_a	2.1_a	4.3_b	p < .01

NOTE: In this, and all following tables, group means marked with subscripts $_{a, b}$ indicate that this group mean did not differ significantly from either means marked "a" or means marked "b".

Although analyses used transformed and standardized scores, the values presented on the table include original scores so they can be interpreted more easily. On Table 3.1, the GVQ and CTS2 scores presented are the severity-weighted, past year violence scores. The three MCMI scores presented are the base rate score for each summary scale we derived; in other words, as on the individual MCMI personality disorder scales, a score of 75 or above may be regarded as representing clinically judged presence of the personality disorder features. Though the subgroups should differ significantly on these measures as they were used to form the clusters, we did conduct ANOVAs to compare the clusters on each descriptive dimension. ANOVAs were followed by post hoc Tukey's HSD tests, and significant group differences are indicated with subscripts.

Cluster 1 consisted of 15 men. This group clearly resembles our hypothesized family only batterer group. Of the four clusters, they scored the lowest on the three MCMI summary scores, scoring well below the clinical levels on these measures. Thus, they did not evidence personality disorders. Their general violence score indicated that they had engaged in almost no violence outside of their relationship in the past year. Finally, they had engaged in the lowest level of marital violence in the past year.

Cluster 2 consisted of 26 men and closely resembles our hypothesized borderline/dysphoric group; we will call them the *dysphoric* cluster (since the borderline MCMI scale was not included in the MCMI summary scores).

Relative to the family only cluster (and similar to the third cluster), this group had somewhat elevated scores on the antisocial and schizoid summary scores. Relative to the other clusters, they had the highest scores on the dysphoric MCMI summary score. Their levels of general and marital violence in the past year were moderate—higher than cluster 1 but lower than cluster 4.

Cluster 3 consisted of 17 men who resembled the Cluster 2 men on several of the descriptive dimensions. One important exception was their low score on the dysphoric summary score, which was closer to that of family only batterers. Also, they had engaged in slightly less marital violence, again more closely resembling the family only batterers. They differed from the family only batterers in their higher scores on the antisocial scale and their higher levels of general violence. This group was not hypothesized in our proposed typology. We have tentatively labeled this group the low-level antisocial group.

Cluster 4 consisted of only 5 of the violent men assessed to date. Therefore, all group comparisons involving this cluster should be interpreted cautiously. However, this group was unique and closely resembles our proposed *generally violent/antisocial* subtype; therefore, we maintained it as a separate cluster. Men in this group had clinically elevated scores on the antisocial summary score, but nonelevated scores on the other two measures of personality disorder. They had engaged in significantly higher levels of both general and marital violence than the other clusters.

Cluster Differences on Other Descriptive Variables

After forming the clusters, we then compared them on other descriptive measures, conducting a series of analyses of variance followed by post hoc Tukey's HSD tests. Given a lack of control for experiment-wise Type I error, caution should be used in interpreting findings. However, as the study is not yet complete and additional participants will eventually provide more statistical power, we discuss nonsignificant trends.

Demographic Variables

Interestingly, as can be seen in Table 3.2, the clusters did not differ significantly on most of our demographic measures. This is consistent with most previous typologies, in which demographic variables have not differentiated subtypes of batterers from one another (Holtzworth-Munroe & Stuart, 1994).

Husband to Wife Abuse Variables

As can be seen in Table 3.3, the groups differed as predicted on other measures of husband abuse. Specifically, men and women were asked to report on: (1) wife injury resulting from husband violence in the past year,

TABLE 3.2 Husband Demographic Variables

Clusters:	Family Only	Dysphoric	Low-Level Antisocial	Generally Violent/ Antisocial	F
Age (years)	34.33	34.54	35.24	36.00	NS
Education (years)	14.87	13.19	13.29	14.80	NS
Monthly Income ($)	$2,425_{a, b}$	$1,613_a$	$1,727_a$	$2,325*_b$	$p < .01$
Ethnicity					NS
% Caucasian	86.7	65.4	52.9	100	
% African American	6.7	26.9	29.4	—	
% Other	6.7	7.7	17.6	—	
Length of Relationship (years)	10.27	8.49	10.22	9.30	NS
Number of Children	1.07	1.15	1.35	1.00	NS

NOTE: * Outlier dropped.

TABLE 3.3 Husband Abuse Behaviors

Clusters:	Family Only	Dysphoric	Low-Level Antisocial	Generally Violent/ Antisocial	F
CTS2—Wife Injury Scale, past year					
H report	.40	3.00	.29	4.00	$p < .11$
W report	1.07_a	4.81_a	1.24a	14.80_b	$p < .02$
Psychological Maltreatment of Women Inventory					
H report	89.87_a	112.28a	101.11_a	143.20_b	$p < .01$
W report	103.33_a	128.96_a	122.06_a	171.60_b	$p < .01$
CTS2—Sexual Abuse Scale, past year					
H report	4.33	6.04	8.18	1.80	NS
W report	$8.35_{a,b}$	1.73_a	$10.27_{a,b}$	27.00_b	$p < .01$
Sexual Experiences Survey, past year					
H report	1.27	9.15	4.12	7.00	NS
W report	1.00_a*	$8.35_{a,b}$	$5.88_{a,b}$	18.00_b	$p < .03$
Husbands—Report of Violence in Past Intimate Relationships on GVQ	2.00	13.73	10.88	28.40	NS

NOTE: * Outlier dropped.

on the CTS2 (CTS2-Wife Injury Scale-past year); (2) husband's psychological abuse, on the Psychological Maltreatment of Women Inventory (Tolman, 1989); and (3) husband's sexual abuse in the past year, on both the sexual abuse subscale of the CTS2 (CTS2-Sexual Abuse Scale) and the Sexual Experiences Survey (Koss & Oros, 1982). In addition, as noted above, on the GVQ, husbands self-reported their use of violence, as adults, against previous intimate female partners (i.e., ex-wives and ex-girlfriends; Husbands' Report of Violence in Past Intimate Relationships on GVQ). Wives of generally violent/antisocial men suffered the most injuries and experienced the highest levels of psychological abuse and, by wife report, of sexual abuse; generally violent/antisocial men had also engaged in the highest levels of violence in past intimate relationships.

Other Measures of Psychopathology and Behavioral Problems

As can be seen in Table 3.4, participants completed additional measures of psychopathology and behavioral problems related to the three descriptive dimensions, in an attempt to further characterize the subtypes of batterers.

First, men completed two measures designed to capture characteristics hypothesized to be unique to the dysphoric batterer: (1) the Borderline Personality Organization (Oldham, Clarkin, Appelbaum, Carr, Kernberg, Lotterman, & Haas, 1985), this measure has been used by Dutton to study batterers whom we assume are similar to dysphoric/borderline batterers (e.g., Dutton & Starzomski, 1993); and (2) the Modified PostTraumatic Stress Disorder Symptom Scale (PTSD; Falsetti, Resnick, Resick, & Kilpatrick, 1993), which measures PTSD symptoms, in a continuous manner, with 18 items corresponding to DSM-III-R symptom criteria for PTSD. In addition to the predicted elevation of the dysphoric group, the generally violent/ antisocial batterers had the highest scores on these measures.

Second, men completed two measures designed to capture the characteristics that we have proposed would be unique to generally violent/ antisocial batterers: (1) the Hare Psychopathy Self-Report Checklist-Revised (Hare Psychopathy; Hare, 1985); and (2) the Criminality Questionnaire (a measure designed for this study; on it men were asked how often they had engaged in each of a list of delinquent and criminal behaviors). As can be seen in Table 3.4, the groups differed as predicted on these measures, with generally violent/antisocial men scoring the highest of the subgroups.

Third, we included measures of substance use and abuse including: (1) husband and wife reports of husband's drinking problems on the Short Michigan Alcoholism Screening Test (SMAST-alcohol; Selzer, Vinokur, & VanRooijen, 1975); (2) husband and wife report of husband's drug use problems on the Drug Abuse Screening Test (DAST-drug; Skinner, 1982); and (3) husband's self-report of the quantity and frequency of both his

TABLE 3.4 Psychopathology and Behavioral Problems

Clusters:	Family Only	Dysphoric	Low-Level Antisocial	Generally Violent/ Antisocial	F
Borderline Personality Organization	44.31$_a$	70.52$_{b,c}$	53.94$_{a,b}$	72.00$_c$	p < .01
PTSD	2.15$_a$	19.43$_{a,b}$	9.25$_{a,b}$	26.00$_b$	p < .01
Hare Psychopathy	57.00$_a$	65.68$_a$	71.53$_a$	95.33$_b$	p < .01
Criminality Questionnaire					
Adult Crime:	35.31$_a$	81.19$_{a,b}$	74.73$_{a,b}$	132.50$_b$	p < .01
Substance Use/Abuse					
SMAST (Alcohol):					
H report	.64$_a$	3.27$_a$	2.35$_a$	9.50$_b$	p < .01
W report	.62$_a$	2.67$_a$	2.19$_a$	8.25$_b$	p < .01
DAST (Drugs):					
H report	1.86	5.23	3.47	6.33	p < .17
W report	1.86$_a$	4.40$_{a,b}$	2.20$_a$	9.50$_b$	p < .02
QFI:					
Alcohol—H	0.72	2.80	2.88	6.85	NS
Drug—H	0.73	0.93	0.25	4.15	p < .10
General Anger;					
Husband Report					
Buss-Perry Hostility:	12.64$_a$	22.64$_b$	16.82$_{a,b}$	22.75$_b$	p < .01
Passive-Aggressive:	−8.93$_a$	5.75$_a$	−7.60$_a$	8.50$_b$	p < .05
STAXI-Trait:	16.36$_a$	21.18$_{a,b}$	18.82$_{a,b}$	29.50$_b$	p < .01
STAXI-Expression:					
Anger In	16.86	17.45	18.65	18.75	NS
Anger Out	14.50$_a$	18.18$_{a,b}$	15.76$_a$	23.25$_b$	p < .01
Anger Control	24.79$_a$	16.64$_b$	23.65$_a$	15.75$_b$	p < .01
Spouse Specific Anger					
Buss-Perry Hostility:					
H Report	14.36	18.90	14.12	20.67	p < .08
W Report	16.57	22.05	19.38	20.00	NS
Passive-Aggressive:					
H Report	−10.93	−6.33	−7.82	2.00	NS
W Report	−2.57	.76	4.13	11.75	p < .20
STAXI-Trait:					
H Report	15.29$_a$	21.10$_{a,b}$	17.88$_{a,b}$	23.00$_b$	p < .01
W Report	18.43$_a$	23.86$_{a,b}$	23.00$_{a,b}$	27.25$_b$	p < .05

(continued)

TABLE 3.4 (Continued)

Clusters:	Family Only	Dysphoric	Low-Level Antisocial	Generally Violent/ Antisocial	F
STAXI-Expression:					
Anger In					
H Report	10.93	11.71	10.94	12.00	NS
W Report	12.14	12.43	12.19	15.50	NS
Anger Out					
H Report	15.07_a	$17.81_{a,b}$	16.00a	21.33_b	p < .05
W Report	16.71	21.38	19.25	22.50	p < .15
Anger Control					
H Report	25.71_a	$20.48_{a,b}$	25.59a,b	18.67_b	p < .01
W Report	23.14_a	15.52_b	16.38b	16.00_b	p < .05

alcohol use in the past year (Quantity-Frequency Index-Alcohol, or QFI-Alcohol; Cahalan, Cisin, & Crossley, 1969) and drug use in the past year (QFI-Drug; adapted from the QFI-Alcohol Index). As can be seen in Table 3.4, as predicted, the generally violent/antisocial men had the highest levels of substance use and abuse and the family only batterers had the lowest levels.

Finally, we included several measures of both general anger and spouse-specific anger. The measures of general anger included husbands' self-reports on: (1) the Buss-Perry Aggression Questionnaire-Hostility Subscale (Buss-Perry Hostility; Buss & Perry, 1992); (2) a Passive-Aggressive Scale designed for this study by combining items from the Buss-Durkee Hostility Inventory Negativism Subscale (Buss & Durkee, 1957) and the Spouse-Specific Aggression Scale Passive-Aggressive Subscale (Rosenbaum & O'Leary, 1981; SSAS items were modified to make them general, not spouse specific)[Note that negative scores were possible on the Passive-Aggressive measure as we z-scored scores on the Buss & Perry and the Rosenbaum & O'Leary measure scores before summing them]; and (3) Spielberger's Anger Trait and Anger Expression Inventories (STAXI; Spielberger, 1988; the three subscales on the Anger-Expression scales measure keeping anger-in, demonstrating anger [anger-out], and controlling one's anger). As can be seen in Table 3.4, as predicted, the generally violent/antisocial men, and on some measures the dysphoric men also, generally scored the highest on measures of general anger and hostility and lowest on measures of anger control.

We also modified each of these anger measures to specifically assess the husband's anger at his wife. We then asked both husbands and wives to complete these spouse-specific anger measures. As can be seen in Table 3.4, when significant group differences emerged, the groups differed in the predicted manner—the generally violent/antisocial, and on many measures the dysphoric batterers, scored the highest on measures of spouse-specific anger and hostility and lowest on measures of controlling anger at one's spouse.

Cluster Differences on Distal
Correlates of Violence from Model

Our developmental model (Holtzworth-Munroe & Stuart, 1994) proposed that the subtypes of men would differ on three distal/historical correlates of violence: genetic and prenatal loading, family of origin experiences, and association with deviant peers. Thus, we conducted a series of ANOVAs, followed by post hoc Tukey's HSD tests, to compare the clusters on measures of these constructs. The findings are presented in Table 3.5.

Family Background/Genetic Loading

First, to examine family background, and as a very inadequate proxy for genetic factors, we asked men to complete the Child Family Home Environment Scale (CFHES). The CFHES was designed for this study as a retrospective report of a man's parents' antisocial behavior (Parent's Antisocial Behavior; i.e., questions regarding criminal behavior and aggression), substance abuse (Parent's Substance Abuse; i.e., alcohol and drugs), and health problems (Parent's Health Problems; i.e., medical and mental). All questions asked about problems severe enough that they had interfered with the parent's functioning and/or involved outside intervention (e.g., hospitalization, imprisonment). As seen in Table 3.5, as predicted, generally violent/antisocial men were the most likely to report having had parents who engaged in antisocial behavior and substance abuse. While not predicted, dysphoric men were the most likely to report having had mothers with health problems (both mental and physical).

Family-of-Origin Home Environment

Second, to measure family-of-origin home environment, with a focus on exposure to violence and parental rejection, men in the study completed the following measures: (1) the Egna Minnen Betraffande Uppfostran (EMBU; Perris, Jacobson, Lindstrom, von Knorring, & Perris, 1980; this scale assesses memories of parental behavior in the participant's childhood; it was developed in Sweden and has been used by Dutton in his research on batterers); (2) the Family-of-Origin Violence Questionnaire (designed for this study; items assessing interparent violence were taken from the CTS2; items assessing parent-to-child violence were taken from the Parent-Child Conflict Tactics Scales; Straus, Hamby, Finkelhor, & Runyan, 1995); and (3) the Childhood Sexual Abuse Questionnaire (designed for this study by borrowing

TABLE 3.5 Distal Correlates

Clusters:	Family Only	Dysphoric	Low-Level Antisocial	Generally Violent/ Antisocial	F

Family Background
(Genetic Loading: Child Family Home Environment Scale)

Parent's Antisocial Behavior (Criminal/Legal Problems and Physical Fights)

	Family Only	Dysphoric	Low-Level Antisocial	Generally Violent/ Antisocial	F
Dad	4.71	5.90	5.71	6.75	NS
Mom	4.14	4.57	4.53	6.00	NS
Total	4.93	7.24	6.94	12.75	p < .16

Parent's Substance Abuse (Drinking Problem and Drug Abuse)

Dad	2.50	3.14	2.94	3.50	NS
Mom	2.07	2.52	2.47	4.00	NS
Total	2.57	4.38	4.12	9.50	p < .17

Parent's Health Problems (Medical and Mental)

Dad	2.93	3.62	2.76	2.75	NS
Mom	2.50	3.52	2.06	2.50	p < .02
Total	4.57	6.86	2.82	3.25	p < .15

Family Background/Violence

EMBU

Mother—warmth	70.93	70.70	68.76	72.00	NS
—rejection	42.07	49.50	46.19	54.00	NS
Father —warmth	68.93	66.50	55.13	45.33	p < .07
—rejection	36.29_a	47.30a	45.88_a	74.50_b	p < .02

Family of Origin Violence

# of Mom-Dad violent incidents	2.43	2.38	2.35	6.33	NS
# of Parent-Subject violent incidents	10.62	11.81	12.00	21.67	p < .12

Childhood Sexual Abuse Questionnaire

	.04	.75 (Outlier included)	.18	0	NS

Association with Deviant Peers

Delinquent Friends Questionnaire

Before Age 15	19.60	19.89	14.07	13.00	NS
Ages 15-18	25.25	43.17	31.33	101.50	p < .07
Adult	6.00_a	38.43a	25.92_a	125.50_b	p < .01

the four items from the sexual abuse scale of the Parent-Child Conflict Tactics Scales; Straus et al., 1995). As seen in Table 3.5, while most of the findings were not statistically significant, they were in the predicted direction. Generally violent/antisocial men came from the most violent homes (both interparent violence and parent-to-child violence) and experienced the most parental rejection and least parental warmth, although this finding was limited to fathers. In contrast, but consistent with the notion of an abusive and traumatic childhood (Dutton, 1995), dysphoric batterers reported experiencing the highest levels of childhood sexual abuse.

Association With Deviant Peers

Third, to measure associations with deviant peers, men completed a measure designed for this study—the Delinquent Friends Questionnaire. On this measure, a variety of delinquent and criminal behaviors were listed. For each age period (i.e., before age 15, ages 15 to 18, and after age 18), men responded to two questions about each delinquent behavior listed—how many of his friends engaged in the behavior, and how often his friends engaged in the behavior. These two responses were multiplied and summed to form a rough index of amount of involvement in deviant/criminal behavior among the man's peers. As can be seen in Table 3.5, as predicted, men in the generally violent/antisocial group had the greatest levels of association with deviant peers; however, this group difference only emerged after the age of 15.

Cluster Differences on Proximal
Correlates of Violence From Model

Our developmental model (Holtzworth-Munroe & Stuart, 1994) also proposed that the subtypes of men would differ on proximal correlates of violence: attachment/dependency, impulsivity, marital and nonmarital social skills, and attitudes (both hostile attitudes toward women and attitudes supportive of violence). Again, we conducted a series of ANOVAs, followed by post hoc Tukey's HSD tests, to compare the clusters on measures of these constructs.

Attachment/Dependency

Men completed the following measures of these constructs: (1) the Spouse-Specific Dependency Scale (Rathus & O'Leary, 1997; it measures the extent to which a person is dependent on his/her spouse); (2) the Revised Rejection Sensitivity Questionnaire (RRSQ; the RSQ was used by Downey & Feldman, 1996, to measure rejection sensitivity of dating men; we modified it to make it appropriate for married men); (3) the Interpersonal Jealousy Scale (Mathes & Severa, 1981); and (4) the Relationship Styles Questionnaire

TABLE 3.6 Proximal Correlates: Attachment/Dependency (All-Husband Report)

Clusters:	Family Only	Dysphoric	Low-Level Antisocial	Generally Violent/ Antisocial	F
Spouse Specific Dependency Scale	$109.14_{a,b}$	$124.73a$	106.25_b	$111.00_{a,b}$	p < .04
Rejection Sensitivity Questionnaire	141.44	181.27	158.46	138.00	NS
Interpersonal Jealousy Scale	$111.14_{a,}$	138.38_b	$123.29a,b$	$130.25_{a,b}$	p < .01
Relationship Styles Questionnaire					
Secure:	25.54_b	$20.59a$	$21.76_{a,b}$	25.25_b	p < .01
Dismissing:	$18.36_{a,b}$	$23.32a,b$	24.65_b	$20.50_{a,b}$	p < .01
Fearful:	19.64_a	26.91_b	$23.76a,b$	28.33_b	p < .05
Preoccupied:	$20.43_{a,b}$	$26.09_{b, c}$	$18.47a$	28.25_c	p < .01

(Bartholomew & Horowitz, 1991; it measures attachment in romantic relationships). As can be seen in Table 3.6, the findings on these measures were generally consistent with predictions, although not all were statistically significant. Relative to the other subtypes, the dysphoric group scored the highest on the SSDS, the RRSQ, and the IJS. In addition, examining just the dysphoric batterers, they received their highest RSQ scores on the subscales of preoccupied and fearful attachment; however, the generally violent/ antisocial men actually scored the highest on these subscales.

Impulsivity

We have gathered behavioral measures of impulsivity but have not yet analyzed these data. However, we do have data available from a self-report measure of impulsivity—the Barratt Impulsivity Scale (Barratt, 1985); we

TABLE 3.7 Proximal Correlates: Impulsivity

Clusters:	Family Only	Dysphoric	Low-Level Antisocial	Generally Violent/ Antisocial	F
Barratt Impulsivity Scale					
H report	45.08	60.71	56.86	66.67	p < .06
W report	48.50_a	$68.67_{a,b}$	$65.20a,b$	72.00_b	p < .03

TABLE 3.8 Proximal Correlates: Marital Skills

Clusters:	Family Only	Dysphoric	Low-Level Antisocial	Generally Violent/ Antisocial	F
Response Incompetency in Hypothetical Marital Situations (high=incompetent)					
H report	25.07	29.05	28.41	32.00	$p < .08$
W report	27.85	30.68	31.82	33.50	$p < .13$
Wife Negative Intentions Questionnaire					
H report	2.37	2.82	2.29	2.99	$p < .17$

asked both husbands and wives to report on husband impulsivity. As can be seen in Table 3.7, and as predicted, the generally violent/antisocial men scored highest on this measure.

Skills

Our measures of social skills in nonmarital situations are not yet ready for analysis. In addition, direct observational measures of marital skills (i.e., coding of videotaped marital problem discussions) are not yet ready. However, we do have initial data on the men's skills in marital conflicts. Specifically, as in our past research (Holtzworth-Munroe & Anglin, 1991; Anglin & Holtzworth-Munroe, 1997), we presented men with 10 hypothetical marital conflict vignettes and asked them what they would say or do in each; these responses were coded for competency level (from 1= competent to 4 = incompetent). In the present study, we also presented the situations to wives and asked them what their husbands would do in each situation. Husband competency was then coded based on both self and partner reports (Response Incompetency in Hypothetical Marital Situations). We also asked men to complete the Negative Intentions Questionnaire (Holtzworth-Munroe & Hutchinson, 1993; Wife Negative Intentions Questionnaire), which measures a husband's attributions of negative intent to his wife following a negative wife behavior, as presented in the hypothetical marital conflicts. As can be seen in Table 3.8, and as predicted, the generally violent/antisocial men provided the most incompetent responses, while both this group and the dysphoric batterers attributed the most negative intent to their wives.

Attitudes

We included measures of both hostile attitudes toward women and attitudes supportive of violence. To measure the first construct, men self-reported

TABLE 3.9 Proximal Correlates: Attitudes

Clusters:	Family Only	Dysphoric	Low-Level Antisocial	Generally Violent/ Antisocial	F
Hostility Towards Women Scale (low score=hostility)					
H Report	165.46$_a$	129.84b	153.11a,b	138.33$_{a,b}$	p < .01
W Report	146.57$_a$	129.68$_{a,b}$	126.40a,b	103.75$_b$	p < .04
Attitudes Toward Violence					
Acceptance of Interpersonal Violence (low score=acceptance)					
H Report	37.64	32.67	32.88	35.50	p < .06
Acceptance of Violence Questionnaire (Male to Female Aggression)					
Acceptance of Aggression					
H Report	1.71	2.90	2.71	4.67	NS
W Report	1.39$_a$	5.95$_{a,b}$	4.63$_{a,b}$	11.00$_b$	p < .02
Aggression is Justified					
H Report	.57	1.10	.82	1.00	NS
W Report	1.57	3.24	2.13	4.25	NS
Aggression Solves Problems					
H Report	.14	.62	1.18	2.33	p < .07
W Report	.23$_a$	2.29$_{a,b}$	1.25a,b	4.00$_b$	p < .03
Aggression: Is it Violence? (low score=minimization)					
H Report	11.00	10.81	11.29	10.67	NS
W Report	9.57$_{a,b}$	8.38$_a$	8.00a,b	4.25$_b$	p < .06

their attitudes, and wives reported what they believed their husband's attitudes to be, on the Hostility Towards Women Scale (Check, Malamuth, Elias, & Barton, 1985). As can be seen in Table 3.9, and as predicted, generally violent men and dysphoric batterers had the most hostile attitudes toward women.

To measure attitudes supportive of violence, men completed two measures regarding their own attitudes: (1) the Acceptance of Interpersonal Violence (Burt, 1980); and (2) the Acceptance of Violence Questionnaire (Riggs & O'Leary, 1996; subscales assess the acceptability of violence, whether aggression is viewed as justified, whether aggression is believed to solve problems, and whether aggression is labeled as violence, as presented in a series of hypothetical descriptions of a man using various forms of physical aggression against his female partner). In addition, wives reported husband attitudes on the AVQ. As can be seen in Table 3.9, and as predicted, on most measures, generally violent/antisocial men had attitudes which were the most supportive of violence.

SUMMARY AND DISCUSSION

Based on a review of previous batterer typologies and our developmental model of husband violence, Holtzworth-Munroe and Stuart (1994) proposed that three batterer subgroups would emerge in research examining three descriptive dimensions (i.e., severity of marital violence, generality of violence, psychopathology/personality disorder). We also proposed that these groups would differ on measures of distal/historical correlates (i.e., genetic/prenatal loading, family-of-origin violence, deviant peer association) and proximal correlates (i.e., attachment, impulsivity, social skills, attitudes) of husband violence.

In the present study, these three groups did emerge along with one additional subgroup, which is discussed later. The three predicted clusters of maritally violent men generally differed as predicted on the three descriptive dimension. family only batterers engaged in the least marital violence, had engaged in almost no general violence, and did not evidence personality disorder; dysphoric men engaged in intermediate levels of marital and general violence and had the highest scores on the dysphoric MCMI summary scale; and generally violent/antisocial men had engaged in the highest levels of marital violence, the most general violence, and scored the highest on the MCMI antisocial summary scale. These groups also generally differed as predicted on related measures of psychopathology and behavior problems. Specifically, generally violent/antisocial men reported the highest levels of involvement in criminal activity, substance use/abuse, psychopathy, and general anger; the dysphoric group had intermediate scores on these measures, while the family only batterers had the lowest scores on these measures. In addition, both the generally violent/antisocial and the dysphoric batterers reported the highest levels of spouse-specific anger. The one exception to our predictions was that both the dysphoric and the generally violent/antisocial groups had the highest scores on the measures of borderline personality and traumatic stress. In retrospect, these findings make sense. First, impulsivity is reflected on measures of both antisocial and borderline personality, so that generally violent/antisocial men may also report impulsive, borderline type behaviors. Second, given the high levels of violence experienced, both in childhood and as adults, by the generally violent/antisocial men, it is not surprising that they report symptoms of PTSD.

In addition, the three groups generally differed as predicted on the distal/historical correlates of violence presented in our developmental model of violence. Generally violent/antisocial men reported having the parents with the highest levels of problems involving criminal behavior, aggression, and substance abuse, having experienced the greatest levels of family-of-origin violence, and (since the age of 15) having the most association with deviant peers. Consistent with trauma theories for the dysphoric group, this group reported the highest levels of sexual abuse as a child, and also reported having mothers with the highest levels of health (including mental health) problems. As predicted, family only batterers scored the lowest on all measures of distal correlates.

Finally, the three groups generally differed as predicted on the proximal correlates of violence presented in our developmental model of violence. Dysphoric men tended to have the most problems with attachment-related issues (e.g., jealousy, spouse dependency, rejection sensitivity). Generally violent/antisocial men were the most impulsive. Generally violent/antisocial men also had the lowest response competency in marital situations. In a manner consistent with our predictions, both the generally violent/antisocial group and the dysphoric group reported the highest levels of hostile attitudes toward women and were the most likely to attribute negative intent to their wife's actions. Generally violent/antisocial men reported the most accepting attitudes toward violence. Again, as predicted, the family only batterers scored the lowest on measures of proximal correlates of violence.

As noted above, an unexpected fourth cluster emerged, which we labeled the "low-level antisocial group," given their somewhat elevated score on the MCMI antisocial summary scale and their moderate levels of marital and general violence. On most measures, this group fell intermediate to the family only batterers and the generally violent/antisocial men. On most measures, family only batterers had the lowest scores, the unpredicted cluster had intermediate scores, and the generally violent/antisocial men had the highest scores. Thus, it is possible to conceptualize these three groups as falling along a continuum—family only batterers had the fewest risk factors for violence and reported the lowest levels of violence and psychopathology, while generally violent/antisocial men had the highest levels, and the new cluster had intermediate levels. If these same groups emerge in our final analyses using the full study sample, we will use statistical analyses to examine these dimensions as continuous variables. In other words, these three clusters may perhaps be best conceptualized as falling along a continuum of antisociality rather than as being distinct groups.

In contrast, the dysphoric group cannot be easily placed along this continuum. It is true that this group falls intermediate to the family only and the generally violent/antisocial group on many measures and resembles the new, low-level antisocial group on many measures. However, this group also scored high on a set of variables that cluster in a theoretically coherent manner. Specifically, the dysphoric group scored highest on the MCMI dysphoric summary score. They also reported the highest levels of childhood sexual abuse. They scored highest on measures of dependency, jealousy, and sensitivity to rejection. They resembled the generally violent/antisocial men in their high scores on measures of spouse-specific anger, attribution of negative intentions to their wives, and hostile attitudes toward women. Thus, as predicted, these men appear to have particular problems with dysphoria, attachment, and hostility toward their partners. In this sense they may form a distinct group that does not fall along a continuum with the other three groups. However, it is also possible that all four clusters could be adequately described if we placed men along two major dimensions (i.e., antisociality and dysphoria) rather than one (i.e., antisociality). Again, exploratory analyses using dimensions rather than clusters will be conducted on the final study sample.

At this point, we plan to finish the present study, repeating the steps presented above with a final, larger sample of maritally violent men. As noted above, we also plan to use statistical approaches that allow us to examine the data in a continuous manner, to examine the relative utility of a dimensional versus categorical approach to understanding the difference among violent husbands. We will compare the subtypes that emerge to the nonviolent comparison samples. These comparisons are especially important to help us to differentiate what uniquely characterizes family only batterers. Relative to the other subtypes, family only batterers look quite "normal," being low on risk factors and measures of psychopathology and behavior problems. Thus, it is important to understand how they differ from men who are not violent toward their wives, particularly men who are unhappy with their marriages but do not use violence. Finally, we have just begun reassessing violent couples 18 months after their initial participation in the study. Doing so will allow us to examine the stability of our time-one typology.

A methodological issue emerging from the data involves the sometimes large differences found between husband and wife reports of the husbands' behaviors, attitudes, and feelings. In many cases, this study represents the first time that wife reports have been gathered on these variables (e.g., husband's spouse-specific anger, impulsivity, competence in hypothetical marital conflict situations, and attitudes toward women and violence). Of course, when differences exist, we do not know which report is accurate; this is particularly the case for wife reports of husbands' feelings and attitudes. Nonetheless, such discrepancies raise questions about the accuracy of using only one spouse's report (e.g., only violent husbands' self-reports) in future research and in clinical settings.

Implications for Research

The present findings have several other implications for future research. First, prospective, longitudinal studies are needed to better identify the developmental pathways resulting in different subtypes of violent husbands. While many of the hypothesized differences between batterer subtypes were confirmed in the present study, these data are cross-sectional and some of the measures involved retrospective reports that may not be accurate. Thus, these findings, while consistent with our developmental model of husband violence, cannot be used to verify our model. Future longitudinal studies should be conducted, examining constructs assumed to predict the use of violence (e.g., the correlates in our model) among young adolescents or children and then observing the relationship between these variables and the emergence of relationship violence as study participants enter intimate relationships. Such research might also have practical implications. Ideally, if differential predictors of violent subtypes can be identified, then early prevention programs could be uniquely designed for each subtype of violence. For example, young men who are at risk to become generally violent/antisocial adults may need intensive interventions designed to improve their home environment, decrease their involvement with deviant peers, and prevent their entry into delinquent and criminal behavior. In contrast, youths who are at risk to become family only violent men may require less intensive interventions; they might benefit from early interventions building relationship skills.

Second, future researchers should examine how various subtypes of violent men respond to different treatment programs. At this point in time, the overall effectiveness of batterers' treatment is not impressive (Rosenfeld, 1992). It has been suggested that this overall lack of effect may be due to the fact that therapists do not match interventions to batterer subtypes (Stuart & Holtzworth-Munroe, 1995). However, one recent study offers hope that treatment efficacy might be improved by batterer-treatment matching. In a post hoc analysis of data from a study comparing traditional cognitive-behavioral-feminist treatment to a new process-psychodynamic treatment designed to help men examine the traumas they have experienced in their lives, Saunders (1996) found that batterers who scored high on an antisocial measure did better in the structured cognitive-behavioral intervention, while batterers who scored high on a measure of dependency did better in the new process-psychodynamic intervention. These findings suggest that matching batterer subtypes to treatments might increase our overall ability to help men end their use of violence against their partners.

Finally, we believe that our research, along with the previous typology research, makes it increasingly clear that researchers must begin to consider subtypes in their studies of violent husbands. It may no longer be adequate to conduct studies comparing violent and nonviolent men; instead, future researchers should identify subtypes of batterers and then compare them to each other and to nonviolent comparison groups on variables of theoretical interest.

REFERENCES

Aldenderfer, M. S., & Blashfield, R. K. (1984). *Cluster analysis* (University paper series on Quantitative Applications in the Social Sciehces). Newbury Park: Sage.

Anglin, K., & Holtzworth-Munroe, A. (1997). Comparing the responses of violent and nonviolent couples to problematic marital and nonmarital situations: Are the skill deficits of violent couples global? *Journal of Family Psychology, 11,* 301-313.

Barratt, E. S. (1985). Impulsiveness subtraits: Arousal and information processing. In
J. T. Spence & C. E. Itard (Eds.), *Motivation, emotion, and personality* (pp. 137-146).
North Holland: Elsevier.

Bartholomew, K., & Horowitz, L. M. (1991). Attachment styles among young adults: A
test of a four-category model. *Journal of Personality and Social Psychology, 61,*
226-244.

Burt, M. R. (1980). Cultural myths and supports for rape. *Journal of Personality and
Social Psychology, 38,* 217-230.

Buss, A. H., & Durkee, A. (1957). An inventory for assessing different kinds of hostility.
Journal of Consulting Psychology, 21, 343-349.

Buss, A. H., & Perry, M. (1992). The aggression questionnaire. *Journal of Personality
and Social Psychology, 63,*452-459.

Cahalan, D., Cisin, I. H., & Crossley, H. M. (1969). *American drinking practices: A
national study of drinking behavior and attitudes.* New Brunswick, NJ: Rutgers
Center of Alcohol Studies.

Check, J. V. P., Malamuth, N. M., Elias, B., & Barton, S. A. (1985, April). On hostile
ground. *Psychology Today,* 56-61.

Downey, G., & Feldman, S. (1996). Implications of rejection sensitivity for intimate
relationships. *Journal of Personality and Social Psychology, 70,* 1327-1343.

Dutton, D. G. (1995). Intimate abusiveness. *Clinical Psychology: Science and Practice,2,* 207-224.

Dutton, D. G., & Starzomski, A. J. (1993). Borderline personality in perpetrators of
psychological and physical abuse. *Violence and Victims, 8,* 327-337.

Falsetti, S. A., Resnick, H. S., Resick, P. A., & Kilpatrick, D. G. (1993). The modified
PTSD symptom scale: A brief self-report measure of posttraumatic stress disorder.
Behavior Therapist, 161-162.

Gottman, J. M., Jacobson, N. S., Rushe, R. H., Shortt, J. W., Babcock, J., LaTaillade,
J. J., & Waltz, J. (1995). The relationship between heart rate reactivity, emotionally
aggressive behavior and general violence in batterers. *Journal of Family Psychology,
9,* 227-248.

Hamberger, L. K., Lohr, J. M., Bonge, D., & Tolin, D. F. (1996). A large sample empirical
typology of male spouse abusers and its relationship to dimensions of abuse. *Violence
and Victims, 11,* 277-292.

Hare, R. D. (1985). Comparison of procedures for the assessment of psychopathy.
Journal of Consulting and Clinical Psychology, 53, 7-16.

Holtzworth-Munroe, A., & Anglin, K. (1991). The competency of responses given by
maritally violent versus nonviolent men to problematic marital situations. *Violence
and Victims, 6,* 257-269.

Holtzworth-Munroe, A., & Hutchinson, G. (1993). Attributing negative intent to wife
behavior: The attributions of maritally violent versus nonviolent men. *Journal of
Abnormal Psychology, 102,* 206-211.

Holtzworth-Munroe, A., Smutzler, N., & Sandin, E. (1997). A brief review of the
research on husband violence. Part II: The psychological effects of husband violence on battered women and their children. *Aggression and Violent Behavior, 2,*
179-213.

Holtzworth-Munroe, A., & Stuart, G. L. (1994). Typologies of male batterers: Three
subtypes and the differences among them. *Psychological Bulletin, 116,* 476-497.

Koss, M. P., & Oros, C. J. (1982). Sexual Experiences Survey: A research instrument investigating sexual aggression and victimization. *Journal of Consulting and Clinical Psychology, 50,* 455-457.

Locke, H. J., & Wallace, K. M. (1959). Short marital adjustment and prediction tests: Their reliability and validity. *Marriage and Family Living, 21,* 251-255.

Mathes, E. W., & Severa, N. (1981). Jealousy, romantic love, and liking: Theoretical considerations and preliminary scale development. *Psychological Reports, 49,* 23-31.

Millon, T. (1983). *Millon Clinical Multiaxial Inventory Manual.* Minneapolis, MN: Interpretive Scoring Systems.

Oldham, J., Clarkin, J., Appelbaum, J., Carr, A., Kernberg, P., Lotterman, A., & Haas, G. (1985). A self-report instrument for borderline personality organization. *The Borderline: Current Empirical Research* (pp. 3-18). Los Angeles: American Psychiatric Association.

Perris, C., Jacobsson, L., Lindstrom, H., von Knorring, L., & Perris, H. (1980). Development of a new inventory for assessing memories of parental rearing behavior. *Acta Psychiatrica Scandinavica, 61,* 265-274.

Rathus, J. H., & O'Leary, K. D. (1997). Spouse-Specific Dependency Scale: Scale development. *Journal of Family Violence, 12,* 159-168.

Riggs, D. S., & O'Leary, K. D. (1996). Aggression between heterosexual dating partners. *Journal of Interpersonal Violence, 11,* 519-540.

Rosenbaum, A., & O'Leary, K. D. (1981). Marital violence: Characteristics of abusive couples. *Journal of Consulting and Clinical Psychology, 49,* 63-71.

Rosenfeld, B. D. (1992). Court-ordered treatment of spouse abuse. *Clinical Psychology Review, 12,* 205-226.

Saunders, D. G. (1996). Feminist-cognitive-behavioral and process-psychodynamic treatments for men who batter: Interactions of abuser traits and treatment model. *Violence and Victims, 4,* 393-414.

Selzer, M. L., Vinokur, A., & VanRooijen, L. (1975). A self-administered Short Michigan Alcoholism Screening Test (SMAST). *Journal of Studies on Alcohol, 36,* 117-126.

Skinner, H. A. (1982). The Drug Abuse Screening Test. *Addictive Behaviors, 7,* 363-371.

Spielberger, C. D. (1988). *Manual for the State-Trait Anger Expression Inventory.* Odessa, FL: Psychological Assessment Resources.

Straus, M. A. (1979). Measuring intrafamily conflict and violence: The Conflict Tactics (CT) Scales. *Journal of Marriage and the Family, 41,* 75-87.

Straus, M. A., & Gelles, R .J. (1990). Societal change and change in family violence from 1975 to 1985 as revealed by two national surveys. In M. A. Straus & R. J. Gelles (Eds.), *Physical violence in American families: Risk factors and adaptations to violence in 8,145 families* (pp. 113-131). New Brunswick, NJ: Transaction Publishers.

Straus, M. A., Hamby, S. L., Boney-McCoy, S., & Sugarman, D. B. (1996). The Revised Conflict Tactics Scales (CTS2): Development and preliminary psychometric data. *Journal of Family Issues, 17,* 283-316.

Straus, M. A., Hamby, S. L., Finkelhor, D., & Runyan, D. (1995). *The Parent-Child Conflict Tactics Scales (PCCTS), Form A.* Durham, NH: Family Research Laboratory, University of New Hampshire.

Stuart, G. L., & Holtzworth-Munroe, A. (1995). Identifying subtypes of maritally violent men: Descriptive dimensions, correlates, and causes of violence, and treatment implications. In S. M. Stith & M. A. Straus (Eds.), *Understanding partner violence: Prevalence, causes, consequences, and solutions* (pp. 162-172). Minneapolis, MN: National Council on Family Relations.

Tolman, R. M. (1989). The development of a measure of psychological maltreatment of women by their male partners. *Violence and Victims, 4,* 159-177.

Ward, J. (1963). Hierarchical grouping to optimize an objective function. *Journal of the American Statistical Association, 58,* 236-244.

4

Limitations of Social Learning Models in Explaining Intimate Aggression

Donald G. Dutton

This chapter examines violence in intimate relationships and analyzes how well social learning theory can account for its key aspects. It discusses the personality features and phasic behavior patterns of spousal batterers, and proposes a triad of traumatic childhood experiences that can lead to an abusive personality. This analysis leads to the conclusion that a trauma model is superior to a social learning theory approach in its ability to account for the features of spousal abusiveness.

In recent decades, social learning models of aggression have enjoyed great prominence in social psychology. All contemporary social psychology texts emphasize the acquisition of aggressive habits or their elicitation through violent cues or media influences (for example, see Baron & Byrne, 1994). The extensive research of Bandura and his colleagues in developing this model has provided a counterpoint to earlier theories of aggression that stressed drives or instincts. In contrast to classical learning theory, social learning models focus on observation as a major factor in the acquisition of aggressive habits (Bandura, 1979). They also stress the cues or instigators that trigger violence and the regulators of violence, including self-reward and self-punishment (such as conscience and the ability to empathize with the victim).

In a social learning theory analysis, aggression is conceptualized as an active response to an "aversive stimulus," in a similar category as assertiveness or achievement. Aggression may follow from a cognitive appraisal that assesses the aversive stimulus as controllable (Bandura, 1979). The differential categorization of aggressive responses versus more passive responses to aversive life events is demonstrated in the social-learning tree-diagram adapted from Turner, Fenn, and Cole (1981). See Figure 4.1.

Social learning theory tends to focus on behavior and on rational cognitive processes, which direct the assessment of controllability and provide mental models of behavioral "solutions" and their imagined consequences. Therefore, it also focuses on social information processing patterns and their acquisition. For example, Dodge, Petit, Bates, and Valente (1995) found that children exposed to physical abuse trauma prior to kindergarten demonstrated externalizing (acting out of aggression), which was mediated by social information processing. Accessing of aggressive mental responses, evaluations of aggressive outcomes, and "hostile attributional biases" (blaming the victim of the subsequent aggression for "causing" the problem) were all found to be sequelae of physical abuse, and also to be predictors of acting out.

When family violence became a focus of social science in the 1970s, social learning analyses were applied to the process that was described as the "intergenerational transmission" of violence (Dutton, 1980, 1988, 1995b; O'Leary, 1988), but with mixed results. On one hand, social learning models for treatment were developed by Ganley (1981), and they fulfilled a need for court-mandated treatment having an orientation toward personal responsibility that was consonant with the criminal justice system's philosophy (see Dutton, 1988, 1995a). On the other hand, social learning predictions about the increased risk for use of violence, given exposure to violence in the family of origin, were only partially confirmed.

For instance, Kalmuss (1984) reviewed studies on the effects of observed parental violence and found that having witnessed parental violence was related to use of violence against one's spouse. Specifically, when parental violence had been observed, the odds of committing spousal violence as an adult doubled. However, no effect for *sex-specific* modeling of violence was found. Exposure to fathers hitting mothers increased the likelihood of spousal aggression by both sexes in the next generation. Moreover, the probability of severe aggression such as punching only increased from 1% if no parental hitting was observed, to 6% if it was observed. Put somewhat differently, the real positive rate (observation associated with severe aggression) was about $1/_{16}$ or a ratio of 6:94 of the false positive rate (observation but no severe aggression).

Kalmuss (1984) did not analyze the effects of exposure to mothers hitting fathers in cases where aggression was not mutual. In her sample of respondents who had witnessed parental violence, only 19% of the cases involved

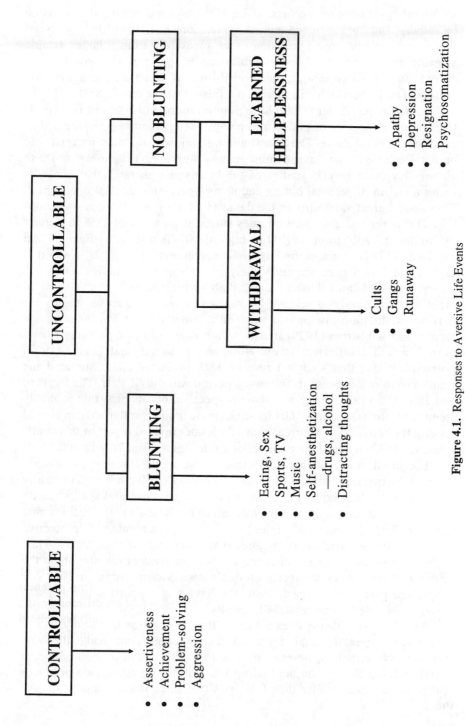

Figure 4.1. Responses to Aversive Life Events

unilateral aggression by mothers, while 45% involved unilateral aggression by fathers, and 36% included mutual aggression. Kalmuss (1984) analyzed this sample of observed-aggression cases separately from a larger sample where both witnessing of and victimization by parental violence had occurred. In the latter sample, the probability of using severe aggression increased to 12%, which still indicated a false positive rate of 88%.

Kaufman and Zigler (1993) have pointed to the huge rate of false positives found in research on children who witnessed parental aggression and/or experienced child abuse. The overwhelming majority of children exposed to parental hitting do not later exhibit spousal aggression themselves. These authors reviewed several studies of the "transmission rate" that connects being a victim of parental hitting and using aggression against one's child. They found great variability in the data, which they attributed to methodological differences. Transmission rates varied from a low of 18% in a study by Hunter and Kihlstrom (1979) to a high of 70% in a study by Egeland and Jacobvitz (1984). A major finding of Kaufman and Zigler (1993) was that high transmission rates are most likely in retrospective studies (i.e., ones where identified child abusers are asked about their history of abusive treatment by their family of origin). In contrast, when prospective studies are performed, the transmission rate obtained is usually lower. For instance, the Hunter and Kihlstrom (1979) study—which examined 282 parents of newborns—was a prospective study. However, Kaufman and Zigler (1993) pointed out that that study's figure of 18% probably underestimated the transmission rate because its follow-up period was only 1 year. The Egeland and Jacobvitz (1984) study was also prospective, but its high rate probably stemmed from its sample—160 high-risk single mothersand from using broad criteria for both past and current abuse. In a later revised report of this study, Egeland (1993) reduced the transmission rate figure from 70% to 40%.

The implications of these findings for the social learning process are twofold: Witnessing parental violence is a risk factor for subsequent family aggression, but the majority of those who do witness parental aggression do not become spouse abusers nor child abusers. Based on the studies that they reviewed, Kaufman and Zigler (1993) reported a number of "protective factors" that prevented intergenerational transmission of child abuse. They included more extensive social support, fewer ambivalent feelings about the birth of the child, better recall of one's own victimization, having one supportive parent in the past, currently having a supportive partner, and currently having fewer stressful life events.

Social learning theory does not argue that observation is the only way of acquiring an aggressive habit, for trial and error learning can lead to the same response. Nevertheless, observational learning has been a cornerstone of social learning theory, and the finding that witnessing aggression produces real positive rates smaller than false positive rates is problematic for the theory.

Dutton (1994, 1995a, 1995b, 1998, in press) has pointed out another problem with the social learning theory analysis of intimate aggression—in its behavioral focus, it has overlooked many of the personality features which sustain intimate aggression and which seem to be acquired through exposure to abusive families of origin. These personality features, such as attributional tendencies to externalize blame and disproportionate emotional reactions to perceived abandonment, are internal events that are not visible for modeling, and therefore they must be acquired by other means. Because they are among the long-term consequences of exposure to trauma, Dutton (1995b, in press) argued that the "abusive personality" was formed as a long-term response to early trauma. He posited that this childhood trauma involves a combination of three aspects—witnessing physical abuse of a parent (as discussed above) and two aspects that are discussed later: being shamed and having insecure attachment so that soothing was not possible.

A key implication of a trauma model for social learning theories of aggression is that aggression may sometimes occur in response to events that are uncontrollable and unbluntable. This form of aggression may not have the rational appraisal characteristics expected by social learning theory. That is, it may occur under extreme arousal states where appraisal is skewed. The arousal in turn stems from earlier traumatic experiences which undermined the person's ability to modulate arousal or soothe oneself. The result is a form of "irrational aggression" that is generated more by internal cues than by cognitive appraisal of external events. The aggression described by social learning analysis is instrumental in character, whereas that described by trauma theory is more impulsive.

PERSONALITY FEATURES
OF INTIMATE ABUSERS

Men who exhibit features of the abusive personality tend to demonstrate cyclical abuse corresponding to the phasic nature of their personalities (cf. Walker, 1979). The first of these phases is a *tension building phase* (Dutton, 1998), during which the perpetrator's perceptions come to resemble what Baumeister (1990) calls deconstructed thinking—a form of "tunnel vision" that departs from normal associative cognition and is concrete and simplistic in form. In the original report of this phenomenon (Walker 1979), female respondents who were partners of batterers described a tension-building phase characterized by the man's emotional withdrawal, escalating verbal and emotional abuse, increasing demands that served to isolate the woman, and "gaslighting" or constant attempts to undermine her reality testing. The woman's response was to attempt to nurture or calm the man, to keep things quiet and orderly around the house, and to keep the kids on their best behavior. Many battered women described this as "walking on eggshells." See Figure 4.2.

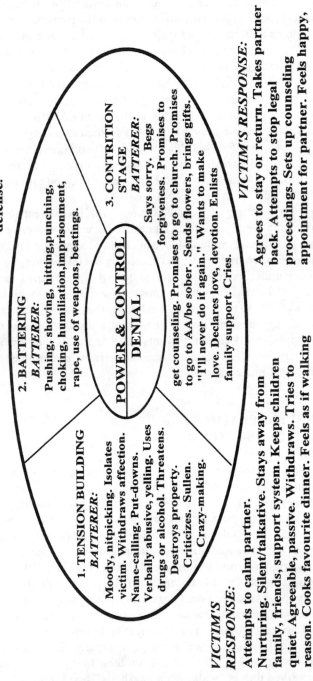

VICTIM'S RESPONSE: Protects self any way possible. Police called by friend, children, neighbour. Tries to calm partner. Leaves. Practices self-defense.

2. BATTERING
BATTERER:
Pushing, shoving, hitting, punching, choking, humiliation, imprisonment, rape, use of weapons, beatings.

3. CONTRITION STAGE
BATTERER:
Says sorry. Begs forgiveness. Promises to get counseling. Promises to go to church. Promises to go to AA/be sober. Sends flowers, brings gifts. "I'll never do it again." Wants to make love. Declares love, devotion. Enlists family support. Cries.

POWER & CONTROL
DENIAL

1. TENSION BUILDING
BATTERER:
Moody, nitpicking. Isolates victim. Withdraws affection. Name-calling. Put-downs. Verbally abusive, yelling. Uses drugs or alcohol. Threatens. Destroys property. Criticizes. Sullen. Crazy-making.

VICTIM'S RESPONSE:
Agrees to stay or return. Takes partner back. Attempts to stop legal proceedings. Sets up counseling appointment for partner. Feels happy, hopeful.

VICTIM'S RESPONSE:
Attempts to calm partner. Nurturing. Silent/talkative. Stays away from family, friends, support system. Keeps children quiet. Agreeable, passive. Withdraws. Tries to reason. Cooks favourite dinner. Feels as if walking on eggshells.

Figure 4.2: Cycle of Violence

However, no matter what the woman would do, the tension erupted into outright physical and/or sexual abuse. This is phase 2—the *battering phase*—which can last from mere seconds to weeks, depending on the individual perpetrator. During this phase, some women are even taken captive inside their own home and terrorized. This is the phase where the police are most likely to be called either by someone inside the house or by a neighbor. If the man owns a gun, a hostage incident may ensue. If the woman survives and flees, she may take shelter with family, friends, or at a transition house.

The third and final phase of the abuse cycle is the *contrition phase,* in which the husband's personality and behavior are distinctly different from prior phases. Now he is contrite. He promises personal reform, promises to go to church, to enter counseling, to join AA. He enlists supports from any available source,—the priest, his mother-in-law, mutual friends. He cries, tells the woman he can't live without her; in some cases he threatens suicide. He points out how all relationships go through "difficult patches." He makes her feel that it's just the two of them against a harsh and unjust world. Many men who refer themselves for batterer treatment do so at this point. Those who drop out prematurely have the highest recidivism risk for more spousal assault, but those who complete treatment have a better prognosis than court-referred men (Dutton, Bodnarchuk, Kropp, Hart, & Ogloff, 1997).

For men in this cyclical process, normal appraisal, as described by social learning theory, is not possible. In the tension building phase, which leads to abusive outbursts, appraisals are skewed in ways not described by social learning theory models. Yet these phases do not resemble what is called "bizarre symbolic control" or psychosis either. They are by-products of a personality that is neither "normal" nor psychotic—one that resembles Gunderson's (1984) description of the borderline personality disorder.

The woman's attempts to prevent the tension explosion are inevitably doomed because the eruption is a response to internal events in the man. These events, which include attachment-based dysphoria, rumination, and escalating rage, are personality features. A person who exhibits such features in this repeated phasic fashion is described as having a borderline personality organization (Dutton, 1994, 1995a, 1995b, 1998, in press). This personality pattern typically is formed by trauma experiences in early childhood (van der Kolk, McFarlane, & Weisaeth, 1996). One of these early experiences is the child's witnessing of violence toward one parent by another. However, as described above, this experience is not a sufficient condition to produce later family violence because, by itself, it has too many false positives in predicting violence. Two other early experiences interact with witnessing of familial violence to produce a person with a *fragile ego,* fearful of rejection and prone to experience anger as a by-product of intimacy. These other experiences are *shaming* and *insecure attachment.* Together with witnessing family violence, they form the trauma triad.

Shaming as a Source of Trauma

Being shamed can be a source of trauma for a child, especially when combined with witnessing abuse and having insecure feelings of attachment. Many authors (e.g., H. B. Lewis, 1987; M. Lewis, 1992; Miller, 1985; Retzinger, 1991; Scheff, 1987; Tompkins, 1987; Wurmser, 1981) have commented on the "soul-destroying" aspects of shame—an attack on the global sense of self; what Shengold (1989) calls "soul murder." Lewis (1987) and others have described shaming experiences as having lasting emotional impact and connoting an inherent and essential "badness" about the self.

Dutton, van Ginkel, and Starzomski (1995) found that recalled shaming actions by the parent (usually the father) were highly related to adult abusiveness. These shaming actions took the form of global attacks (e.g., "You'll never amount to anything"), public humiliation, or random punishment (conveying the message that the child was being punished for who he was, not what he did). Shame can convert instantly to rage—a process that Scheff (1987) called the "shame-rage spiral," which is an attempt to protect the self from what feels subjectively like looming annihilation. Dutton et al. (1995) found that there was a strong connection between having been shamed and having suffered physical abuse in the family of origin—a correlation of +.61 ($p < .001$). Moreover, they reported that when shaming behaviors were partialled out of the correlation between parental abuse victimization and current abusiveness, the correlation dropped from +.35 ($p < .05$) to +.18 (ns). Similarly, partialling out physical abuse from the correlation of parental shaming and current abusiveness also reduced this correlation to nonsignificance, suggesting an interactive or "emergent" effect of the combination of physical abuse victimization and experiences of being shamed, which act together to produce adult abusiveness. The combined effect of this joint exposure, especially when secure "soothing" attachment is not available, can constitute a trauma source.

Insecure Attachment as a Source of Trauma

Bowlby (1969, 1973, 1977) described secure attachment as a necessary buffer against trauma. In his conceptualization, a distressed child engages in proximity-seeking behaviors to the "attachment other" in order to reduce the impact of a traumatic experience. Furthermore, expectations about the outcome of relationships and the ability to self-soothe to reduce trauma effects are both consequences of attachment. Securely attached persons have more positive expectations, more optimism, even a more benign theology (Kirkpatrick & Shaver, 1992). Conversely, individuals with poor attachments, produced by parental abuse or neglect, have poor trauma resolution skills (Cicchetti & Toth, 1995; van der Kolk & Fisler, 1995).

The relationship of secure attachment to psychological functioning was sufficiently recognized to merit a special issue on attachment and psychopathology in 1996 in the *Journal of Consulting and Clinical Psychology.* In it, Jones (1996, p. 6) summarized that "the studies in this special section demonstrate that an overwhelming number of individuals who are clinically diagnosable will be classified as having insecure attachments . . . attachment research is currently one of the most promising avenues in development and clinical research to the understanding of psychological antecedents of disordered behavior." In the same issue, Lyons-Ruth (1996, p. 64) reviewed attachment-related studies of risk factors for early aggression, finding that attachment patterns, family adversity, and parental hostility "were already evident in infancy and predictive of later aggression before the onset of coercive child behavior." She concluded that "one of the best documented findings in the area of child psychopathology is the consistent relation between harsh and ineffective parental discipline and aggressive behavioral problems." As van der Kolk put it (1987, p. 31), "the essence of trauma is the loss of faith that there is order and continuity in life."

Physiological factors in stress reactions have been studied in relation to attachment styles. One risk factor for early aggression has been found to be elevated cortisol levels when a child is separated from the parent—an indicator of a stress reaction. Klein (1980), noting that both panic attacks and depression in humans respond to treatment with tricyclic antidepressants and MAO inhibitors, postulated that both conditions are rooted in "neurobiological sensitivity to abandonment precipitated by early life experiences" (van der Kolk, 1987, p. 46). Similarly, van der Kolk (1987) demonstrated that secure attachment is essential for the development of core neurobiological functions in the primate brain.

The connection between attachment and neural development has been most fully explicated in Schore's (1994) monograph, *Affect Regulation and the Origin of the Self.* In this work, Schore developed a psychobiological model linking maternal behaviors (such as attunement) to neural development in the child, specifically to those neural mechanisms that regulate emotion (such as the limbic system). Of note is Schore's observation that "shame is a powerful modulator of interpersonal relatedness" and has the capacity to "rupture the dynamic attachment bond" (p. 242). Recovery from shaming experiences involves both a seeking out of other attachments and psychobiological processes. Schore stated:

> If the caregiver is sensitive, responsible and emotionally approachable, especially if she reenters into affect-regulating mutual gaze visuoaffective (as well as tactile and auditory affect modulating) truncations, the dyad is psychobiologically reattuned, the object relations link (attachment bond) is reconnected, the arousal deceleration is inhibited, and shame is metabolized and regulated. (p. 243)

Maternal touch inhibits an accelerating hypothalamic-pituitary-adrenocortical stress response as well as secretion of glucocorticoids as a stress response (Schore, 1994). Developmental endocrinological studies have shown that increased levels of touch and other somesthetic sensory modalities have both immediate and long-term beneficial effects (Denenberg & Zarrow, 1971). In 1987 van der Kolk showed that in a variety of species the separation-distress call is mediated by endogenous opioids. Low doses of opioid receptor agonists powerfully modified both the distress call and the maternal response to it.

In a group of batterers, Dutton, Saunders, Starzomski, and Bartholomew (1994) found that those with a "fearful" (insecure) attachment style self-reported the highest chronic levels of stress symptoms ($r = +.51$, $p = .00001$). Men who were in treatment for wife assault had high chronic trauma level scores of 26 (sd = 9.8) on the Trauma Symptom Checklist (TSC-33), compared to 16 (sd = 7.9) for demographically matched controls. Dutton (1995b) found that all of the men's self-report subscales of the TSC-33 (anxiety, depression, sleep disturbance, dissociative states, and "post sexual abuse trauma—hypothesized") correlated with wives' reports of men's abusiveness. One of the mechanisms through which secure attachment may function to buffer trauma is through affect regulation. Both insecure attachment and trauma generate affect dysregulation; the effect of both in concert (e.g., in children abused by their parents) is to produce extreme dysregulation (van der Kolk et al., 1996).

Combined Trauma Sources

Although witnessing parental violence, being shamed, and being insecurely attached are each sources of trauma in and of themselves, the combination of the three over prolonged and vulnerable developmental phases constitutes a dramatic and powerful traumatic source. The child has no secure attachment source to turn to for soothing, yet the need created by the shaming and exposure to violence triggers enormous emotional and physiological reactions requiring soothing. Furthermore, as Pynoos (1994, p. 88) pointed out, traumatic exposure in childhood can occur during critical periods of personality formation "when there are ongoing revisions of the inner model of the world, self and other . . . these internal models, once organized, operate outside conscious awareness . . . they may result in isolated areas of decision making or behavior that is inconsistent with other personality attributes." It is for this reason that the personalities of wife assaulters are often described as incongruent with their everyday persona.

These personality features of assaulters include extreme jealousy and fear of abandonment, tendencies to project blame, and a high chronic level of trauma symptoms. In a series of empirical studies assessing the personalities of abusive men and their spouses' reports of abusiveness, Dutton found this constellation to be related to borderline personality organization (BPO) in men. This pattern was found in convicted and self-referred wife abusers, nonphysically abusive working-class controls, male university students, clinical outpatients, and gay males. Figure 4.3 demonstrates this pattern of correlations for the spouse abusers (Dutton, 1994; Dutton et al., 1994). Similar patterns were obtained for samples of college males, clinical outpatients, working-class controls, and gay males. The form of abusiveness varied in these groups (from physical to exclusively verbal), but not the constellation of factors related to abusiveness.

It is important to note that BPO is a phasic personality that repeatedly undergoes three phases similar to the behavioral descriptions given by Walker's respondents (Dutton, 1994, 1998). Each stage corresponds to an internal anxiety state (e.g., the tension-building phase corresponds to a dysphoric stalemate where intimacy needs are unmet and unexpressed, and instead the batterer "arches away angrily" from his partner). In the contrition phase the preoccupation is with avoiding aloneness through extreme reconciliation attempts.

Dutton (1998) emphasized that many of these personality features are internal processes which are unobservable for modeling and therefore must have been acquired through the traumatic processes described above. Based on retrospective reports of adult wife abusers, the modal picture of the family of origin for men who have abusive personalities is a family where the father was physically abusive and shaming, and the mother was perceived as ambivalent toward the boy (i.e., she was rated as high on both warmth and rejection). This combination constitutes the basis of early trauma for these men.

TRAUMA MODELS

Trauma models have the advantage that they account for the associated features of abusiveness better than do social learning models. Recent research on the sequelae of trauma (Schore, 1994; van der Kolk et al., 1996) shows that trauma produces not only aggression but also an inability to modulate arousal, an unstable sense of self, insecure attachment, high chronic anger, and a tendency to externalize blame, especially when the trauma had a shaming component (Lewis, 1971). Dutton (in press) posited that, in social learning terms, a traumatic event was an aversive stimulus that was perceived as both uncontrollable and unbluntable (see Figure 4.1). He argued that, contrary to social learning theory, exposure to such events does not always produce passive coping strategies but can produce aggression. This occurs because the combination of high arousal, externalization, and attachment rage found in children traumatized by intrafamilial events overrides the more rational appraisal processes posited by a social learning model.

The conclusion of this line of reasoning is that intimate aggression may represent a paradigm-breaking type of event for social learning theory.

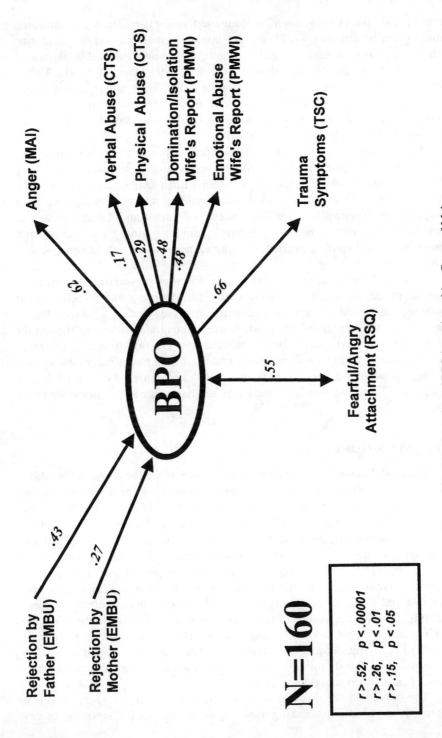

Figure 4.3: The Centrality of BPO in an Assaultive Group of Males

Anger (MAI)

Verbal Abuse (CTS)

Physical Abuse (CTS)

Domination/Isolation
Wife's Report (PMWI)

Emotional Abuse
Wife's Report (PMWI)

Trauma
Symptoms (TSC)

Rejection by
Father (EMBU)

Rejection by
Mother (EMBU)

Fearful/Angry
Attachment (RSQ)

BPO

.62

.17

.29

.48

.48

.66

.43

.27

.55

N=160

r > .52,   p < .00001
r > .26,   p < .01
r > .15,   p < .05

FAMILY OF ORIGIN	ADULT DEFICITS
• Physical Abuse	
– between parents	– cognitive problem resolution deficits
– directed at child	– violent response repertoire
• Parental Rejection	
– shaming	– externalizing/blaming attributional style
• public punishment	– high chronic anger
• random punishment	
• global criticism	
• Insecure Attachment	– rejection sensitivity
	– ambivalent attachment style
	– disturbed self schema
	• inability to self soothe
	• anxiety depression

Figure 4.4: Trauma Model of Abusiveness

Although wife assaulters may react to a proximal stimulus, victim-witness reports indicate that this stimulus was trivial, imagined, or would not have produced the same disproportionate response the preceding week (prior to the build-up of internal tension). All these features indicate a more perpetrator-driven, less reactive model of aggression than that suggested by social learning theory. This model, in turn, has etiological aspects clarified through knowledge of trauma reactions. The resulting trauma model of abusiveness is depicted in Figure 4.4 and shows how developmental experiences may produce adult deficits that cannot be acquired through observation or modeling.

REFERENCES

Bandura, A. (1979). The social learning perspective: Mechanisms of aggression. In H. Toch (Ed.), *Psychology of crime and criminal justice* (pp. 298-336). New York: Holt, Rinehart & Winston.

Baron, R. A., & Byrne, D. (1994). *Social psychology: Understanding human interaction* (7th ed.). Boston: Allyn & Bacon.

Baumeister, R. F. (1990). Suicide as an escape from self. *Psychological Review, 97,* 90-113.

Bowlby, J. (1969). *Attachment and loss (Vol. 1) Attachment.* New York: Basic Books.

Bowlby, J. (1973). *Attachment and loss (Vol. 2). Separation.* New York: Basic Books.

Cicchetti, D., & Toth, S. L. (1995). A developmental psychopathology perspective on child abuse and neglect. *Journal of American Academy of Child Adolescent Psychiatry, 34,* 541-565.

Denenberg, V. H., & Zarrow, M. X. (1971). Effect of handling in infancy upon adult behavior and adrenocortical activity: Suggestions for a neuroendocrine mechanism. In D. N. Walcher & D. L. Peters (Eds.), *Early childhood: The development of self-regulatory mechanisms* (pp. 40-74). San Diego: Academic Press.

Dodge, K., Petit, G. S., Bates, J. E., & Valente, E. (1995). Social information-processing patterns partially mediate the effect of early physical abuse on later conduct problems. *Journal of Abnormal Psychology, 104,* 632-643.

Dutton, D. G. (1980). Some social psychological research of relevance to an understanding of domestic violence. In C. T. Griffiths & M. Nance (Eds.), *The female offender* (pp. 81-92). Simon Fraser University Press.

Dutton, D. G. (1988). Profiling wife assaulters: Some evidence for a trimodal analysis. *Violence and Victims, 3*(1), 5-30.

Dutton, D. G. (1994). Behavioral and affective correlates of borderline personality organization in wife assaulters. *International Journal of Law and Psychiatry, 17,* 265-279.

Dutton, D. G. (1995a). *Domestic assault of women: Psychological and criminal justice perspectives* (2nd ed.). Vancouver: University of British Columbia Press.

Dutton, D. G. (1995b). Trauma symptoms and PTSD profiles in perpetrators of abuse. *Journal of Traumatic Stress, 8,* 299-315.

Dutton, D. G. (1998). *The abusive personality: A trauma model.* New York: Guilford.

Dutton, D. G. (in press). Traumatic origins of intimate rage. *Aggression and Violent Behavior.*

Dutton, D. G., Bodnarchuk, M., Kropp, R., Hart, S., & Ogloff, J. (1997). Wife assault treatment and criminal recidivism: An eleven year follow-up. *International Journal of Offender Therapy and Comparative Criminology, 41*(1), 9-23.

Dutton, D. G., Saunders, D., Starzomski, A. J., & Bartholomew, K. (1994). Intimacy-anger and insecure attachment as precursors of abuse in intimate relationships. *Journal of Applied Social Psychology, 24,* 1367-1386.

Dutton, D. G., van Ginkel, C., & Starzomski, A. J. (1995). The role of shame and guilt in the intergenerational transmission of abusiveness. *Violence and Victims, 10,* 121-131.

Egeland, B. (1993). A history of abuse is a major risk factor for abusing the next generation. In R. J. Gelles & D. R. Loseke (Eds.), *Current controversies on family violence.* Newbury Park, CA: Sage.

Egeland, B., & Jacobvitz, D. (1984). *Intergenerational transmission of parental abuse: Causes and consequences.* Paper presented at conference on biosocial perspectives on abuse and neglect, York, ME.

Ganley, A. (1981). *Participant's manual: Court-mandated therapy for men who batter—A three day workshop for professionals.* Washington, DC: Center for Women's Policy Studies.

Gunderson, J. G. (1984). *Borderline personality disorder.* Washington, DC: American Psychiatric Press.

Hunter, R. S., & Kihlstrom, N. (1979). Breaking the cycle in abusive families. *American Journal of Psychiatry, 136,* 1320-1322.

Jones, E. E. (1996). Introduction to the special section on attachment and psychopathology: Part 1. *Journal of Consulting and Clinical Psychology, 64,* 5-7.

Kaufman, J., & Zigler, E. (1993). The intergenerational transmission of abuse is overstated. In R. J. Gelles & D. R. Loseke (Eds.), *Current controversies on family violence.* Newbury Park, CA: Sage.

Kalmuss, D. S. (1984). The intergenerational transmission of marital aggression. *Journal of Marriage and the Family, 46,* 11-19.

Kirkpatrick, L. A., & Shaver, P. (1992). An attachment-theoretical approach to romantic love and religious belief. *Personality and Social Psychology Bulletin, 18,* 266-275.

Klein, D. F. (1980). Anxiety reconceptualized. *Comprehensive Psychiatry, 6,* 411-427.

Lewis, H. B. (1971). *Shame and guilt in neurosis.* New York: International Universities Press.

Lewis, H. B. (1987). Shame and the narcissistic personality. In D. Nathanson (Ed.), *The many faces of shame* (pp. 233-255). New York: Guilford.

Lewis, M. (1992). *Shame: The exposed self.* Hillsdale, NJ: Erlbaum

Lyons-Ruth, K. (1996). Attachment relationships among children with aggressive behavior problems: The role of disorganized early attachment patterns. *Journal of Consulting and Clinical Psychology, 64,* 64-73.

Miller, S. (1985). *The shame experience.* Hillsdale, NJ: Erlbaum.

O'Leary, K. D. (1988). Physical aggression between spouses: A social learning perspective. In V. B. Van Hasselt, R. Morrison, A. S. Bellack, & M. Hersen (Eds.), *Handbook of family violence.* New York: Plenum.

Pynoos, R. S. (1994). *Posttraumatic stress disorder: A clinical review.* Lutherville, MD: Sidran.

Retzinger, S. M. (1991). *Violent emotions: Shame and rage in marital quarrels.* Newbury Park, CA: Sage.

Scheff, T. J. (1987). The shame-rage spiral: A case study of an interminable quarrel. In H. B. Lewis (Ed.), *The role of shame in symptom formation* (pp. 109-149). Hillsdale, NJ: Erlbaum.

Shengold, L. (1989). *Soul murder: The effects of childhood abuse and deprivation.* New Haven, CT: Yale University Press.

Schore, A. N. (1994). *Affect regulation and the origin of the self.* Hillsdale, NJ: Erlbaum.

Tompkins, S. S. (1987). Shame. In D. Nathanson (Ed.), *The many faces of shame* (pp. 128-137). New York: Guilford.

Turner, C., Fenn, M., & Cole, A. (1981). A social psychological analysis of violent behavior. In R. B. Stuart (Ed.), *Violent behavior: Social learning approaches.* New York: Brunner/Mazel.

van der Kolk, B. (1987). *Psychological trauma.* Washington, DC: American Psychiatric Press.

van der Kolk, B., & Fisler, R. (1995). Dissociation and fragmentary nature of traumatic memories: Overview and exploratory study. *Journal of Traumatic Stress, 8,* 505-525.

van der Kolk, B., McFarlane, A. C., & Weisaeth, L. (1996). *Traumatic stress.* New York: Guilford.

Walker, L. (1979). *The battered woman.* New York: Harper & Row.

Wurmser, L. (1981). *The mask of shame.* Baltimore: Johns Hopkins University Press.

PART II

Correlates of Violence

The Interpersonal and Communication Dynamics of Wife Battering

Sally A. Lloyd

The frequent occurrence of violence in marriage and the family is no longer a surprising phenomenon. Even using the most conservative estimates, it is tragic how very frequently women and children are hit, slapped, pushed around, or beaten by a person who purports to love them. And if more "nebulous" phenomena are assessed, such as emotional control and psychological aggression, the numbers skyrocket.

Looking just at physical violence, we know that nearly one in six wives reports experiencing some type of physical violence at the hands of their husbands, and nearly one in fifteen reports the presence of violent behaviors likely to result in an injury (Straus & Gelles, 1990). Indeed, Johnson (1995) argued that enough couples suffer from occasional episodes of physical violence that the term "common couple violence" is warranted.

Physical violence against wives is no longer an "understudied topic." We know a great deal about the personalities, backgrounds, and demographic characteristics of victims and of perpetrators of physical violence. Fortunately, we are also learning more about the interpersonal and communication dynamics that surround husbands' use of physical violence, since much evidence suggests that interpersonal and communication factors are integral to understanding the dynamics of violence in marriage (Margolin, John, & Gleberman, 1988; Stets, 1992).

The purpose of this chapter is to review the literature on the interpersonal and communication dynamics of husbands' use of physical violence against their wives. This review begins with a conceptualization of violence as a gendered, communicative act designed to enact control in relationships; this is the "underlying framework" that I bring to the analysis of the literature. I then summarize five broadly defined areas of research on interpersonal dynamics: social skill and problem solving deficits, conflict patterns, "everyday" marital interaction, negative affect and reciprocity in laboratory observations, and patterns of dominance and power dynamics. The chapter concludes with a final note on the longitudinal course of battering.

COMMUNICATIVE ACTS, GENDER, AND CONTROL

Physical violence has been conceptualized as a communicative act along a variety of dimensions: violence as an action which leads to the achievement of instrumental, relationship and identity goals (Cahn, 1996); violence as a potent conflict negotiation strategy (Lloyd & Emery, 1994); and violence as a component of marital conflict enactment (Burman, Margolin, & John, 1993). Infante, Chandler, and Rudd (1989, p. 174) emphasized that a communication approach is "illuminating because it reveals that when violence occurs it is not an isolated event in people's lives, but is embedded firmly in the process of interpersonal communication which people use to regulate their daily lives."

Communication perspectives emphasize the ways that physical violence is embedded within transactional patterns in the relationship; for example, violence is seen as emanating from patterns of enmeshment, power dynamics, and/or escalated conflict (Babcock, Waltz, Jacobson, & Gottman, 1993; Bograd, 1984; Cahn 1996; Planalp, 1993). Violence is also conceptualized as the product of a set sequence of interactions such as negative reciprocity (Burman et al., 1993; Sabourin, 1995), and of a marital system that is marked by clear relational patterns such as rigidity or competitive symmetry, a pattern of one partner responding to the other's attempt at dominance with another dominance attempt (Gage, 1988; Rogers, Castleton, & Lloyd, 1996).

However, conceptualizing violence solely in transactional terms has been roundly criticized, for at times these frameworks have been applied in such a way as to render the violent behavior, and the gendered nature of violence, invisible (Bograd, 1984; Margolin & Burman, 1993; Yllö, 1994). For instance, the victim may be blamed inadvertently (she was nagging, she provoked the violence), and the aggressor may be excused (he was insecure; he was trying to regain his rightful place in the relationship). The works of Bograd (1984) and of Goldner, Penn, Sheinberg, and Walker (1990) are illuminating here, for they remind us that the use transactional perspectives should not ignore issues of context, including who holds the more powerful position in the relationship and in society, who initiates violence, and who is physically injured and psychologically harmed by violence.

Although there is consistent evidence that both men and women engage in physically violent behavior during courtship and marriage (Straus & Gelles, 1990; Stets & Henderson, 1991), it is overly simplistic to assert that men and women are "equally violent" without a close examination of the context and consequences that surround the use of violence in intimate relationships (Bograd, 1990).

First, women's use of violence occurs largely in self-defense—that is, in response to males' use of violence (Bograd, 1990; Jacobson, Gottman, Waltz, Rushe, Babcock, & Holtzworth-Munroe, 1994; Yllö, 1994). Second, women are clearly at much greater risk of injury, due to the greater size and strength of men, and males' use of more harm-inducing tactics of violence (Morse, 1995; Stets & Straus, 1990). Indeed, women sustain the vast majority (more than 95%) of the injuries that occur in situations of domestic violence (Schwartz, 1987). Finally, the overall context of romantic relationships is one in which men are empowered to hold dominance over women (Dobash & Dobash, 1979; Lloyd, 1991). While it is important to acknowledge that women behave violently in relationships and may even be the sole aggressor (see for example, Emery & Lloyd, 1994), the most likely dynamic is that of a male aggressor and female victim (Bograd, 1990). It is the latter dynamic that is the focus of this chapter.

In addition to paying attention to the gendered, communicative aspects of violence, it is also useful to examine violence as a tactic of control. Gortner, Gollan, and Jacobson (1997, p. 347) state that "the primary intent and function of battering is the intimidation and control of another." This control may entail literal physical control of her person (e.g., holding her down, locking her in a room), as well as psychological or symbolic control (e.g., fear, ridicule, degradation, denial of her independence of thought and/or behavior; Goldner et al., 1990; Kirkwood, 1993; Marshall, 1994; Stets & Pirog-Good, 1990). Physical violence and verbal aggression may be used as tactics to strike fear into the victim, to intimidate her, to retaliate against her autonomous actions, and to maintain "order" (Emery & Lloyd, 1994; Jacobson & Gottman, 1998). Indeed, male batterers have a unique ability to use the fear of physical violence as a mechanism of psychological control of their wives (Jacobson et al., 1994, p. 986).

Male aggressors describe a variety of control-related "reasons" for their violence, including the need to dominate the female, fear of her gaining independence, fear of abandonment, her failure to live up to the obligations of being a "good woman," jealousy over her interaction with other males or family members, spending decisions, or sexual denial (Dutton, 1988; Dutton & Golant, 1995; Ferraro, 1988; Maynard, 1993; Stamp & Sabourin, 1995; Stets, 1988). Over time, control tactics may form a vicious web, as the control of the abuser is strengthened by the victim's lowered self-esteem, loss of separate identity, hopelessness, and depression (Kirkwood, 1993).

My emphasis on aggression as an act of control is not meant to ignore the simultaneously highly expressive nature of an act of violence. Indeed, aggressive men often speak of losing control, of not even remembering what occurred in a "blind rage" or "drowning in a red tide" of anger (Dutton & Golant, 1995; Goldner et al., 1990; Stets, 1988). Aggression often occurs in a context of volatile, negative interaction, and is accompanied by hostility and anger, all of which clearly speak to its expressive side (Lloyd, 1996). I disagree, however that violence is sometimes only an uncontrollable emotional outburst (see Spitzberg, 1997, for a thoughtful argument along these lines). Rather, like Goldner et al. (1990), I argue that aggression is simultaneously an expressive and instrumental action; even when aggression is experienced by the man as a frightening loss of emotional control, his aggression has an instrumental control-based underlying intent.

Ultimately, then, my view is that "gender matters" when examining the interpersonal and communication dynamics of violence in marriage. Although there is not a clearly defined link between the patriarchal underpinnings of our culture with why a particular man does or does not engage in wife battering (Dutton, 1994), the literature on marital interaction and violence continues to demonstrate that issues of male dominance and control are an integral part of the dynamics that result in men's use of physical violence and verbal aggression against the women they purport to love. Thus, my review of the literature emphasizes gender dynamics whenever possible (however, where necessary, my terminology changes as a result of reporting on different studies that have assessed "violent husbands" versus "violent marriages").

This chapter now turns to the examination of five key arenas of research that address the role of interpersonal and communication dynamics in marital violence.

SOCIAL SKILL AND PROBLEM SOLVING DEFICITS

The first area of research to be examined is the role of social skills and problem solving deficits. Holtzworth-Munroe (1992) presented a compelling argument for examining the social information processing skills of maritally violent men. The emphasis in this line of research is on the deficits in behavioral, cognitive, and emotional skills that violent men display in both marital and nonmarital situations. Anglin and Holtzworth-Munroe (1997) studied deficits in problem solving skills in a sample of 58 married couples, 35 of whom reported the presence of violence in the marriage. The authors proposed that violent spouses lack the skills needed to generate and enact constructive responses to marital conflicts, and this contributes to a heightened risk for escalated conflict and violence. They found that, compared to nonviolent distressed and nonviolent nondistressed spouses, spouses in violent distressed marriages produced less competent responses to standardized vignettes of marital and nonmarital situations, and they concluded that husbands and wives demonstrated deficits in both marital and general skills which contribute to problem solving difficulties.

Holtzworth-Munroe and Smutzler (1996) examined emotional reactions and behavioral intentions in a group of 97 men, 46 of whom were violent and distressed. The men rated their reactions to a set of standard written and videotaped scenarios of wife behaviors that were irritated versus dysphoric, and aggressive versus distressed. Particularly in response to wife aggressive behaviors, the violent men reported fewer reactions of support and sympathy, fewer inclinations to discuss the subject, and more reactions of feeling irritated and angry as well as increased inclinations to act negatively. However, violent men had similar reactions to written and videotaped scenarios depicting wife distress, defined as self-denigration and complaints. Holtzworth-Munroe and Smutzler (1996) concluded that these results were in keeping with the unpredictability of men's violence: Not only are they likely to respond negatively to the spouse's attempts to influence them, but they are also likely to respond negatively to her expression of emotional distress.

Hostile attributions may play a key role in the cycle of information processing deficits. Violent men in particular were more likely to attribute hostile intent to the actions of their wives (Holtzworth-Munroe & Hutchinson, 1993; Stamp & Sabourin, 1995). The situations most likely to elicit attributions of negative intentions were jealousy, rejection, and potential public embarrassment of the husband. Holtzworth-Munroe and Hutchinson (1993) hypothesized that these situations of perceived wife abandonment or rejection are also the most likely to result in the husbands' use of violence.

Additional deficiencies in communication skills are apparent among violent couples. Infante, Chandler, and Rudd (1989) characterized violent couples as being low in argumentativeness—that is, they demonstrated poor skills in presenting and defending their positions on issues. This type of argumentativeness was not the same as staunchly and belligerently defending a position; rather Infante et al. (1989) defined it as competence in defending one's views without resorting to hostility.

Overt verbal hostility and passive aggression have been conceptualized as key precursors to physical violence (Murphy & O'Leary, 1989; O'Leary, Malone, & Tyree, 1994; Sabourin, 1996); in particular, husbands' verbally aggressive messages which entail character attacks, curses, and threats have been hypothesized to be the most catalytic (Infante, Sabourin, Rudd, & Shannon, 1990). Physically violent husbands also have been characterized by low levels of general problem solving and communication skills, as well as higher levels of reciprocity of verbal aggression and spouse-specific anger and hostility (Boyle & Vivian, 1996; Infante, Sabourin, Rudd, & Shannon,

1990; Sabourin, Infante, & Rudd, 1993). Finally, Choice, Lampke, and Pittman (1995) have demonstrated that ineffective marital conflict resolution skills played a mediational role between men's witnessing parental violence and men's later involvement in battering.

Violent men's deficits in behavioral, emotional, and cognitive skills may be most evident in situations that are perceived as threatening; for example, violent husbands reported less socially competent responses than their non-violent counterparts to situations involving rejection by the wife (Holtzworth-Munroe & Anglin, 1991) and more anger and verbal aggression in situations of perceived wife abandonment (Dutton & Browning, 1998). Ferraro (1988) emphasized the role of threats to the self as catalytic to the use of physical violence; such feelings of threat occur when the husband perceives the wife to have violated his need for loyalty (as evident in her interaction with friends and family) and/or control (as evident in her attempts to resist his domination).

CONFLICT PATTERNS

A second fruitful arena of research on the interpersonal dynamics of men's physical violence toward their wives is conflict patterns. Couples reporting high levels of conflict in their marriages were more likely to report high levels of physical violence (Straus, Gelles, & Steinmetz, 1980); conflict levels also predicted premarital violence, particularly for men (Riggs & O'Leary, 1996). Violence may be the result of highly escalated conflict; it is enacted when conflicts spiral to particularly hostile levels, and/or when the perpetrator attempts to gain control over the situation or partner (Jacobson et al. 1994; Lloyd & Emery, 1994; Margolin, John, & O'Brien, 1989).

Margolin, John, and O'Brien (1989) examined the course of conflictual interactions among 75 married couples (16 physically violent) using the interaction record method developed by Peterson (1979). Spouses identified the most important interaction of the day; their descriptions of these interactions were read to a researcher over the phone on a daily basis. Records characterized as conflictual were content-analyzed for five categories of affect: affection/affiliation, calm/neutrality, aggression/disapproval, withdrawal, and distress/dysphoria.

The authors conducted sequential analyses on the conflictual interaction records, and discovered greater patterning and structure in the interaction of couples with a physically violent husband. Escalation to physical violence was encouraged through the mechanism of reciprocity; an initial act of aggression/disapproval followed by aggression/disapproval from the partner increased the likelihood of a third action of aggression/disapproval, and so on. Margolin, John, and O'Brien (1989) concluded that the many sequential contingencies of the physically violent couple's conflict interactions were indicative of highly reactive and ritualized behavior.

Lloyd (1990) examined conflict types and strategies in violent versus nonviolent marriages. Using a telephone self-report method, her sample of 78 couples (39 physically violent) described 200 conflicts that had occurred over the course of 6 days. These conflicts were classified using the dimensions of stability of the issue, level of conflict resolution, and escalation of the conflict. Both violent nondistressed and violent distressed couples reported lower levels of "everyday squabbles" (conflicts that were low in stability, escalation, and resolution) than did their nonviolent counterparts. In addition, nondistressed couples reported a higher proportion of problem solving and a lower proportion of stable heated arguments than did distressed couples. Lloyd (1990) speculated that the lower level of squabbles seen in the conflicts of couples with a violent husband may be similar to the patterns of conflict described by Vuchinich (1987). Vuchinich found that having a proportion of family conflicts of short duration with no resolution was adaptive; thus, in healthy families, letting some issues drop without a resolution seemed to work to air grievances in a nonthreatening atmosphere. Perhaps violent couples are not as good at "letting things drop." In addition, issues of dominance and control may lead to striving to win all arguments.

Lloyd (1990) also analyzed couples' descriptions of the course of a "typical intense argument." Both violent distressed and violent nondistressed couples reported heightened levels of anger and verbal attack. Violent distressed couples reported the lowest levels of negotiation and apology. Nonviolent distressed couples were the least likely to mention the use of direct negotiation strategies, nonviolent nondistressed couples were the most likely group, and the two violent groups fell in between. This may reflect withdrawal on the part of the nonviolent distressed couples, and a tendency for the violent couples to go ahead and engage in conflict. Ultimately, while violent couples may strive for a resolution to arguments, their use of verbal attack, anger, and withdrawal, and lack of negotiation, may ensure that resolution is unlikely.

EVERYDAY MARITAL INTERACTION

Several recent investigations have examined "everyday" marital interaction (i.e., the daily exchange of positive and negative behaviors, discussions of everyday things, or the events of a "typical" day) in violent and nonviolent marriages. Langhinrichsen-Rohling, Smutzler, and Vivian (1994) studied a clinical group of distressed spouses using the Structured Marital Interview. The interview protocol asked about recollections of everyday discussions of positive things and caring gestures. Both husbands and wives in the severely violent group reported less frequent and lower quality positive interactions than did the nonviolent group. Compared to nonviolent husbands, severely violent husbands also reported fewer caring gestures from their wives, although their wives reported no differences in their own or their husbands' caring gestures as a function of violence in the marriage. Langhinrichsen-Rohling et al. (1994) noted that among distressed husbands, the violent ones were more likely than the nonviolent ones to see themselves as "doing more and getting less," and they concluded that violent men may be overplaying their own caring gestures and underplaying the caring gestures of their wives.

Langhinrichsen-Rohling, Schlee, Monson, Ehrensaft, and Heyman (1998) also assessed positivity in marriage through the use of extensive questionnaire assessments. In this portion of the study, there were no differences between the distressed couples who were nonviolent and distressed couples with violent husbands in their reports of positivity in marriage.

Sabourin and Stamp (1995) examined everyday interaction in a sample of 10 abusive and 10 nonabusive couples. The definition of "abusive couple" in this study was broader than most, and included the presence of marital and/or parent-to-child violence as assessed by self-referral for treatment of spouse or child abuse. The authors used an interview technique wherein husbands and wives talked to each other about a "typical day." Sabourin and Stamp (1995) examined both the content of the interview and the relational data apparent in the couple's communication patterns during the interview. They noted several thematic differences in the couples' talk about their typical day. Abusive couples gave overall "vague" and stagnant descriptions of their day; their talk also revealed more conflict over relational issues, more expressed frustration and angry interference, complaints, a lack of a sense of how they might effectively change what they did not like, and a lack of cooperation. Sabourin and Stamp (1995) ultimately characterized the abusive couples as less balanced in their management of changes/stability and autonomy/connection in the family.

Lloyd (1996) described differences in everyday marital interaction in a sample of 78 married couples from the community. Using the behavioral self-report telephone method developed by Huston to assess positive and negative behaviors in marriage (see Huston, Robins, Atkinson, & McHale, 1987), she assessed the frequency of 9 positive and 9 negative behaviors across 6 days. There were significant differences in negative daily interaction as a function of both distress and violence. Looking at main effects, distressed couples displayed significantly more negative interaction than did nondistressed couples, and violent couples displayed significantly more negative interaction than did nonviolent couples. There were also significant distress-by-violence interaction effects for both positive and negative behaviors. Violent distressed couples reported the highest levels of negative interaction; violent nondistressed, nonviolent nondistressed, and nonviolent distressed couples did not differ in their reports of negative daily interaction. Surprisingly, however, violent distressed couples were also characterized by levels of positive interaction that were as high as their nonviolent nondistressed counterparts. The nonviolent distressed marriages were the marriages characterized by the lowest levels of positive interaction.

Although the results of Lloyd (1996) on positivity among nonviolent-distressed marriages differ from those of Langhinrichsen-Rohling et al. (1994 & 1998), these differences stem from the differences in samples and in measurement techniques. However, these studies resulted in similar conclusions about the everyday dynamics of the violent marriage. Lloyd (1996) speculated that the high levels of positive interaction seen in her sample of violent distressed marriages indicated the presence of intense attachments. Langhinrichsen-Rohling et al. (1998) did find key differences in the reasons given for staying together; violent couples in which the husband was distressed emphasized love as the reason for staying in the marriage, whereas nonviolent distressed couples emphasized family responsibilities, children, and the hope that the marriage would improve. Langhinrichsen-Rohling et al. (1998) concluded that distressed husbands in violent marriages may be characterized by strong but insecure attachments. Both conclusions are in keeping with the work of Murphy, Meyer, and O'Leary (1994), who noted excessive dependency among maritally violent men; they also noted that the violent men kept a focus on the relationship that was equivalent to that of nonviolent nondistressed men.

NEGATIVE AFFECT AND RECIPROCITY IN LABORATORY OBSERVATIONS OF MARITAL INTERACTION

One of the most fruitful arenas of investigation of the interpersonal dynamics involving a violent husband has been in laboratory observations of marital interaction. Margolin and her colleagues have been seminal in this arena. Margolin, John, and Gleberman (1988), and Burman, John, and Margolin (1992) discussed the results of their laboratory observation of 79 couples during a marital discussion; data were coded using a variety of marital interaction coding systems. Their study involved the comparison of four types of couples: nondistressed and three distressed groups; those who were physically violent, verbally violent, and withdrawing. Physically violent husbands enacted higher levels of threat, blame, and other offensive negative behaviors such as signs of dismissal, pointing one's finger, waving arms, or negative physical contact and (in contrast to defensive negative behaviors, such as head hanging, lack of eye contact, and leaning away). Husbands and wives in physically violent marriages enacted fewer positive behaviors than did spouses in nonviolent marriages; they also exhibited patterns that increased the likelihood of further anger responses. In addition, both physically violent and verbally violent couples showed patterns of engaging in cycles of attack and defense (Margolin et al., 1988; Burman et al., 1992).

Videotaped observations of couples enacting "typical conflicts" in their own homes has yielded additional information about physically violent marriages. Violent couples have been observed to be high in overt hostility and defensiveness, low in problem-solving skills, and have been characterized by a pattern of increasing withdrawal and despair, and decreasing warmth over the course of a marital discussion (Margolin, Burman, & John, 1989). In other research (Burman, Margolin, & John, 1993), physically violent husbands and wives displayed rigid, highly contingent behavior patterns; in particular, hostile, angry behavior from one spouse was likely to trigger hostile, angry behavior by the other spouse. In addition, physically violent couples were characterized by anger-reactivity; after the expression of anger, spouses were less likely to express positive, neutral, or nonhostile negative behavior (Burman et al., 1993).

Margolin and her colleagues hypothesized that the withdraw/defense pattern and the negative affective patterns of violent husbands, particularly when accompanied by nonconstructive problem-solving skills, might be a precursor to escalated violent behavior in the marriage (Burman et al., 1992; Margolin et al., 1988). Specifically, these lead to "long-standing frustrations, a build-up of unsolved problems, and more serious displays of anger, including aggression" (Burman et al., 1993, p. 37). Nondistressed couples, on the other hand, although exhibiting some similar negative behaviors, demonstrated a clear ability to de-escalate their conflicts and break out of patterns of negativity (Burman et al., 1993).

Not surprisingly, the wives of violent husbands were quick to respond to their husband's anger with anger of their own, an understandable reaction to living in an abusive environment (Burman et al., 1993). It is also interesting that the violent husbands were characterized to a greater extent by the more overtly "self-defending" negative behaviors (offensive) than were men in the conflictual but nonviolent marriages. Although Margolin and her colleagues did not specifically examine dominance patterns, their findings are consistent with power and control as core issues for violent husbands.

The findings of Margolin and her colleagues have been corroborated by observational studies by Cordova, Jacobson, Gottman, Rushe, and Cox (1993) and Jacobson, Gottman, Waltz, Rushe, Babcock, and Holtzworth-Munroe (1994). Using the Marital Interaction Coding System (Weiss & Summers, 1983), Cordova et al. (1993) studied the marital interaction of 57 couples. They observed higher levels of aversiveness (e.g., criticism, disagreement, put-downs) and lower levels of facilitation (e.g., approval, accepting responsibility, smiling, paraphrasing) by the violent distressed couples than by the nonviolent distressed couples. Further, violent distressed spouses were more likely to reciprocate negative behavior. Cordova et al. (1993) characterized the wives as "standing up to" their husbands; clearly, they had not been beaten down by the battering. Interestingly, the nonviolent distressed and nonviolent nondistressed couples did not differ in aversive behavior or in negative reciprocity.

Jacobson et al. (1994) studied 60 violent distressed and 32 nonviolent distressed couples, utilizing both the Specific Affect Coding System

(Gottman & Krokoff, 1989) and assessments of cardiovascular arousal. They found that violent husbands used highly provocative forms of anger, including belligerence and contempt; they were also more controlling, and unlikely to acknowledge that there was anything wrong with their behavior. Their wives, in contrast, while showing intense anger, also displayed the highest levels of fear, tension, and sadness. Jacobson et al. (1994) characterized the wives as simultaneously hostile and frightened.

Gottman et al. (1995) have extended the psychophysiological study of batterers to examine different types of battering men. They examined the marital interaction and background characteristics of 61 couples with a violent husband. Assessments included five measures of physiology taken during a taped discussion of two problem areas in the marriage. The tapes were analyzed with the SPAFF coding system with particular emphasis on the anger codes. The sample was divided into two types of batterers—Type I and Type II—on the basis of heart rate reactivity. Type I men reduced their heart rates over the first third of the marital interaction discussion, and Type II men increased their heart rates. In terms of marital affect, Type I men exhibited more provocative and abusive anger; this emotional aggression decreased over the course of the problem-solving discussion. The emotional abusiveness of the Type II men increased over the course of the interaction; however, it did not reach the initial level of Type I men's emotional aggression. Wives of Type I husbands showed less anger and more sadness during the discussion than did wives of Type II husbands; for both groups of wives, anger increased over time.

Analysis of prior violence histories and psychopathology for the men also revealed differences between the two types of batterers. The Type I batterers were much more likely to have been violent with others (friends, strangers, coworkers), and much more likely to report having observed their fathers behaving violently toward their mothers (Gottman et al., 1995). Type I men also were more severely violent toward their wives; they were more likely to have threatened or used a weapon, and to have kicked, bitten, or hit her with fists than were Type II husbands (Jacobson, Gottman, & Shortt, 1995). Finally, Type I men were more likely to have been assessed as antisocial, drug-dependent, and aggressive-sadistic (Gottman et al., 1995).

Gottman et al. (1995) concluded that Type I batterers may be characterized by "focused attention" aimed at control of the wife. Their belligerent and contemptuous control seemed successful at restraining the wife's expression of anger and maximizing her feelings of fear. The authors speculated that this control was enacted in response to the wives' reasonable requests for cooperation and respect. In their 1998 book *When Men Batter Women,* Jacobson and Gottman named these Type I batterers "cobras" to highlight their sense of entitlement to get whatever they want by whatever means necessary. Ultimately, they will not be controlled.

Type II men, on the other hand, responded with loss of emotional control to their wives' greater independence moves; they became abusive in an attempt to keep the wife from pulling away emotionally (Gottman et al., 1995). Jacobson and Gottman (1998) have labeled these Type II batterers "pit bulls," because their fear of abandonment produces jealous rages which escalate into violence. They were characterized by the slow burn and the quick temper.

As several of the previous studies demonstrate, an important issue in the study of marital interaction and physical violence is the behavior of husband versus wife. Jacobson et al. (1994, p. 987) emphasize that in the course of violent arguments and violent relationships, it is "the men who are driving the system." Indeed, they contrast their findings on violent marriages with previous work on distressed marriages. While wives in distressed marriages exhibit more negative affect and demand more change than do their husbands, this gender difference disappears when the distress is accompanied by violence. In violent marriages, husbands are highly likely to exhibit negative affect and verbal aggression.

This emphasis on the battering male as the "driver of the system" leads us to the fifth section of this review, an examination of additional studies which assess patterns of dominance and power.

PATTERNS OF DOMINANCE AND POWER DYNAMICS

Several investigators have specifically examined the issues of dominance and power in marriages with a violent husband. Three very distinct types of studies will be reviewed here: studies of relational control, a study of male rejection of female influence, and studies of demand/withdraw patterns.

Relational control refers to the process of establishing joint and individual rights to direct the action of the dyad (Millar & Rogers, 1987). Three studies demonstrate that a struggle for relational control may characterize physically violent marriages. In an analysis of abusive couples' initial counseling discussions of their latest incident of abuse, Gage (1988) found an overwhelming proportion of competitive symmetry (one partner's attempt to assert definitional rights is followed by the other partner's attempt to assert definitional rights). The struggle for relational control clearly dominated these interactions, with strong patterns of nonacceptance of the other's directive assertions. Sabourin (1995) found high rates of competitive symmetry and nonsupport statements, and a tendency toward negative reciprocity among violent couples.

In addition to these studies of more extreme situations of abuse and distress, Rogers et al. (1996) focused on minor violence among relatively satisfied, nonclinical couples. In a context of moderate marital satisfaction, physically violent husbands tended to use more one-up messages (attempts to assert definitional rights) than did their nonviolent counterparts. Violent husbands also displayed the highest levels of nonconstructive communication patterns, including nonsupport messages and competitive symmetry, and they were somewhat more domineering and dominant than their wives. In contrast, nonviolent husbands and wives were very similar in their use of one-up control (responding to a negative message from the partner with a positive or neutral message), and egalitarian patterns of dominance.

Coan, Gottman, Babcock, and Jacobson (1997) examined a particularly interesting facet of dominance patterns. They were specifically interested in the degree to which battering men "reject influence" from women. In watching the interaction of violent men with their wives, these researchers noted a "bat-em-back" tendency—the batterers reminded them of baseball batters at automatic pitching machines who hit back every pitch. Specific to marital interaction, every low-level negative affect from the wife (complaint, sadness, anger) seemed to be batted back, with an "in-your-face" quality of contempt, belligerence, or defensiveness. The violent husbands were also noted to rarely say anything conciliatory.

Coan et al. (1997) specifically tested the "bat-em-back" tendency in 94 couples (again using the SPAFF coding system) by looking at sequences of low-intensity negative affect that were escalated to high intensity by the husband. They found that, particularly for Type I batterers (the "cobras"— batterers whose heart rates declined over the course of a discussion), there were heightened levels of reciprocation with high-intensity negative affect. Their wives responded with both acceptance and rejection of the negative affect, once again reflecting a pattern of both fear and resistance to the husband's domination. Coan et al. (1997) speculated that these Type I batterers were locked into an "honor code" which equated accepting influence from the wife with being unmasculine. They may feel compelled to reject all attempts at influence on the part of their wives, not only because of a pathological desire to control their wives, but also as part of the belief that it is their right to do so. On the other hand, Type II batterers (the "pit bulls") rejected only the highly negative interactions from their wives; they appeared to be threatened by the independence of their wives and fearful of abandonment.

A study by Babcock et al. (1993) on power processes and demand/ withdraw patterns (i.e., one spouse makes a demand, and the other spouse withdraws) is relevant here. The authors hypothesized that a husband's lack of power would be related to increased risk of violence in the marriage. They developed the Behavioral Observation of Communication Skill Coding System to assess communication during a systematic interview. A total of 95 married couples were assessed with the BOCS and a variety of measures of power processes and outcomes.

Babcock et al. (1993) demonstrated that battering husbands exhibited higher levels of demand/withdraw interaction patterns than did nonbattering men. Indeed, both spouses reported engaging in the demand/withdraw pattern, resulting in the potential for numerous power struggles. Further, when both husband and wife were low in communication ability, and when the husband was in a less powerful position relative to his wife, there was an increased risk of more severe physical violence by the husband. Babcock et al. (1993) concluded that violence may be enacted in an attempt to make up for lack of power in the marriage, and/or as a tactic to ensure winning verbal arguments despite low communication skills.

In my study of daily marital interaction (the method is described in detail in Lloyd, 1996), I also utilized the Christensen and Sullaway (1984) demand/ withdraw measure, which was included in the 18-month follow-up data collection. My findings corroborate those of Babcock et al. (1993); distressed marriages with a violent husband were characterized by the highest levels of *both* husband demand/wife withdraw and wife demand/husband withdraw, whereas nonviolent distressed marriages were characterized by less husband demand/wife withdraw than wife demand/husband withdraw behaviors.

SUMMARY

The studies reviewed in this chapter provide an emerging picture of the interpersonal and communication dynamics of wife battering. Understanding these interpersonal dynamics requires consideration of a complex set of factors, from the social skills deficits of the husband to the male honor code of control of women. The model depicted in Figure 5.1 attempts to summarize the research reviewed here and to depict the way in which these interpersonal (and societal) dynamics are interwoven. This model emphasizes the importance of attending to the interplay of four factors in understanding the communication dynamics in marriages with a battering husband: social skills, control, climate, and interaction. *Social skills deficits* that make a person prone to violence can include low levels of argumentativeness, hostile attributions for the wife's behavior, and nonconstructive problem solving skills. These skills deficits interact with *a context of control,* which is characterized by a belief in a male honor code that emphasizes the importance of the rejection of female influence, perceived threat to the husband's control of the wife and marriage, and the efficacy of the use of aggression as a tactic of control. Both social skills deficits and the context of control interact with the *marital climate* that make possible violent interaction; such a climate is characterized by dependency and enmeshment, volatility and intensity, and long-standing frustrations. This marital climate both influences and is influenced by violence-promoting *marital interaction,* which is characterized by rigid and sequenced patterns of communication, negative affect, belligerence on the part of the husband, resistance and fear on the part of the wife, and patterns of demand/withdraw. It is the interplay of these factors, rather than any one characteristic alone, which is most useful in understanding the communication dynamics that surround wife battering.

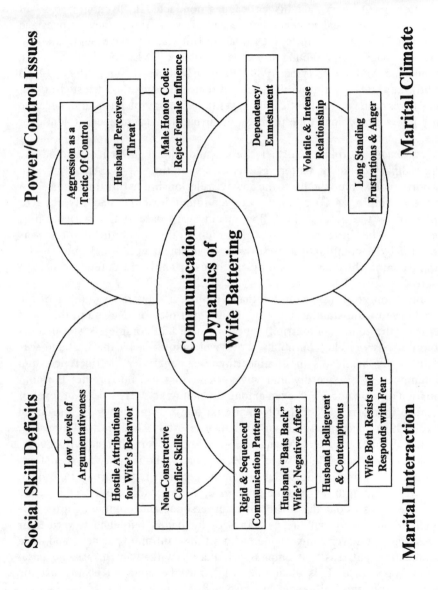

Figure 5.1: Communication Dynamics of Wife Battering

WHAT HAPPENS TO MARRIAGES WITH
A VIOLENT HUSBAND OVER TIME?

Several investigators have addressed the question of the longitudinal course of battering. O'Leary and his colleagues conducted a 36-month study of the course of physical violence before and after marriage; they emphasized the role of marital discord, overt verbal hostility, and passive aggression toward the spouse in predicting subsequent violence (O'Leary, Barling, Arias, Rosenbaum, Malone, & Tyree, 1989; O'Leary, Malone, & Tyree, 1994). Lloyd (1996), in an 18-month follow-up, found that marriages that desisted in violence across time were significantly lower in husband violence and in negative daily interaction at one time than were marriages that remained violent over time.

Jacobson, Gottman, Gortner, Berns, and Shortt (1996) examined the longitudinal course of battering over a 2-year time span. An impressive proportion of women did leave the abusive relationship in this time span: 38% of their sample of 60 couples with a violent husband had divorced or separated by the time of the follow-up, in every case at the instigation of the wife. The best prediction of which couples would divorce was achieved by a combination of severity of husband emotional abuse, wife dissatisfaction, husband physiological arousal, and wife defending herself assertively.

Jacobson et al. (1996) noted that although a significant number of the men showed a substantial decrease in the level of violence (more than half of those who remained married), only one man had completely stopped his violent behavior. The continuation of severe violence by the husband was predicted by his levels of domineeringness, negativity, belligerence, and contempt; it is noteworthy that wives' behaviors did not predict the continuation of violence. And, even among the men who decreased their level of violence in marriage, levels of emotional abuse remained high. Jacobson et al. (1996) speculated that, once control is established in a relationship, emotional abuse may serve to maintain it without overt physical violence.

Jacobson et al. (1996) were very cautionary about applying their findings to therapy and public policy, given the preliminary nature of their data. However, their findings, and the findings of all the studies reviewed here, do speak volumes about the utility of interpersonal and communication perspectives in teasing out the dynamics of husbands' violence toward their wives. Early intervention with men who hit their intimate partners, and male socialization patterns that emphasize equality with women, assume paramount importance. It is clear that what must be changed is not just the pattern of physical violence, but also a dynamic of negative interaction, emotional abuse, unresolved conflict, and male domination of the relationship.

REFERENCES

Anglin, K., & Holtzworth-Munroe, A. (1997). Comparing the responses of maritally violent and nonviolent spouses to problematic marital and nonmarital situations: Are the skills deficits of physically aggressive husbands and wives global? *Journal of Family Psychology, 11,* 301-313.

Babcock, J. C., Waltz, J., Jacobson, N. S., & Gottman, J. M. (1993). Power and violence: The relation between communication patterns, power discrepancies, and domestic violence. *Journal of Consulting and Clinical Psychology, 61,* 40-50.

Bograd, M. (1984). Family systems approaches to wife battering: A feminist critique. *American Journal Of Orthopsychiatry, 54,* 558-568.

Bograd, M. (1990). Why we need gender to understand human violence. *Journal of Interpersonal Violence, 5,* 132-135.

Boyle, D. J., & Vivian, D. (1996). Generalized versus spouse-specific anger/hostility and men's violence against intimates. *Violence and Victims, 11,* 293-317.

Burman, B., John, R. S., & Margolin, G. (1992). Observed patterns of conflict in violent, nonviolent and nondistressed couples. *Behavioral Assessment, 14,* 15-37.

Burman, B., Margolin, G., & John, R. S. (1993). America's angriest home videos: Behavioral contingencies observed in home reenactments of marital conflict. *Journal of Consulting and Clinical Psychology, 61,* 28-39.

Cahn, D. D. (1996). Family violence from a communication perspective. In D. D. Cahn & S. A. Lloyd (Eds.), *Family violence from a communication perspective* (pp. 1-19). Thousand Oaks, CA: Sage.

Choice, P., Lampke, L. K., & Pittman, J. F. (1995). Conflict resolution strategies and marital distress as mediating factors in the link between witnessing interparental violence and wife battering. *Violence and Victims, 10,*107-120.

Christensen, A., & Sullaway, M. (1984). *Communication patterns questionnaire.* Unpublished manuscript, University of California, Los Angeles.

Coan, J., Gottman, J. M., Babcock, J., & Jacobson, N. (1997). Battering and the male rejection of influence from women. *Aggressive Behavior, 23,* 375-388.

Cordova, J. V., Jacobson, N. S., Gottman, J. M., Rushe, R., & Cox, G. (1993). Negative reciprocity and communication in couples with a violent husband. *Journal of Abnormal Psychology, 102,* 559-564.

Dobash, R. E., & Dobash, R. P. (1979). *Violence against wives: A case against patriarchy.* New York: Free Press.

Dutton, D. G. (1994). Patriarchy and wife assault: The ecological fallacy. *Violence and Victims, 9,* 167-182.

Dutton, D. G. (1988). *The domestic assault of women.* Boston: Allyn & Bacon.

Dutton, D. G., & Browning, J. J. (1988). Concern for power, fear of intimacy, and aversive stimuli for wife assault. In G. T. Hotaling, D. Finkelhor, J. T. Kirkpatrick, & M. A. Straus (Eds.), *Family abuse and its consequences: New directions in research* (pp. 163-175). Newbury Park, CA: Sage.

Dutton, D. G., & Golant, S. K. (1995). *The batterer: A psychological profile.* New York: Basic Books.

Emery, B. C. , & Lloyd, S. A. (1994). A feminist perspective on the study of women who use aggression in close relationships. In D. L. Sollie & L. A. Leslie (Eds.),

Gender, families, and close relationships: Feminist research journeys (pp. 237-262). Thousand Oaks, CA: Sage.

Ferraro, K. J. (1988). An existential approach to battering. In G. T. Hotaling, D. Finkelhor, J. T. Kirkpatrick & M. A. Straus (Eds.), *Family abuse and its consequences: New directions in research* (pp. 126-138). Newbury Park, CA: Sage.

Gage, R. B. (1988). *An Analysis of Relational Control Patterns in Abusive Couples.* Unpublished doctoral dissertation, Seton Hall University.

Goldner, V., Penn, P., Sheinberg, M., & Walker, G. (1990). Love and violence: Gender paradoxes in volatile attachments. *Family Process, 29,* 343-364.

Gortner, E. T., Gollan, J. K., & Jacobson, N. S. (1997). Psychological aspects of perpetrators of domestic violence and their relationships with their victims. *Psychiatric Clinics of North America, 20,* 337-352.

Gottman, J. M., Jacobson, N. S., Rushe, R. R., Shortt, J. W., Babcock, J., La Taillade, & Waltz, J. (1995). The relationship between heart rate reactivity, emotionally aggressive behavior, and general violence in batterers. *Journal of Family Psychology, 9,* 227-248.

Gottman, J. M., & Krokoff, L. J. (1989). Marital interaction and satisfaction: A longitudinal view. *Journal of Consulting and Clinical Psychology, 57,* 47-52.

Holtzworth-Munroe, A. (1992). Social skills deficits in maritally violent men: interpreting the data using a social information processing model. *Clinical Psychology Review, 12,* 605-617.

Holtzworth-Munroe, A. & Anglin, K. (1991). The competency of responses given by maritally violent versus nonviolent men to problematic marital situations. *Violence and Victims, 6,* 257-269.

Holtzworth-Munroe, A., & Hutchinson, G. (1993). Attributing negative intent to wife behavior: The attributions of maritally violent versus nonviolent men. *Journal of Abnormal Psychology, 102,* 206-211.

Holtzworth-Munroe, A., & Smutzler, N. (1996). Comparing the emotional reactions and behavioral intentions of violent and nonviolent husbands to aggressive, distressed and other wife behaviors. *Violence and Victims, 11,* 319-340.

Infante, D., Chandler, T. A., & Rudd, J. E. (1989). Test of an argumentative skill deficiency model of interspousal violence. *Communication Monographs, 56,* 163-177.

Infante, D. C., Sabourin, T. C., Rudd, J. E., & Shannon, E. A. (1990). Verbal aggression in violent and nonviolent marital disputes. *Communication Quarterly,38,* 361-371.

Huston, T. L, Robins, E., Atkinson, J., & McHale, S. M. (1987). Surveying the landscape of marital behavior: A behavioral self-report approach to studying marriage. In S. Oskamp (Ed.), *Family Processes and Problems* (Vol. 7, pp. 45-71). Newbury Park, CA: Sage.

Jacobson, N. S., & Gottman, J. M. (1998). *When men batter women: New insights into ending abusive relationships.* New York: Simon & Shuster.

Jacobson, N. S., Gottman, J. M., Gortner, E., Berns, S., & Shortt, J. W. (1996). Psychological factors in the longitudinal course of battering: When do the couples split up? When does the abuse decrease? *Violence and Victims, 11,* 371-392.

Jacobson, N. S., Gottman, J. M., & Shortt, J. W. (1995). The distinction between type I and type II batterers: Reply to Ordnuff et al. (1995), Margolin et al. (1995), and Walker (1995). *Journal of Family Psychology, 9,* 272-279.

Jacobson, N. S., Gottman, J. M., Waltz, J., Rushe, R., Babcock, J., & Holtzworth-Munroe, A. (1994). Affect, verbal content, and psychophysiology in the arguments of couples with a violent husband. *Journal of Consulting and Clinical Psychology,62,* 982-988.

Johnson, M. P. (1995). Patriarchal terrorism and common couple violence: Two forms of violence against women. *Journal of Marriage and the Family, 57,* 283-294.

Kirkwood, C. (1993). *Leaving abusive partners.* Newbury Park, CA: Sage.

Langhinrichsen-Rohling, J., Schlee, K. A., Monson, C. M., Ehrensaft, M., & Heyman, R. (1998). What's love got to do with it?: Perceptions of marital positivity in H-to-W aggressive, distressed, and happy marriages. *Journal of Family Violence,13,* 197-212.

Langhinrichsen-Rohling, J., Smutzler, N., & Vivian, D. (1994). Positivity in marriage: The role of discord and physical aggression against wives. *Journal of Marriage and the Family, 56,* 69-79.

Lloyd, S. A. (1990). Conflict types and strategies in violent marriages. *Journal of Family Violence, 5,* 269-284.

Lloyd, S. A. (1991). The dark side of courtship. *Family Relations, 40,* 14-20.

Lloyd, S. A. (1996). Physical aggression and marital distress: The role of everyday marital interaction. In D. D. Cahn & S. A. Lloyd (Eds.), *Family violence from a communication perspective* (pp. 177-198). Thousand Oaks, CA: Sage.

Lloyd, S. A., & Emery, B. C. (1994). Physically aggressive conflict in romantic relationships. In D. Cahn (Ed.), *Conflict in personal relationships* (pp. 27-46). New York: Erlbaum.

Margolin, G., & Burman, B. (1993). Wife abuse versus marital violence: Different terminologies, explanations and solutions. *Clinical Psychology Review, 13,* 59-73.

Margolin, G., Burman, B., & John, R. S. (1989). Home observations of married couples reenacting naturalistic conflicts. *Behavioral Assessment, 11,* 101-118.

Margolin, G., John, R. S., & Gleberman, L. (1988). Affective responses to conflictual discussions in violent and nonviolent couples. *Journal of Consulting and Clinical Psychology, 56,* 24-33.

Margolin, G., John, R. S., & O'Brien, M. (1989). Sequential affective patterns as a function of marital conflict style. *Journal of Social and Clinical Psychology, 8,* 45-61.

Marshall, L. L. (1994). Physical and psychological abuse. In W. R. Cupach & B. H. Spitzberg (Eds.), *The dark side of interpersonal communication* (pp. 281-311). Hillsdale, NJ: Erlbaum.

Maynard, M. (1993). Violence towards women. In D. Richardson & V. Robinson (Eds.), *Thinking Feminist* (pp. 99-122). New York: Guilford Press.

Millar, F. E., & Rogers, L. E. (1987). Relational dimensions of interpersonal dynamics. In M. E. Roloff & G. Miller (Eds.), *Interpersonal processes: New directions in communication research* (pp. 117-139). Newbury Park, CA: Sage.

Morse, B. J. (1995). Beyond the conflict tactics scale: Assessing gender differences in partner violence. *Violence and Victims, 10,* 251-272.

Murphy, C. M., Meyer, S. L., & O'Leary, K. D. (1994). Dependency characteristics of partner assaultive men. *Journal of Abnormal Psychology, 103,* 729-735.

Murphy, C. M., & O'Leary, K. D. (1989). Psychological aggression predicts physical aggression in early marriage. *Journal of Consulting and Clinical Psychology, 57,* 579-582.

O'Leary, K. D., Barling, J., Arias, I., Rosenbaum, A., Malone, J., & Tyree, A. (1989). Prevalence and stability of physical aggression between spouses: A longitudinal analysis. *Journal of Consulting and Clinical Psychology, 57,* 263-268.

O'Leary, K. D., Malone, J., & Tyree, A. (1994). Physical aggression in early marriage: Prerelationship and relationship effects. *Journal of Consulting and Clinical Psychology, 62,* 594-602.

Peterson, D. R. (1979). Assessing interpersonal relationships by means of interaction records. *Behavioral Assessment, 1,* 221-236.

Planalp, S. (1993). Communication, cognition and emotion. *Communication Monographs, 60,* 3-9.

Riggs, D. S., & O'Leary, K. D. (1996). Aggression between heterosexual dating partners: An examination of a causal model of courtship aggression. *Journal of Interpersonal Violence, 11,* 519-540.

Rogers, L. E., Castleton, A., & Lloyd, S. A. (1996). Relational control and physical aggression in satisfying marital relationships. In D. D. Cahn & S. A. Lloyd (Eds.), *Family violence from a communication perspective* (pp. 218-239). Thousand Oaks, CA: Sage.

Sabourin, T. C. (1996). The role of communication in verbal abuse between spouses. In D. D. Cahn & S. A. Lloyd (Eds.), *Family violence from a communication perspective* (pp. 199-217). Thousand Oaks, CA: Sage.

Sabourin, T. C. (1995). The role of negative reciprocity in spouse abuse: A relational control analysis. *Journal of Applied Communication, 23,* 271-283.

Sabourin, T. C., Infante, D. C., & Rudd, J. E. (1993). Verbal aggression in marriages: A comparison of violent, distressed but nonviolent, and nondistressed couples. *Human Communication Research, 20,* 245-267.

Sabourin, T. C., & Stamp, G. H. (1995). Communication and the experience of dialectical tensions in family life: An examination of abusive and nonabusive families. *Communication Monographs, 62,* 213-242.

Schwartz, M. D. (1987). Gender and injury in spousal assault. *Sociological Focus, 20,* 61-75.

Spitzberg, B. H. (1997). Violence in intimate relationships. In W. R. Cupach & D. J. Canary (Eds.), *Competence in interpersonal conflict* (pp. 175-201). New York: McGraw-Hill.

Stamp, G. H., & Sabourin, T. C. (1995). Accounting for violence: An analysis of male spousal abuse narratives. *Journal of Applied Communication Research, 23,* 284-307.

Stets, J. E. (1992). Interactive processes in dating aggression: A national study. *Journal of Marriage and the Family, 54,* 165-177.

Stets, J. E. (1988). *Domestic violence and control.* New York: Springer Verlag.

Stets, J. E., & Henderson, D. A. (1991). Contextual factors surrounding conflict resolution while dating: Results from a national study. *Family Relations, 40,* 29-36.

Stets, J. E., & Pirog-Good, M. A. (1990). Interpersonal control and courtship aggression. *Journal of Social and Personal Relationships, 7,* 371-394.

Stets, J. E., & Straus, M. A. (1990). Gender differences in reporting marital violence and its medical and social consequences. In M. A. Straus & R. J. Gelles (Eds.), *Physical violence in American families* (pp. 151-166). New Brunswick, NJ: Transaction.

Straus, M. A., & Gelles, R. J. (1990). How violent are American families? Estimates from the national family violence resurvey and other studies. In M. A. Straus & R. J.

Gelles (Eds.), *Physical violence in American families* (pp. 95-112). New Brunswick, NJ: Transaction.

Straus, M. A., Gelles, R., & Steinmetz, S. K. (1980). *Behind Closed Doors*. Garden City, NY: Doubleday.

Vuchinich, S. (1987). Starting and stopping spontaneous family conflicts. *Journal of Marriage and the Family, 49,* 591-601.

Weiss, R. L., & Summers, K. J. (1983). Marital interaction coding system III. In E. Filsinger (Ed.), *Marriage and family assessment* (pp. 35-115). Beverly Hills, CA: Sage.

Yl18, K. (1994). Reflections of a feminist family violence researcher. In D. A. Sollie & L. A. Leslie (Eds.), *Gender, families, and close relationships: Feminist research journeys* (pp. 213-236). Thousand Oaks, CA: Sage.

Alcohol Use and Husband Marital Aggression Among Newlywed Couples

Kenneth E. Leonard

Researchers and practitioners concerned with marital violence have frequently commented upon the prevalence of alcoholism among domestically violent men, and the co-occurrence of alcohol intoxication and domestic violence since the earliest recognition of wife abuse as an important social issue. For example, Gelles (1974) reported that alcohol consumption accompanied marital violence in approximately 50% of the violent couples in this sample. Roy (1982) reported that 35% of 4,000 women who called an abuse hotline indicated that their husbands were "problem alcoholics." These published reports were often accompanied by the caution that the alcohol was not the cause of violence. Instead, alcohol's association with marital aggression was viewed either as a spurious association or the result of the violent man seeking an "excuse" for his violence. Indeed, the empirical literature at that time was suggestive of an association between alcohol and marital violence, but was so limited that nothing beyond this association could be

AUTHOR'S NOTE: This research was supported by grant R01-AA08128 awarded to Kenneth E. Leonard. Address correspondence to: Kenneth E. Leonard, Research Institute on Addictions, 1021 Main Street, Buffalo, New York 14203, Telephone, (716) 887-2509. Fax (716) 887-2510, E-mail address: Leonard@RIA.ORG. I am grateful to Lalee Backus for preparation of this manuscript and Rob Marczyzinski for graphics support.

asserted. The potential causal influence of alcohol on domestic violence was often viewed as one of the "myths that undermine understanding of family violence" (Gelles & Cornell, 1985, pp. 13-19).

Recent research has found that both excessive alcohol consumption (e.g., frequency of intoxication, average daily alcohol consumption) and alcohol abuse (e.g., excessive consumption and the occurrence of problems associated with consumption) are significantly related to marital aggression (Coleman & Straus, 1983; Fagan, Stewart, & Hansen, 1983; Leonard & Blane, 1992; Leonard, Bromet, Parkinson, Day, & Ryan, 1985). For example, Leonard and Blane (1992) found that problematic alcohol use was associated with marital aggression after controlling for sociodemographic factors, hostility, self-consciousness, and marital satisfaction. Similarly, Reider, Zucker, Noll, Maguin, and Fitzgerald (1988) reported that, among alcoholic husbands and their wives, the severity of alcohol problems on the part of the husband was significantly related to the husband's cumulative violence toward his wife, after controlling for husband antisocial behavior, husband perception of family conflict, and husband and wife age.

These studies were of importance in that they began to address the conceptual-methodological problems that have plagued this area and to substantiate the association between alcohol and domestic violence (Leonard & Jacob, 1988). For example, these studies have utilized clear criteria for both the alcohol variables and the marital aggression variables; the samples have not been clinic samples, but rather community and representative samples; the studies have utilized implicit comparisons of subjects with heavy versus lighter alcohol use; and they have controlled for potentially confounding sociodemographic, personality, and family factors.

Despite the progress made by these studies, a variety of important issues remained. First, virtually all of these studies were cross-sectional analyses. As stated by Gelles (1993), "it is at least plausible that drinking . . . that is correlated with violence commenced *after* the onset of the violent and abusive behavior" (p. 193, italics in the original). Consequently, the absence of prospective studies of alcohol and marital violence was a serious problem.

Second, many of the studies had not been attentive to the different stages of family development and to the possibility that alcohol might be important during some developmental period, but less important during other periods. Alcohol may be an important factor primarily during the initiation of violence, and may be a less important influence once that aggression has been established. Our own interest focused on the marriage transition and the early years of marriage for several reasons. First, the rates of marital violence are highest among young couples (Suitor, Pillemer, & Straus, 1990), and evidence suggests that many instances of violence actually precede marriage (O'Leary et al., 1989). Second, frequent heavy drinking and alcohol problems reach their highest rate among men and women in their early twenties (Blane, 1978; Clark & Midanik, 1982; Hilton, 1991a, 1991b); they decline somewhat in the late twenties, and decline markedly in the thirties and forties. For example, in the most recent national survey, Hilton (1991a) reported that 33% of men age 18 to 29 have a weekly or more frequent episode of heavy drinking (five drinks on a single occasion). Consequently, by virtue of the base rates of heavy drinking and marital aggression, young couples were an obvious and important population. Moreover, focusing on newlywed couples allowed us to observe the relationship between alcohol and violence in a sample, before any influence of these two variables on marital dissolution could have occurred.

The third important issue concerned the lack of an appropriate theoretical model for understanding how alcohol use and/or alcohol abuse might influence marital violence. In developing a model such as Figure 6.1, one of the primary issues to be addressed was the differential levels of explanation embedded in the constructs of alcohol use and alcohol abuse. Specifically, one set of variables that had often been studied were distal variables, variables that were more or less constant in the individual and were viewed as important in domestic violence because they discriminated violent from nonviolent men. For example, trait anger and hostility are often viewed as important to domestic violence. These variables "reside" in the individual, are used to explain differences between violent and nonviolent men, and are presumed to "come into play" in some way at the occurrence of the violence. In contrast, variables that operate in the potentially violent episode are referred to as proximal variables. These variables may distinguish violent from nonviolent individuals, but may also distinguish between instances of violence and instances of nonviolent behavior among violent men. In the case of trait anger, the proximal representation of this variable might be state anger. Note that the presence of an association between the occurrence of violence and trait anger is not necessarily supportive of the occurrence of anger at the time of the violent episode. Rather, the findings at the distal level are taken to suggest the importance of the variables at the proximal level, though this distinction is rarely discussed. However, in the case of alcohol, the potential disjunction between the distal variable, a pattern of heavy drinking, and the proximal variable, acute alcohol use, is more evident. That is, alcohol abusers are not under the influence of alcohol at all times, and in fact, many alcohol abusers may drink in an episodic fashion.

There are many aspects to the model depicted in Figure 6.1. For the purposes of this chapter, we will focus on only those relevant to the potential contribution of alcohol. Specifically, we will address the following issues: (1) What is the relationship between the distal drinking pattern of husbands and wives and the occurrence/frequency of marital aggression, and what factors moderate this relationship; (2) What is the relationship between the distal factor of drinking patterns and the proximal factor of drinking during episodes of violence?; (3) What is the relationship between the proximal drinking factor and the occurrence/severity of marital aggression?

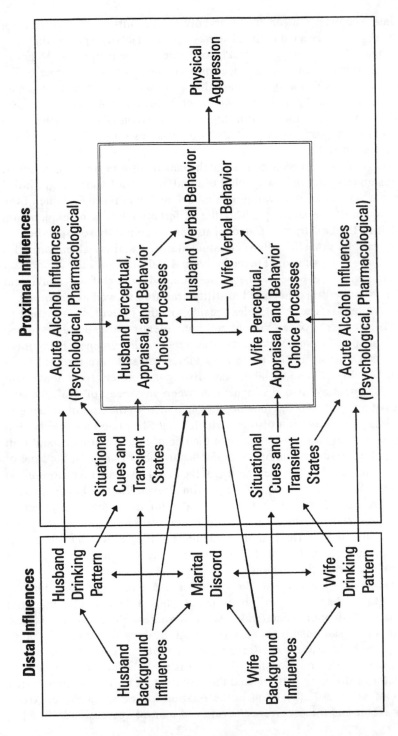

Figure 6.1: Heuristic Model of Alcohol and Marital Aggression

116

THE BUFFALO NEWLYWED STUDY

Design and Procedure

In order to address these issues, we began the Buffalo Newlywed Study (BNS) in 1987. The BNS is a three-wave longitudinal study of newly married couples conducted over the first 3 years of marriage. A full description of the methodology is presented in Leonard and Senchak (1996). Briefly, couples applying for a marriage license who indicated that this was the first marriage for both husband and wife, and that the husband was between the ages of 18 and 29 inclusive, were recruited for a brief screen. These couples were then interviewed separately by a same-gender interviewer concerning socio-demographic and drinking variables and then recruited for the longitudinal study. Couples who agreed to participate (842 or 90% of those recruited) were each given a questionnaire packet and a separate postage-paid envelope in which to return the questionnaire. The couples were instructed to complete the questionnaires in private, to return them within two weeks, and not to discuss the questionnaires until both of them had completed and mailed them back. Complete data were collected from 647 couples, or approximately 77% of the couples who agreed to participate. African American couples were less likely to complete the assessment than other racial/ethnic groups. Completion rates were higher for younger couples, couples living together prior to marriage, couples with higher husband income, and couples in which the wife was unemployed.

The second data collection of the project involved the 1-year follow-up assessment of couples (T + 1). This assessment involved separate interviews with husbands and wives as well as completion of the same questionnaire battery used before. Of the 647 couples who provided complete data at the time of marriage (T0), at least one questionnaire or one interview was completed for 543 couples (84%), and both questionnaires and interviews were completed for 494 couples (76%). Despite the relatively good rates of follow-up, certain subgroups manifested somewhat lower rates. In particular, follow-up rates were higher among older couples, white couples, and higher socioeconomic status couples. However, complete and incomplete couples at T + 1 did not differ with respect to premarital aggression, or husband or wife frequent heavy drinking.

At the 3-year anniversary (T + 3), all of the complete couples at T0 were targeted for follow-up. At T + 3, we collected full information (husband and wife questionnaires and interviews) for 62% (N = 400) of the complete T0 couples, and partial information for an additional 9% (N = 58)

Description of the Sample

The couples successfully recruited for the newlywed study represent a large, heterogeneous sample. The average age of couples in the sample closely approximated the average age of couples at marriage nationally. Husbands were approximately 24 years old, and wives were 1 year younger on the average. Reflecting the urban area in which the couples resided, approximately 70% of the sample were Caucasian, and approximately 25% were African American. Only about 5% were Hispanic, with a few subjects of Oriental or American Indian descent. The sample was predominantly Catholic (50%). Protestant denominations (Episcopal, Lutheran, Methodist) and fundamentalist Protestant denominations (e.g., Baptist, Pentecostal) were endorsed by 15% and 23%, respectively. Only 10% reported no religious affiliation. The rates of other religions, including Judaism, were negligible in this sample. Approximately one third had completed high school or a G.E.D. and had gone no further with their education, but only 12% reported not completing high school. One third had some college or occupational training. An additional 25% were college graduates. Wives had educational levels similar to the husbands. One of the most surprising statistics was that 32% of this sample of first marriages already had children and that 14% were currently pregnant. However, other representative samples of newlyweds have reported similar findings (Crohan & Veroff, 1989).

Scope of the Assessments

Couples were involved in a brief screening interview when they applied for their marriage license, a large battery of self-report questionnaires and some spouse-report questionnaires that were administered at T0, T + 1, and T + 3, and individual interviews focused on occurrences of marital conflict at T + 1 and T + 3. The screening interview focused on sociodemographic factors, such as the education and occupation of both the husband and wife, race/ethnicity, religion, and employment situation (full-time, part-time, un-employed, student, housewife, military). In addition, questions concerning the drinking behavior of the husband and wife were asked, as well as several questions derived from the Conflict Tactics Scale to assess premarital aggression in the couples. The core questionnaires, which were identical for husband and wife and across T0, T + 1, and T + 3, focused on four general domains: alcohol consumption patterns, alcohol expectancies, personality factors, and relationship functioning factors.

Alcohol Consumption Patterns

Several important issues were addressed in the measurement of alcohol consumption patterns. First, quantity-frequency variability questions based on the work of Cahalan, Cisin, and Crossley (1969) were asked of couples with respect to the past year. Additional questions asked the husband and wife about the frequency of drinking six or more drinks per occasion and the frequency of drinking to intoxication. The Alcohol Dependence Scale (Skinner & Allen, 1982) was also used. This is a 25-item scale that was derived through the use of factor analysis of the Alcohol Use Inventory (Wanberg, Horn, & Foster, 1977).

Alcohol Expectancies

Two aspects of alcohol expectancies were of interest: the subject's belief concerning the effects of alcohol intoxication, and tolerance of deviant behaviors performed by intoxicated persons. The Alcohol Effects Questionnaire (AEQ) developed by Rohsenow (1983) was used in the present study. Since expectancies appear to differ as a function of the amount of alcohol consumed (Southwick, Steele, Marlatt, & Lindell, 1981), subjects were asked their beliefs with respect to the effects of enough alcohol to become intoxicated on people in general. The second aspect of expectancy was the tolerance for intoxicated behavior, assessed with the Permissiveness in Respect to Aggression While Intoxicated Scale devised by Bruun (1959).

Personality Factors

Dispositional hostility is commonly considered to be a complex affective response which predisposes individuals to behave in an aggressive fashion. In the present study, the 10-item Spielberger Trait Anger Scale (STAS) (Spielberger et al., 1979) assessed anger, and the assault subscale of the Buss-Durkee Hostility Inventory (Buss & Durkee, 1957) assessed the individual's report of behavioral tendencies with respect to actual physical aggression. Given the potential importance of gender roles in violence, gender role identity was assessed with the Personal Attributes Questionnaire (Spence, Helmreich, & Stapp, 1974), which consists of two separate scales balanced for socially desirable items measuring masculinity (instrumental behavior) and femininity (expressive behavior).

Relationship Functioning

According to the model guiding this project, marital problems and dissatisfactions serve as instigations to aggress, and some evidence has been presented that cross-sectionally, marital dissatisfaction is related to marital violence (Leonard et al., 1985). The Family Assessment Measure (FAM; Skinner, Steinhauer, & Santa-Barbara, 1984) is a self-report instrument of family strengths and weaknesses. Applied to the marital dyad, it reflects the spouse's evaluation of the partner's functioning on a variety of different marital tasks. The Margolin Conflict Inventory (Margolin, 1980) is a 26-item scale devised to determine an individual's typical response to conflict in the marriage. Three factors have been derived from this scale, Verbal Aggression,

Problem Solving, and Withdrawal. The Miller Social Intimacy Scale (Miller & Lefcourt, 1982) is a 17-item scale which taps the degree of closeness, affection, and personal disclosure in the marriage.

At the T + 1 and T + 3 assessments, separate interviews were conducted with husbands and wives to determine the absence/presence, extent, and severity of marital violence within the first year of marriage. For this purpose, the Conflict Tactics Scale (CTS; Straus, 1979) was administered to both members of the couple. This scale consists of 18 items describing behaviors which the respondent may have displayed within the context of a marital conflict situation. Although some of these behaviors are adaptive (i.e., "discussed the conflict calmly"), most describe different degrees of verbal and physical aggression (ranging from "argued heatedly but short of yelling" to "used a knife or gun"). Husbands and wives reported on their own behavior, as well as the behavior of their spouse. For analyses of distal elements of the model, husband and wife scores were combined by taking the maximum report of husband aggression. Supplementing and extending this assessment procedure was an interview designed to describe important characteristics of the first episode of violence, the most severe marital argument, the most severe episode of violence, and episodes of violence in general. Some of the characteristics which were of importance were drinking, drunkenness, and drug use by either the husband or the wife; the perceived interaction preceding the violence; and the attributions of causality relative to the episode. This interview was administered only to respondents acknowledging some degree of verbal or physical aggression within the past year, or approximately 90% of the sample. Moreover, because the husband and wife may have described different episodes, analyses based on the proximal elements were necessarily conducted at the individual level of reporting (in contrast to the couple report of aggression used in the distal model).

DISTAL DRINKING PATTERNS
AND MARITAL AGGRESSION

The Cross-Sectional and Longitudinal Relationship
Between Drinking Patterns and Marital Aggression

One of the primary findings of importance has been that a pattern of heavy drinking among these newlywed husbands was strongly associated with premarital aggression, and that this association could not be attributed to husband or wife hostility, marital satisfaction, conflict styles, or other personality or sociodemographic factors. In the initial analysis of these data, Leonard and Senchak (1993) examined the cross-sectional association between premarital drinking by both the husband and the wife and premarital aggression, both assessed during the screening interview. In terms of the simple bivariate correlations, the frequency of premarital aggression (average of husband and wife report of husband aggression) correlated with both husband's heavy drinking (r = .24, p .01) and wife's heavy drinking (r = .11, p .01) (defined on the basis of the Alcohol Dependence Scale and the frequency of intoxication and frequency of six or more drinks at a time). In the regression analyses, husband and wife heavy drinking predicted 1.6% of the unique variance after controlling for sociodemographic, personality, and relationship functioning variables. However, examination of the regression weights indicated that husband heavy drinking was significantly associated with the frequency of violence, but that wife heavy drinking was not.

This cross-sectional association basically replicates several other studies (Pan, Neidig, & O'Leary, 1994; Kaufman Kantor, & Straus, 1990) demonstrating that husband's drinking is related to marital aggression. As noted above, there have been very limited data concerning the longitudinal relationship between drinking and marital violence. Leonard and Senchak (1996) evaluated the relationship between T0 husband and wife drinking and T + 1 husband-to-wife violence, controlling for premarital violence. As in the earlier paper, sociodemographic factors, relationship factors (including perceived power), and personality factors were controlled in the analyses. In addition, the potential importance of a history of family violence was assessed. As before, husband, but not wife, heavy drinking was longitudinally predictive of the frequency of husband-to-wife violence. Importantly, this study replicates the study by Heyman, O'Leary, and Jouriles (1995), which found that indicators of husband heavy drinking at the time of marriage were predictive of marital violence at 6 and 18 months after marriage.

It is worth noting that, while husband drinking has been consistently associated with the frequency of husband-to-wife aggression, wife drinking has not. However, in some analyses (Leonard & Roberts, 1998a), in which a weighted severity index was utilized as the criterion variable, husband and wife heavy drinking were both significantly associated with the violence measure. This finding raises the possibility that wife drinking may not be related to the occurrence of husband to wife violence, but may be related to the severity of such aggression when it occurs. More detailed analyses are needed to examine this possibility.

Moderated Effects in the Cross-Sectional and Longitudinal Prediction of Marital Aggression

From the perspective of identifying high risk couples and understanding the distal relationship between heavy drinking and the occurrence of violence, we have examined whether husband (or wife) drinking interacts with theoretically relevant variables to predict marital aggression. Social learning models of alcohol and aggression have suggested that alcohol may lead to aggression because drinking alcohol serves as a discriminative cue that aggressive and other antinormative behavior would be unlikely to be socially punished. This model has most often been conceptualized as an "alcohol expectancy" model, in which the critical operative variable is the belief that alcohol causes aggression or that alcohol excuses aggression. While this expectancy is viewed as allowing aggression to occur when an individual has been drinking, it does not address the motivation for aggression. Consequently, we have hypothesized (Leonard & Senchak, 1993) that heavy drinking would interact with alcohol expectancies and with hostility or marital conflict to predict marital aggression. In the cross-sectional analysis presented by Leonard and Senchak (1993), there was evidence that husband heavy drinking interacted with relationship dissatisfaction in a theoretically congruent fashion. That is, heavy drinking was associated with premarital aggression among the maritally dissatisfied men, but not among the maritally satisfied men. Similarly, the interaction of heavy drinking and alcohol/ aggression expectancy was significant, with heavy drinking being associated with premarital aggression only among men who believed that alcohol caused aggression.

Although the moderation analysis was supportive of the social learning theory emphasizing alcohol expectancies, the cross-sectional nature of this analysis presents the same difficulty as any cross-sectional analysis, namely the inability to determine which came first–marital aggression or alcohol expectancy. As stated by Leonard and Senchak (1993, p. 106) "having engaged in premarital aggression while drinking might influence one's beliefs concerning the effects of alcohol." Consequently, we have recently examined these moderation analyses longitudinally (Quigley & Leonard, 1999). This analysis focused on the frequency of severe violence. Unlike the cross-sectional analyses, there was no evidence that alcohol expectancies moderated the relationship between heavy drinking and marital aggression. However, there was a significant interaction between marital conflict styles and heavy drinking in prospectively predicting marital aggression after controlling for premarital aggression. Heavy drinking was significantly and positively associated with marital aggression among those who scored high on the conflict styles measure, indicative of high levels of husband and wife verbal aggression. In contrast, heavy drinking was not significantly associated with marital aggression among couples who scored low on husband and wife verbal aggression. These findings are suggestive that excessive drinking might facilitate aggression primarily among couples who are already engaging in high levels of verbal conflict, but might not impact couples who are not in such conflict.

THE LINK BETWEEN DISTAL AND PROXIMAL ALCOHOL VARIABLES

The Proximal Presence of Alcohol in Episodes of Marital Aggression

As discussed previously, the association between the distal variable of drinking patterns and severe marital aggression does not ensure that there is an association between the proximal variable of acute alcohol use and the occurrence or severity of an episode of aggression. In fact, the distal relationship does not even suggest that any episode of aggression was accompanied by drinking. As we attempt to understand the relationship between the distal drinking variable and the proximal variable of drinking prior to marital aggression, it is important to begin with a simple description of the extent to which alcohol accompanies marital aggression. As described previously, at the first anniversary we interviewed the husband and wife about the occurrence of any verbal or physical aggression. Individuals who acknowledged verbal aggression were asked whether the husband and/or wife had been drinking prior to the most severe episode that did not include physical aggression. Individuals who acknowledged physical aggression were also asked about the most severe episode of verbal aggression that did not include physical aggression. In addition, they were asked about drinking prior to the first episode of physical aggression and the most severe episode.

The rates of drinking for the verbal episodes of nonaggressive couples and for the verbal, first and most severe physical aggression episodes are displayed in Table 6.1. Across both husband and wife reports, it is clear that drinking among the women was uncommon, ranging from 3% to 12%. It also appears that drinking during verbal episodes is somewhat more common among aggressive men (15% to 21%) than among nonaggressive men (9% to 11%). Furthermore, drinking was less common among verbal aggression events than among the physical aggression events among aggressive couples, although this difference was more marked among the wives' reports than among the husbands' reports. Among the relatively few individuals who indicated a second, more severe episode, husband drinking was even more marked. Even so, husband alcohol consumption was involved in, at most, a minority of episodes of aggression. It is also important to recognize that, while only a minority of couples indicated that the husband was drinking prior to the first episode, the proportion who indicated that the husband was drinking prior to at least one episode was higher. For example, among women who had experienced any husband to wife aggression, 45% indicated that their husband had been drinking prior to at least one aggressive episode, 20% indicated that he was drinking prior to at least two episodes, and 4% indicated he was drinking prior to three episodes. Only 31% indicated that their

TABLE 6.1 Percentages of Drinking During Episodes of Verbal or Physical
Aggression

	Nonaggressive Couples		Aggressive Couples	
	Verbal Episodes (n = 212)	Verbal Episodes (n = 113)	First Physical (n = 118)	Most Severe Physical (n = 25)
Wife Report				
Wife Drinking	3%	4%	12%	10%
Husband Drinking	9%	21%	37%	44%
	(n = 219)	(n = 104)	(n = 108)	(n = 12)
Husband Report				
Wife Drinking	3%	6%	11%	8%
Husband Drinking	11%	15%	23%	42%

husband aggressed only while sober. Among men who acknowledged any
husband to wife aggression, the corresponding figures were 35% (one episode
or more), 9% (two or more episodes), and 2% (three or more episodes). More
than half (54%) of the men acknowledged only sober aggression. It is also
important to recognize that approximately 50% of husbands who acknowledged drinking prior to one or more episodes also acknowledged engaging in
at least one episode of sober aggression. The figures were comparable for
wives. Applied to the overall prevalence rates, this suggests that among
newlywed couples, 16% to 18% (depending on wife versus husband report)
will experience violence only when the husband is sober, 5% to 6% will
experience violence only when the husband is drinking, and 5% to 7% will
experience violence both when the husband is sober and when he has been
drinking. It is important to remember that these rates reflect individual reports
of aggression rather than couples' reports. As a result, these estimates probably represent minimum rates.

The Link Between Drinking Patterns and
Drinking in Aggressive Episodes

As noted earlier, it is important to draw the distinction between distal
predictors and the proximal aspects of domestic violence. With respect to

alcohol, this means distinguishing between general drinking patterns (i.e., frequency of drinking, frequency of heavy drinking, usual quantity of alcohol consumed) and whether alcohol consumption accompanied incidents of domestic violence. This conceptual distinction should not be interpreted to suggest that these constructs are orthogonal. In fact, a drinking pattern characterized by frequent alcohol consumption significantly enhances the probability that, by chance alone, some episode of domestic violence will be accompanied by drinking. There is, however, little information available concerning the actual strength of this relationship.

One of the few sources of information regarding the relationship between drinking patterns and drinking in violent episodes is Kaufman Kantor and Straus (1990). This analysis of the 1985 National Violence Survey (Straus & Gelles, 1990) classified respondents as abstinent, low, low moderate, high moderate, high, and binge drinkers. They found that drinking by the husband, wife, or both prior to the violent event was very strongly related to the drinking classification. For example, they stated that "the percent drinking at the time of the violence increased from 19% for the low drinking categories, to 21% for the high moderates, 47% for the highs, and 48% for the binge drinkers" (p. 211). Although these authors did not describe which of these groups differed from each other, some comparisons are noteworthy. Binge drinkers and high moderate drinkers were both defined as drinking from less than once a month up to one to two times a week, but they were differentiated by the binge drinkers consuming a much higher quantity. Although by no means definitive, this suggests that the different rates of alcohol involvement in violence between high moderate (21%) and binge drinkers (48%) would be attributable to their different quantities of typical alcohol consumption. High drinkers, who drank up to twice as frequently as binge drinkers, had very similar rates of violence. These findings highlight the fact that, while there may be some coincidental occurrences of violence and drinking, the overall association of drinking patterns and drinking in violent events cannot be entirely attributed to probabilistic overlap.

In the Buffalo Newlywed Study, we focused more specifically on the relationship between the frequency of drunkenness and the occurrence of alcohol-related marital aggression. Figure 6.2 displays the association between the husbands' frequency of intoxication (less than monthly, monthly, or weekly) and the reports of sober versus alcohol-related aggression. Two aspects of this figure are worth noting. First, there was a strong relationship between frequency of intoxication and the occurrence of one or more than one episode of alcohol-related violence. However, some alcohol-related violence was apparent even among individuals who rarely got intoxicated. Further, there were some individuals who got intoxicated very frequently, yet reported violence only when sober. These results were very similar when the wife's report of aggression was examined.

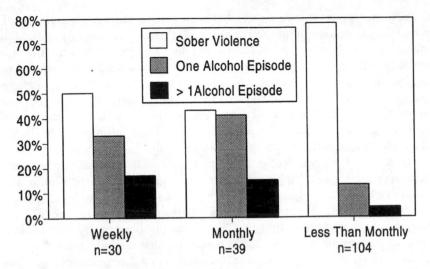

Figure 6.2: Distribution of Violent Episodes as a Function of Husband Frequency of Drunkenness

PROXIMAL DRINKING AND THE OCCURRENCE AND SEVERITY OF MARITAL AGGRESSION

The Importance of Alcohol in Conflict Episodes

In the examination of distal patterns of drinking and marital violence, the traditional focus has been on prediction of the frequency of marital aggression, or in some instances on its simple occurrence (frequency of one or more episodes) versus nonoccurrence (no episodes). The questions with respect to the proximal influence of alcohol require a slight shift in focus because, by definition, the proximal influence of alcohol on an aggressive episode is undefined for individuals with no episodes of physical aggression. Consequently, one question that can be asked is whether drinking is more common in physical aggression episodes than in other conflict episodes that do not culminate in physical aggression, such as verbal aggression and arguments. In addition, one may also ask whether alcohol is more common in more severe episodes of physical aggression than in less severe episodes.

It is also of importance to recognize that these questions can be addressed either between subjects or within subjects. Between-subjects approaches are relevant when some subjects have experienced one type of event, verbal aggression, and other subjects have experienced the other type of event, physical aggression. In such an analysis, it is critical to remember that subjects who have and have not experienced physical aggression differ in many of the distal variables, and controlling for these variables is essential.

It is also important to remember that proximal factors other than alcohol may be related to the occurrence of physical versus verbal aggression, and that these should also be controlled.

Several studies have utilized a between-groups strategy for examining the role of situational variables in the occurrence of aggressive events (e.g., Bard & Zacker, 1974; Fagan, Stewart, & Hansen, 1983). The most sophisticated and representative of these studies were conducted by Pernanen (1991), and Martin and Bachman (1997). Pernanen (1991) interviewed a random community sample and identified a sample of individuals whose most recent victimization involved a spouse. The injury rate was 13% for victims of sober violence and 26% for victims of intoxicated violence. Given the relatively small sample of subjects whose last victimization was from a spouse, this difference was not significant. Nonetheless, it is suggestive that alcohol use by the perpetrator may have increased the severity of the marital aggression. Martin and Bachman (1997) examined drinking and aggression severity with data from the National Crime Victimization Survey for 1992 and 1993 (Bureau of Justice Statistics, 1993). A significant association between assailant alcohol use and severity of aggression was observed for instances of intimate violence toward women; 54% of alcohol-involved assaults were severe (i.e., assault with injury), but only 43% of the sober assaults were severe. Of importance, this association remained significant after controlling for victim marital status and age, and for whether or not the incident took place in a public place.

The second approach to event data is a within-subjects analysis. This analysis focuses on individuals who have experienced both the target event (e.g., physical aggression) and an appropriate control event (e.g., verbal aggression). Inasmuch as the same individuals have been involved in verbal and physical aggression, the distal predictors are essentially controlled in these analyses (though there is the possibility of distal factors interacting with proximal factors and/or drinking in the event). However, the situational factors that might distinguish the two types of events are of importance to consider. To date, this approach has not been utilized in the literature on alcohol and marital violence.

Between-Subjects Analysis

Our analyses of the Buffalo Newlywed Study (Leonard & Quigley, in press) provided similar evidence that acute alcohol consumption is associated with the occurrence and severity of marital aggression. For the between-groups analysis of events, the interview at the first anniversary was utilized to develop the following measures: (1) the severity of the most severe event, with three different levels: verbal aggression, mild physical aggression (push, grab, or shove), and serious physical aggression (slap, hit with fist, beat-up); (2) the husband's use of alcohol in the most severe event; (3) the wife's use of alcohol in the most severe event; (4) the presence of others during the most severe event; and (5) the location of the most severe event (in home versus out of home). These variables were constructed separately for husband report and wife report.

Initially, we examined the bivariate relationships between drinking and episode type with a series of chi-square analyses. These analyses demonstrated that both husband and wife drinking were associated with the occurrence of physical aggression, with the most significant alcohol involvement being observed in the severe aggression episodes. For example, husbands reported that they were drinking in 3% of verbal aggression episodes, in 11% of moderate physical episodes, and 38% of severe physical episodes. Similarly, wives reported that their husbands were drinking in 10% of verbal episodes, 27% of moderate physical episodes, and 43% of severe physical episodes. Wives' drinking was also associated with the occurrence of physical aggression, primarily in the severe episodes. Husbands indicated that their wives were drinking in 12% of verbal episodes, 2% of moderate physical episodes, and 18% of severe physical episodes. The wife's report on her own drinking strongly substantiated these findings, with 3% of wives acknowledging alcohol use prior to verbal episodes, 2% prior to moderate physical events, and 18% prior to severe physical events.

The finding that wife's drinking was significantly associated with the occurrence of severe aggression is potentially very important. However, it is essential to remember that husband and wife drinking are not independent factors. Drinking is a social activity, and in the context of a marriage, it is also a marital activity. For example, Leonard and Das Eiden (in press) have reported that husbands' and wives' initial drinking levels are substantially correlated with each other. At a more event-based level, 43% of the husbands indicated that they drank with their wives once a month or more often. Similarly, 36% of wives indicated drinking with their husbands at this frequency. This issue can also be examined in the context of aggressive episodes. In the physically aggressive episodes that involved wife drinking, husbands were also reported to be drinking between 63% (husband report of severe violence) and 100% of the time (both husband and wife report of moderate aggression). Consequently, it is important, though not always possible, to try to separate the effects of husband's drinking from the effects of wife's drinking.

In addition to examining the independent effects of husband and wife drinking in the event, it is also of importance to control for the fact that different kinds of people may have engaged in moderate and severe aggression than engaged only in verbal aggression. The factors identified by Leonard and Senchak (1996) as being related to the frequency of aggression were examined to determine if they were related to the severity of aggression (verbal vs. moderate vs. severe). Most of these factors were associated with the occurrence of physical aggression in contrast to the occurrence of verbal aggression, including age, education, racial background, self-reports of husband's and wife's verbal aggressive styles, and premarital aggression. There were also, as expected, differences with respect to husband and wife drinking patterns (e.g., scores on the Alcohol Dependence Scale, average daily alcohol consumption, and frequency of intoxication). With respect to the occurrence of moderate versus. severe violence, considerably fewer factors were significant (wife education, wife verbal aggressive style, premarital aggression, wife problem solving style, wife hostility, husband average daily consumption).

Finally, the other situational factors that might be differentially present in verbal versus physical, or moderate versus severe aggression were examined. Two contextual variables were evaluated, the location of the episode and the presence of other individuals during the episode. At the simple bivariate level, the presence of other people was associated with whether the event was a verbal or physical aggression event according to both husband and wife report. Surprisingly, it was *more* likely for a physical aggression event to occur in the presence of other people (including children) than for other people to be present during the most serious verbal event. According to the wife's report, it was also *more* likely for a severe physical aggression event than a moderately aggressive event to occur in the presence of other people. One potential contribution to the relationship between aggression and the presence of other people was the presence of children. Among couples who indicated that other people were present, a sizable percentage indicated that they were the couple's children. Furthermore, couples with children were more likely to have experienced physical aggression than couples with no children. Consequently, it would be erroneous to conclude that the presence of other people facilitates aggression without controlling for children in a more explicit fashion. In controlling for contextual differences, however, this issue is not a major concern and it will not be pursued here. With respect to location, there was a trend for husbands to report that severe as opposed to moderate aggression was more likely to occur at home. However, according to both husband and wife, physical and verbal aggression occurred outside the home with equal frequency.

In order to examine the effects of alcohol in the episode on the kind of episode, several logistic regression analyses were conducted. The first series examined whether verbal episodes could be differentiated from physical episodes by the presence of alcohol. The results indicated a relationship between husband drinking and the occurrence of physical aggression that was significant according to both husband and wife report, and remained significant after controlling for wife drinking. The results were quite different with respect to wife drinking. According to the husband's report, after controlling for husband drinking, wife drinking was more common in verbal than in physical events. When the wife's report of her own drinking was examined, her drinking was not associated with physical or verbal aggression after controlling for husband drinking.

One final aspect of the logistic regression analyses is important to mention. In the above analyses, the distal construct of husband drinking was associated with the occurrence of physical aggression in both husband and wife reports of aggression. This was expected inasmuch as the earlier cross-sectional and longitudinal analyses supported the association between distal drinking patterns and marital aggression frequency. However, when the proximal variable of husband drinking was entered into the logistic regression, the distal drinking variables were no longer significantly related to the occurrence of violence. This suggests that with respect to the occurrence of aggression, the drinking in the episode mediates the relationship between distal drinking patterns and the occurrence of aggression. Logistic regression analyses were conducted with moderate versus severe episode of aggression. After controlling for the spouse's alcohol use, neither husband nor wife drinking significantly differentiated moderate and severe episodes. However, the direction of the findings was that drinking was more associated with severe episodes than moderate episodes. While it is important to control for the spouse's drinking to try to tease apart the effects of husband and wife drinking, it is plausible that both of these might contribute to the severity of aggression, and that controlling for one might obscure the impact of the other. In order to examine this, an additional analysis was conducted for the present chapter. This analysis examined whether drinking (by husband, wife, or both) versus no drinking (neither husband nor wife drinking) was associated with severe versus moderate episodes. As with the other analyses, this analysis controlled for the relevant individual difference and contextual variables. The results indicated that any drinking was more common among severe episodes than among moderate episodes according to the husband's report, but not according to the wife's report. This suggests that any drinking in the aggressive situation might increase the severity of the episode.

Within-Subjects Analysis

Participants with both verbal aggression and at least one episode of physical aggression were considered for the within-group analysis. For this analysis, we constructed the following variables separately for the most serious verbal event and for the most serious physical event: (1) the husband's use of alcohol; (2) the wife's use of alcohol; (3) the presence of others during the event; and (4) the location of the event (in home vs. out of home).

The within-subjects analysis addressed the potential confounds in a different manner than the between-groups analysis. First, because the same individuals were reporting on a physical and a verbal episode, all of the couples were classified as physically aggressive. Therefore, the need to correct for different people being involved in the verbal versus physical event was entirely obviated. However, any observed differences in alcohol involvement between the verbal and physical events could be attributed to contextual difference between verbal and physical episodes, such as the location of the episode and the presence of other people. In order to examine this possibility, we examined the relationship between these context variables and verbal vs. physical aggression. Across husband and wife report, there was no association between the location or the presence of other people and the verbal or physical nature of the episode. Given that these variables were not differentially present in verbal versus physical episodes, any association between drinking and the nature of the episode cannot be attributable to these two context variables.

The overall alcohol involvement reported in physical aggression (31% for husband report and 41% for wife report) was nearly twice the level reported in verbal aggression (17% for husband report and 21% for wife report). The husband's report of husband drinking indicated a marginally greater involvement of alcohol in physical (27%) versus verbal episodes (16%). The wife's report of husband drinking indicated that alcohol was significantly more involved in physical (38%) than verbal episodes (20%). Analyses of the wife's drinking in physical (11%) and verbal episodes (5%) failed to reveal a significant effect in the husband's report. However, according to the wife's report, wives were more likely to be drinking in the physical episodes (12%) than in the verbal aggression episodes (4%).

CONCLUSIONS AND DIRECTIONS FOR FURTHER INQUIRY

The results of this program of research are consistent with the hypothesis that alcohol has a role in the occurrence of domestic violence among newly married couples. The distal drinking pattern of the husband is associated with and predictive of the frequency of marital aggression episodes. This relationship cannot be attributed to demographic, personality, or relationship factors, though it does appear to be moderated by a verbally aggressive marital conflict style. That is, the husband's drinking is predictive of marital aggression among couples who report high levels of verbal aggression in conflict interactions. The distal drinking pattern is associated with the presence of alcohol in marital aggression episodes. In addition, the presence of alcohol, and in particular, husband drinking, is associated with the occurrence of physical rather than verbal aggression, and this proximal relationship appears to account for the relationship between the distal drinking pattern and marital aggression.

The above pattern of findings suggests that acute alcohol consumption may be one factor that has the impact of facilitating the transition from a verbal conflict to a physically aggressive episode. The results are less clear on, but nonetheless consistent with, the further suggestion that alcohol consumption might intensify the extent and severity of an aggressive episode.

The relationship between distal drinking patterns and aggression appears to arise, in part because the heavy drinking patterns reflect multiple instances of heavy drinking, which increase the likelihood that an aggressive episode will occur if other conditions permit (e.g., verbal conflict, an in-home location). This distal relationship is also due, in part, to the relationship between drinking patterns and hostility or verbally aggressive conflict styles. In sum, verbally aggressive heavy drinkers appear to engage in more frequent marital aggression because they are more frequently exposed to the acute influences of alcohol and these acute influences increase the likelihood that some of their many verbal conflicts will escalate to physical aggression.

It is beyond the scope of this chapter to review the processes by which acute alcohol consumption might facilitate the transition to physical aggression. Experimental research has focused on two primary hypotheses, the Expectancy Hypothesis (Lang, Goeckner, Adesso, & Marlatt, 1975) and the Cognitive Disruption Hypothesis (Pernanen, 1976; Taylor & Leonard, 1983; Steele and Josephs, 1988). As noted above, the Expectancy Hypothesis suggests that the consumption of alcohol may serve as a discriminative cue that aggression is permissible and will not be subject to social sanctions. The Cognitive Disruption Hypothesis suggests that the deleterious impact of alcohol on cognition results in a focused attention on the most salient contextual characteristics. When those characteristics are of a threatening, provocative, or otherwise aggression-instigating nature, alcohol would be expected to focus attention on these cues, and thereby facilitate aggressive behavior. The failure of alcohol expectancies to prospectively moderate the relationship between drinking patterns and marital aggression in this study is not consistent with the Expectancy Hypothesis. For the most part, however, the results described in this chapter do not address these hypotheses in a definitive manner. Other research building on the Buffalo Newlywed Study (Leonard & Roberts, 1998b) has attempted to address this issue in an experimental framework, and has presented evidence that is more supportive of the Cognitive Disruption Hypothesis than the Expectancy Hypothesis. Clearly more focused research on these processes is warranted.

Despite the support that the current research program has provided for a causal role of alcohol on marital aggression, it would be a mistake to overstate this role. Alcohol is neither a necessary nor a sufficient cause of marital aggression. As described earlier, the majority of aggressive episodes occur without alcohol, and men who have behaved aggressively with alcohol have often behaved aggressively without alcohol as well. The role of alcohol, at least in the context of this broad population of newlyweds, appears to be one of a facilitative nature, a contributing cause. Whether alcohol has a comparable role in other populations, or at other developmental stages, or whether it has a more or less important role, needs to be more thoroughly examined.

Such research may be of critical importance to future prevention and treatment efforts.

REFERENCES

Bard, K. A., & Zacker, J. (1974). Assaultiveness and alcohol use in family disputes. *Criminology, 12,* 281-292.

Blane, H. T. (1978). Middle-aged alcoholics and young drinkers. In H. T. Blane & M. E. Chafetz (Eds.), *Youth, alcohol, and social policy* (pp. 5-58). New York: Plenum.

Bruun, K. (1959). Significance of role and norms in the small group for individual behavior changes while drinking. *Quarterly Journal of Studies on Alcohol, 20,* 53-64.

Bureau of Justice Statistics (1993). *Criminal Victimization in the United States, 1992.* Washington, DC: Bureau of Justice Statistics.

Buss, A. H., & Durkee, A. (1957). An inventory for assessing different kinds of hostility. *Journal of Consulting and Clinical Psychology, 21,* 343-349.

Cahalan, D., Cisin, I. H., & Crossley, H. (1969). *American drinking practices: A national study of drinking, behavior and attitudes* (Monograph No. 1). New Brunswick, NJ: Rutgers Center of Alcohol Studies.

Clark, W. B., & Midanik, L. (1982). Alcohol use and alcohol problems among U.S. adults: Results of the 1979 national survey. In National Institute on Alcohol Abuse and Alcoholism, *Alcohol and Health Monograph No. 1: Alcohol Consumption and Related Problems* (DHHS Publication No. ADM 82-1190, pp. 3-52). Washington, DC: U.S. Government Printing Office.

Coleman, D. H., & Straus, M. A. (1983). Alcohol abuse and family violence (pp. 104-124). In E. Gottheil, K. A. Druley, T. E. Skoloda, & H. M. Waxman (Eds.). *Alcohol, drug abuse, and aggression.* Springfield, IL: Charles C Thomas.

Crohan, S. E., & Veroff, J. (1989). Dimensions of marital well-being among white and black newlyweds. *Journal of Marriage and the Family, 51,* 373-384.

Fagan, J. A., Stewart, D. K., & Hansen, K.V. (1983). Violent men or violent husbands: Background factors and situational correlates. In D. Finkelhor, R. J. Gelles, G. T. Hotaling, & M. A. Straus (Eds.), *The dark side of families* (pp. 49-67). Beverly Hills, CA: Sage.

Gelles, R. J. (1993). Alcohol and other drugs are associated with violence—they are not its cause. In R. J. Gelles and D. R. Loseke (Eds.), *Current controversies on family violence* (pp. 183-196). Newbury Park, CA: Sage.

Gelles, R. J. (1974). *The violent home.* Beverly Hills, CA: Sage.

Gelles, R. J., & Cornell, C. P. (1985). The youngest victims: Violence toward children. In R. J. Gelles & C. P. Cornell (Eds.), *Intimate violence in families* (pp. 41-61). Beverly Hills: Sage.

Heyman, R. E., O'Leary, K. D., & Jouriles, E. N. (1995). Alcohol and aggressive personality styles: Potentiators of serious physical aggression against wives? *Journal of Family Psychology, 9,* 44-57.

Hilton, M. E. (1991). The demographic distribution of drinking patterns in 1984. In W. B. Clark & M. E. Hilton (Eds.), *Alcohol in America: Drinking practices and problems* (pp. 73-86). Albany, NY: State University of New York Press.

Hilton, M. E. (1991). The presence of alcohol in four social situations: Survey results from 1964 and 1984. In W. B. Clark & M. E. Hilton (Eds.), *Alcohol in America: Drinking practices and problems* (pp. 280-289). Albany, NY: State University of New York Press.

Kaufman Kantor, G. A., & Straus, M. A. (1990). The "Drunken Bum" theory of wife beating. In M. A. Straus & R. J. Gelles (Eds.), *Physical violence in American families: Risk factors and adaptations to violence in 8,145 families* (pp. 203-224). New Brunswick, NJ: Transaction.

Lang, A., Goeckner, D., Adesso, V., & Marlatt, G. (1975). Effects of alcohol on aggression in male social drinkers. *Journal of Abnormal Psychology, 84,* 508-518.

Leonard, K. E., Bromet, E. J., Parkinson, D. K., Day, N. L., & Ryan, C. M. (1985). Patterns of alcohol use and physically aggressive behavior in men. *Journal of Studies on Alcohol, 46,* 279-282.

Leonard, K. E., & Blane, H. T. (1992). Alcohol and marital aggression in a national sample of young men. *Journal of Interpersonal Violence, 7,* 19-30.

Leonard, K. E., & Das Eiden, R. (1999). Husbands and wives drinking: Unilateral or bilateral influences among newlyweds in a general population sample. *Journal of Studies on Alcohol* (Suppl. 113), 130-138.

Leonard, K. E., & Jacob, T. (1988). Alcohol, alcoholism, and family violence. In V. B. Van Hasselt, R. L. Morrison, A. S. Bellack, & M. Hersen (Eds.), *Handbook of family violence* (pp.383-406). New York: Plenum.

Leonard, K. E., & Quigley, B. M. (in press). Drinking and marital aggression in newlyweds: An event-based analysis of drinking and the occurrence of husband marital aggression. *Journal of Studies on Alcohol.*

Leonard, K. E. & Roberts, L. J. (1998a). Marital aggression, quality, and stability in the first year of marriage: Findings from the Buffalo Newlywed Study. In T. N. Bradbury (Ed.), *The developmental course of marital dysfunction* (pp. 44-73). New York: Cambridge University Press.

Leonard, K. E., & Roberts, L. J. (1998b). The effects of alcohol on the marital interactions of aggressive and nonaggressive husbands and their wives. *Journal of Abnormal Psychology, 107*(4), 602-615.

Leonard, K. E., & Senchak, M. (1996). The prospective prediction of husband marital aggression among newlywed couples. *Journal of Abnormal Psychology, 105,* 369-380.

Leonard, K. E., & Senchak, M. (1993). Alcohol and premarital aggression among newlywed couples. *Journal of Studies on Alcohol, 11,* 96-108.

Margolin, G. (1980). *The conflict inventory.* Unpublished manuscript.

Martin, S. E., & Bachman, R. (1997). The relationship of alcohol to injury in assault cases. In M. Galanter (Ed.), Recent developments in alcoholism. *Alcohol & Violence, 13,* 41-56.

Miller, R. S., & Lefcourt, H. M. (1982). The assessment of social intimacy. *Journal of Personality Assessment, 46,* 514-518.

O'Leary, D. K, Barling J., Arias I., Rosenbaum A., Malone J., & Tyree A. (1989). Prevalence and stability of physical aggression between spouses: A longitudinal analysis. *Journal of Consulting and Clinical Psychology, 57,* 263-268.

Pan, H. D., Neidig, P. H., & O'Leary, K. D. (1994). Predicting mild and severe husband-to-wife physical aggression. *Journal of Consulting and Clinical Psychology, 62,* 975-981.

Pernanen, K. (1991). *Alcohol in human violence.* New York: Guilford.

Pernanen, K. (1976). Alcohol and crimes of violence. In B. Kissin & H. Begletier (Eds.), *The biology of alcoholism: Social aspects of alcoholism 4* (pp. 351-444). New York: Plenum.

Quigley, B. M., & Leonard, K. E. (1999). Husband alcohol expectancies, drinking, and marital conflict styles as predictors of severe marital violence among newlywed couples. *Psychology of Addictive Behaviors, 13*(1), 49-59.

Reider, E. E., Zucker, R. A., Noll, R. B., Maguin, E. T., & Fitzgerald, H. E. (1988, August). *Alcohol involvement and family violence in a high risk sample.* Paper presented at the annual Meeting of the American Psychological Association, Atlanta, GA.

Rohsenow, D. J. (1983). Drinking habits and expectancies about alcohol's effects for self verses others. *Journal of Consulting and Clinical Psychology, 51,* 752-756.

Roy, M. (1982). Four thousand partners in violence: A trend analysis. In Moy (Ed.), *The abusive partner: An analysis of domestic battering* (pp. 17-35). New York: Van Nostrand Reinhold.

Skinner, H. A., & Allen, B. A. (1982). Alcohol dependence syndrome: Measurement and validation. *Journal of Abnormal Psychology, 91,* 199-209

Skinner, H. A., Steinhauer, P. D., & Santa-Barbara, J. (1984). *The family assessment measure: Administration and interpretation guide.* Toronto: Canada, Addiction Research Foundation.

Southwick, K., Steele, C., Marlatt, A., & Lindell, M. (1981). Alcohol-related expectancies: Defined by phase of intoxication and drinking experience. *Journal of Consulting and Clinical Psychology, 49,* 713-721.

Spielberger, C. R., Jacobs, G., Crane, R., Russell, S., Westberry, L., Baker, L., Johnson, E., Knight, J., & Marks, E. (1979). *Preliminary manual for the State Trait Personality Inventory (STPT).* Tampa: University of South Florida, Human Resources Institute.

Spence, J. T., Helmreich, R. L., & Stapp, J. (1974). The personal attributes questionnaire: A measure of sex role stereotypes and masculinity-femininity. *JSAS Catalog of Selected Documents in Psychology, 4,* 127.

Steele, C. M., & Josephs, R. A. (1988). Drinking your troubles away II: An attention allocation model of alcohol's effect on psychological stress. *Journal of Abnormal Psychology, 97,* 196-205.

Straus, M. A. (1979). Measuring intrafamily conflict and violence: The conflict tactics (CT) scales. *Journal of Marriage and the Family, 41,* 75-88.

Straus, M. A. & Gelles, R. J. (Eds.). (1990). *Physical violence in American families: Risk factors and adaptations to violence in 8,145 families.* New Brunswick, NJ: Transaction Publishers.

Suitor, J. J., Pillemer, K., & Straus, M. A. (1990). Marital violence in a life course perspective. In M. A. Straus & R. J. Gelles (Eds.). *Physical violence in American families: Risk factors and adaptations to violence in 8,145 families* (pp.305-320). New Brunswick, NJ: Transaction.

Taylor, S. P., & Leonard, K. E. (1983). Alcohol and human physical aggression. In R. G. Geen & E. I. Donnerstein (Eds.), *Aggression: Theoretical and empirical reviews* (pp. 77-101). New York: Academic Press.

Wanberg, K. W., Horn, J. L., & Foster, F. M. (1977). A differential assessment model for alcoholism. *Journal of Studies on Alcohol, 38,* 512-543.

PART III

Consequences of Violence

Women's Responses to Physical and Psychological Abuse

Ileana Arias

Mental health professionals devoted little empirical or theoretical attention to intrafamily violence until the 1960s. Publication of an article in 1962 by Kempe, Silverman, Steele, Droegmueller, and Silver on the battered child syndrome drew immediate attention and interest, and prompted empirical efforts to establish the prevalence and etiology of intrafamily violence in our society. Much of this earlier work was limited to investigations of child abuse. However, detection of widespread child abuse among American families generated interest in violence among other family members. Results of a nationwide study of family violence conducted by Straus and his colleagues in 1975 (Straus, Gelles, & Steinmetz, 1980) shocked professional and lay circles alike by showing that approximately 28% of married couples experienced physical violence at some time during the course of their marriage, and 16% experienced violence during the year preceding the study. Family scholars' interest in this unexpectedly widespread family characteristic came to focus on establishing accurate estimates of the incidence, prevalence, and etiology of marital violence.

Initial empirical responses to issues of family functioning and stability, including domestic violence, primarily were the domain of sociologists and family studies scholars. The major emphasis of this original work was on the assessment of family quality and satisfaction, and macrosystemic variables, such as socioeconomic status, with potential etiological significance (Burgess & Locke, 1953; Terman & Wallin, 1949). However, during the 1970s, there was a rapid increase in psychologists' interests in family and marital functioning. O'Leary (1987) attributed this unprecedented increase to three major factors: (1) the increasing rate of divorce and its documented destructive effects on individual functioning; (2) the emergence of sex therapy as a legitimate and important area of research and practice; and (3) child psychologists' inability to understand and influence child psychopathology adequately without taking marital factors into account. Psychological research on assessment and treatment of family and marital dysfunction shifted the focus of scrutiny from the traditional sociological, or macrovariables to microvariables, such as intrapersonal characteristics and interpersonal interactions. Accordingly, psychological research on marital violence has concentrated first on establishing the consequences of marital violence for victims' psychological adjustment, and then on identifying etiological or maintaining factors that can guide the development of effective interventions and prevention strategies.

PHYSICAL ABUSE

Consequences

Although both men and women in intimate relationships have been shown to be victims of their partners' violence, research on the consequences of abuse has been almost entirely limited to female victims since women are expected to suffer more severe physical and psychological consequences. Men, relative to women, have the potential to cause more physical damage, to protect themselves more effectively from harm, and to escape an abusive attack more easily because of their size and strength advantages (Straus et al., 1980). Further, women's greater social and economic dependence often prevents them from escaping abusive relationships thereby exposing them to increasing levels of violence frequency and severity over time relative to men (Dobash & Dobash, 1979). Negative consequences of marital violence to women have been found to include physical injury (Fagan, Stewart, & Hansen, 1983; Goldberg & Tomlanovich, 1984; Straus, 1986), divorce (Levinger, 1966), and increased risk for homicide (Federal Bureau of Investigation, 1982). Various symptoms of psychological distress have also been associated with women's victimization, such as fear, terror, nightmares (Hilberman & Munson, 1977–1978); inability to trust (Carmen, Reiker, & Mills, 1984); low self-esteem (Carmen et al., 1984; Cascardi & O'Leary, 1992; Walker, 1979); anxiety (Hilberman & Munson, 1977–1978; Walker, 1979); depression (Carmen et al., 1984; Cascardi & O'Leary, 1992; Hilberman & Munson, 1977-1978; Rounsaville & Lifton, 1983); helplessness (Walker, 1984); guilt (Ferraro & Johnson, 1983; Walker, 1979); shame, feelings of inferiority, loneliness, pessimism (Ferraro & Johnson, 1983); low ego strength, shyness, introversion, tension (Star, Clark, Goetz, & O'Malia, 1979); suspiciousness (Walker, 1979); increased risk for suicide (Carmen et al., 1984; Stark, Flitcraft, & Frazier, 1983); and psychophysiological complaints such as fatigue, backache, headache, general restlessness (Walker, 1979); and insomnia (Hilberman & Munson, 1977–1978; Walker, 1979). Additionally, victimized women are characterized by greater alcohol use and abuse and drinking problems than nonvictimized women (Miller, Downs, & Testa, 1993).

Walker (1984) suggested that the psychological symptoms frequently experienced and reported by battered women overlap greatly with symptoms comprising the diagnostic criteria for posttraumatic stress disorder (PTSD; APA, 1994). Assessment of PTSD among battered women indicates that, indeed, PTSD is commonly found among battered women, with prevalence estimates ranging from a low of 33% (Astin, Lawrence, & Foy, 1993; Cascardi, O'Leary, Lawrence, & Schlee, 1995) to a high of 84% (Kemp, Rawlings, & Green, 1991). The variability in prevalence estimates appears to be a function of differences across studies in the method of diagnostic assessment, the population sampled, and the length of time since the traumatic violent episode(s). Higher rates are more likely to result from self-report assessments, made among shelter women, and conducted immediately (e.g., 1 to 2 days) after a violent event. Although a variety of negative psychological sequelae have been associated with women's victimization, the high prevalence of PTSD among battered women merits special attention. PTSD may interfere with a woman's functioning after she leaves her abusive partner and attempts to live on her own. Additionally, PTSD symptomatology may be stressful enough to interfere with women's attempts to escape abusive relationships.

Although women are the direct victims of marital violence, children exposed to interparental violence have been shown to suffer from psychological and social adjustment problems during childhood and adulthood as well. Children from violent homes exhibit a wide range of externalizing and internalizing behavior problems at higher frequencies than children from nonviolent homes (Cummings, Zahn-Waxler, & Radke-Yarrow, 1981; Emery, 1989; Fantuzzo et al., 1991; Fantuzzo & Lindquist, 1989; Jaffe, Wolfe, Wilson, & Zak, 1986; Jouriles, Murphy, & O'Leary, 1989). Specifically, children from violent homes relative to those from nonviolent homes are characterized more frequently by significant levels of depression (Forstrom-Cohen & Rosenbaum, 1985; Silvern et al., 1995), aggression (Hughes & Barad, 1983), and low self-esteem (Hughes, 1988). Children in families characterized by spouse abuse are frequently abused themselves (Straus et al., 1980) and it is often difficult to distinguish the impact of witnessing marital violence from that of being abused by a parent. However, children from maritally violent homes who have not been abused by a parent themselves likewise exhibit greater levels of emotional and psychological difficulties than children from nonviolent homes (Hughes & Barad, 1983; Jouriles et al., 1989; Wolfe, Jaffe, Wilson, & Zak, 1985).

The detrimental impact of exposure to interparental violence on children may be a direct result of such exposure or may be mediated by parental psychopathology. Abused wives exhibit higher levels of depression and anxiety than their nonabused counterparts (Cascardi & O'Leary, 1992), and maternal depression is a significant predictor of negative child outcomes (Downey & Coyne, 1990; Hammen, Gordon, Burge, Adrian, Jaenicke, & Hiroto, 1987). Haskett, Myers, Pirello, and Dombalis (1995) found that the effects of maternal psychological adjustment on child behavior was totally mediated by their parenting. Thus, the detrimental impact of interparental violence on children may be mediated by parental psychological adjustment and related deficits in parenting patterns.

Etiology

Because marital violence has been documented as having significant negative consequences for the physical and psychological adjustment of both its direct and indirect victims, it has become important to understand and account for the development and maintenance of marital violence. Such attempts have focused on the identification of sociocultural, intrapersonal, and interpersonal variables, primarily of perpetrators. Characteristics or correlates of victim status such as low self-esteem and depression have been identified and were described above. However, it is difficult to assess the extent to which such characteristic differences are antecedents or consequences of marital violence. Hotaling and Sugarman (1990) argued that the existing data indicate that the best predictor of whether or not a woman will be battered is whether or not she has a violent partner.

Sociocultural Factors

Marital violence has been shown to be more common among young spouses (Pagelow, 1981; Straus et al., 1980); those with low occupational status and income, unemployment, and job dissatisfaction (Gelles & Cornell, 1985; Straus et al., 1980); and among African American (Hampton, Gelles, & Harrop, 1989) and acculturated Mexican American and Puerto Rican American families (Kaufman Kantor, Jasinski, & Aldarondo, 1994). Cohabitation relative to marriage is associated with higher rates of relationship aggression (Hotaling & Sugarman, 1986). Rates of violence are higher among spouses who report no religious affiliation (Straus et al., 1980). Among those who do report some religious affiliation, the lowest rates of violence are found among Jewish husbands while the highest rates are found among husbands who are members of nonmainstream fundamentalist religious groups (Straus et al., 1980). Social isolation (Pagelow, 1981), a greater number of dependent children in the home (Straus et al., 1980), and violence in the family of origin (Kalmuss, 1984; Malone, Tyree, & O'Leary, 1989) are associated with an increased risk for marital violence.

Intrapersonal Factors

Violent husbands have been found to be characterized as experiencing a high frequency of stressful events in their lives (Straus et al., 1980); they are also characterized by low levels of self-esteem and self-efficacy (Prince & Arias, 1994), and unassertiveness with their partners (Rosenbaum & O'Leary, 1981). Higher rates of alcohol and drug use and abuse are found among violent men (Fagan et al., 1983; Leonard & Senchak, 1993). Violent, relative to nonviolent, men are more likely to make dysfunctional and blaming attributions for their partners' behavior (Holtzworth-Munroe & Hutchinson, 1993), exhibit high levels of pathological jealousy (Walker, 1979), narcissism (Hastings & Hamberger, 1988), and anger (Heyman, O'Leary, & Jouriles, 1995; Maiuro, Cahn, & Vitaliano, 1988), and are more approving of violence (Straus, 1980).

Interpersonal Factors

Interpersonal factors that have been found to distinguish violent from nonviolent couples include interpersonal conflict and relationship dissatisfaction (O'Leary, Barling, Arias, & Rosenbaum, 1989), poor communication skills (Jacobson, Gottman, Waltz, Rushe, Babcock, & Holtzworth-Munroe, 1994; Margolin, John, & Gleberman, 1988), and one-sided allocation of decision-making responsibilities (Straus et al., 1980). Margolin et al. (1988) were the first to demonstrate that during conflictual discussions violent spouses, especially husbands, show greater negative affect and arousal, and greater reciprocity of negative affect than do nonviolent couples. Babcock and colleagues (1993) further demonstrated that violent couples, relative to dissatisfied-nonviolent and satisfied-nonviolent couples, are more likely to be characterized by a pattern of communication wherein the husband demands and pursues the wife while she withdraws from him during conflictual discussions. Straus and colleagues (1980) have shown that violence is most likely in households where decision-making power is solely in the hands of the husband and least likely in democratic homes.

PSYCHOLOGICAL ABUSE

Empirical attempts to illustrate the consequences of marital violence and establish its causes have focused primarily on physical violence. Relatively little attention has been devoted to psychological abuse, which can be defined as, "verbal and nonverbal acts which symbolically hurt the other, or the use of threats to hurt the other . . ." (Straus, 1979, p. 77).

Psychological abuse has been shown to covary significantly with physical abuse among married couples (Follingstad, Rutledge, Berg, Hause, & Polek, 1990), dating high school students (Molidor, 1995), and pregnant teenage and adult women (Parker, McFarlane, Soeken, Torres, & Campbell, 1993). However, there is evidence that psychological abuse is not only a correlate of physical abuse, but also a precursor to it (Murphy & O'Leary, 1989). The occurrence of physical abuse has been conceptualized as a developmental process in which psychological abuse necessarily occurs first (Stets, 1990). Using data from the 1985 National Family Violence Re-Survey, Stets (1990) found that 65% of White American men and 56% of African American men were verbally and psychologically abusive but not physically aggressive against their partners. On the other hand, only 0.2% of White American men and none of the African American men were physically but not psychologically aggressive. Results from probit analyses were consistent with Stets' hypothesis that men progress from a state of no aggression to one of psychological aggression and later to one of physical aggression. Ronfeldt, Kimerling, and Arias (1998) supported Stets' hypothesis and, additionally, demonstrated that progression from the use of psychological abuse to physical abuse was more likely among men who grew up in homes characterized by husband-to-wife physical abuse.

Significance of Psychological Abuse

The relative lack of empirical research on the occurrence and impact of psychological abuse on women's physical and mental health is surprising. Psychological abuse appears to be a precursor to other forms of abuse, including life-threatening behavior, and to accompany physical abuse. Psychological abuse may exacerbate or otherwise moderate the destructive impact of physical abuse (Follingstad et al., 1990). Accordingly, it is important to understand the role of psychological abuse in assessing and modifying the impact of physical abuse. It is also important to understand the occurrence of psychological abuse and victims' responses to it in order to develop effective physical abuse prevention strategies.

Additionally, psychological abuse appears to occur frequently among women who are not physically battered. However, research and intervention efforts are designed primarily or exclusively for physically abused women. Thus, an important population of women who are experiencing psychological abuse and its negative consequences are probably overlooked since the absence of physical assault prevents researchers and practitioners from labeling them as victims or appropriate targets of research and intervention.

The traditional lack of empirical attention to psychological abuse of women may be in part due to the need to respond to the severe and sometimes life-threatening consequences of physical battering. Further, there may be an expectation that psychological abuse will have fewer, less severe, and more transient consequences than physical abuse. Additionally, as Vitanza, Vogel, and Marshall (1995) suggested, difficulties in operationalizing and measuring psychological abuse have posed notable obstacles.

Although there is some agreement on some of the behaviors that constitute psychological abuse, researchers and practitioners have not been able to agree on a complete operational definition of psychological abuse. Some proposed definitions focus on the topography of behaviors that constitute psychological abuse, such as humiliation and threats (Straus, 1979). Other researchers focus on the psychological impact, such as fear or anxiety, of the behaviors in question (Follingstad et al., 1990), while others focus on the function of those behaviors, such as control and coercion of the victim (Walker, 1979). Definitions of psychological abuse that focus on the emotional impact or the function of the behaviors are especially problematic since, by definition, the extent to which a behavior is abusive is subjectively determined by the recipient or victim.

Interestingly, although differences in definitions may interfere with researchers' and practitioners' agreement on the occurrence of psychological abuse, spouses do not appear to have difficulties identifying it. In their examination of interpartner agreement on the occurrence of abusive behaviors by either partner, Moffitt and colleagues (1997) expected that spouses would agree less on the occurrence of psychological abuse relative to physical abuse because of the greater level of subjectivity in the former. However, they found that interpartner agreement on the occurrence of psychological abuse did not differ from their agreement on the occurrence of physical abuse.

Psychological and Physical Consequences

Notwithstanding variability of definitions and lack of consensus, there has been some empirical attention devoted recently to assessment of psychological abuse and its impact on women's physical and mental health. Aguilar and Nightingale (1994) employed a sample of 48 battered and 48 nonbattered women to examine the impact of physical abuse on women's self-esteem. As expected, battered women were characterized by significantly lower levels of self-esteem relative to nonbattered women. However, psychological abuse was the only significant predictor of low self-esteem within the battered subsample. A similar pattern of results was found among female adolescents in dating relationships (Jezl, Molidor, & Wright, 1996). That is, exposure to psychological abuse lowered the self-esteem of battered women still further.

In a sample of 234 women with a history of battering, Follingstad and her colleagues (1990) found that only three of the participants had never experienced any form of psychological abuse. Of the women in this sample, 72% reported that they experienced psychological abuse more negatively than μhysical abuse. Women who experienced psychological abuse more negatively, relative to those who experienced physical abuse more negatively, reported more fear of the partner, shame, loss of self-esteem, depression, and anxiety. Interestingly, there were no differences between women who experienced psychological abuse more negatively and those who experienced physical abuse more negatively on the severity or frequency of the physical abuse they endured.

More recently, Marshall (1996) examined the physical and psychological correlates of psychological abuse among a sample of 578 women who volunteered to participate in a study of women in dysfunctional and unsatisfying relationships. Only 13% of Marshall's sample had never been physically assaulted by the partner, and 3% had never experienced an incident of psychological abuse. Higher frequencies of psychological abuse were related to higher frequencies of serious or chronic illness and visits to a physician; more frequent use of psychotherapeutic services and psychotropic medication; lower levels of relationship satisfaction and more frequent attempts to leave the partner; and lower levels of perceived power and control.

The studies reviewed above derived samples of women who were battered, residing in shelters, or otherwise characterized by dissatisfying, conflictual relationships. It is not clear to what extent concomitant factors influenced the relationships between psychological abuse and emotional and physical factors. In order to overcome some of these potential confounds, Arias, Street, and Brody (1996) studied a community sample of families to assess the detrimental impact of psychological abuse on women's psychological adjustment and related functioning. Specifically, we hypothesized that: (1) as is true among physically abused women (Miller et al., 1993), psychological abuse would be related to depression and problematic drinking; (2) the relationship between psychological abuse and problematic drinking would be mediated by levels of depressive symptomatology; and (3) social support would moderate or interfere with the impact of depression on problematic drinking (see Figure 7.1).

The 232 women in this community sample were all married and living with their spouses at the time of the assessment. Participating women had an average of 2.44 children living at home. On average, they were 38.6 years old, were employed outside the home, and had some college education or more. The sample included 76% European American, while the remaining 24% were African American. As predicted, psychological abuse of the women by their husbands was a significant predictor of both the women's depressive symptomatology and problematic drinking, and depressive symptomatology was a significant predictor of problematic drinking. Although depression was predictive of alcohol problems, it did not totally mediate the effects of psychological abuse on alcohol problems. That is, psychological abuse had a significant impact on problematic drinking and alcohol problems independent of the significant intervening effects of depression. Thus, it appeared

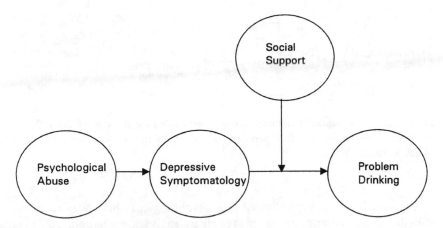

Figure 7.1: Hypothesized Relationships Among Psychological Abuse, Depression, Social Support, and Problematic Drinking (Arias, Street, & Brody, 1996).

that psychological abuse has both direct and indirect effects, via depression, on women's alcohol abuse and related problems. As predicted, social support did exert a significant moderating effect on the relationship between depression and drinking problems. Examination of the moderating effect revealed that the association between depression and problematic or symptomatic drinking was significant only for women who reported low levels of social support in their communities. Alternatively, women who were characterized by high levels of social support did not respond to their depressive symptomatology with alcohol abuse and related problems. Our moderation results are important in illustrating that although psychological abuse has direct and indirect effects on problematic outcomes, such as problematic drinking, the negative impact of abuse can be offset by social support. Eliminating abuse is often difficult and abused women frequently are unable or unwilling to leave abusive partners (Strube, 1985). Under such circumstances, identifying variables that are amenable to intervention and change would improve women's functioning and is critical. Our research suggests that social support may be such a variable.

Consequences for Children

Given the apparent relationships of women's psychological adjustment on their parenting and, subsequently, on their children's adjustment (Haskett et al., 1995), it appears important to examine the role of women's psychological abuse in child outcomes. Using the same sample employed by Arias, Street, and Brody (1996), Arias and Street (1996) explored the effects of children's exposure to their mother's psychological abuse by the father. Arias,

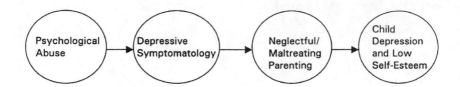

Figure 7.2: Hypothesized relationships among psychological abuse of mothers, their depressive symptomatology, their parenting, and their children's internalizing problems (Arias & Street, 1996).

Street, and Brody (1996) showed that psychological abuse was associated with depression among women. In the current analyses, we hypothesized that: (1) psychological abuse of the mother would be associated with neglectful/ maltreating parenting practices (such as ignoring child success and good behavior, belittling, and nagging), and child internalizing problems, namely, depression and low self-esteem; (2) depressive symptomatology of the mother would be associated with her negative parenting and child internalizing problems; (3) neglectful/maltreating parenting would be related to child internalizing problems; and (4) the association between psychological abuse and child outcomes would be mediated by mother depression and negative parenting (see Figure 7.2).

In order to minimize method error, reports from multiple and independent respondents were employed. Specifically, (1) husbands reported on their own use of psychological abuse against their wives, (2) women reported on their own levels of depressive symptomatology, and (3) children reported on their mother's parenting behaviors and their own levels of depressive symptomatology and self-esteem. Women's psychological abuse was a significant predictor of their levels of depressive symptomatology, their neglectful and maltreating parenting, and both their sons' and daughters' depressive symptomatology and low self-esteem. Women's depressive symptomatology, in turn, was a significant predictor of neglectful, maltreating parenting behaviors and of children's depression and low self-esteem; and neglectful and maltreating parenting was predictive of children's depression and low self-esteem. As hypothesized, the relationship between psychological abuse and children's depression and low self-esteem was mediated by maternal depression, and the impact of maternal depression on children was partly mediated by dysfunctional parenting. This pattern of associations remained significant after controlling for the effects of the children's exposure to interparental physical abuse and of the use of physical maltreatment by mothers and both psychological and physical maltreatment by fathers. Thus, in this study, psychological abuse had a negative impact on women's psychological adjustment which, in turn, compromised their parenting skills and abilities, placing their children at risk for depression and low self-esteem.

Independent Effects of Psychological Abuse

The preponderance of the available data suggests that psychological abuse has a negative impact on women's physical and psychological health. However, past studies frequently fail to control for the effects of physical abuse when examining the effects of psychological abuse. Because both forms of abuse frequently co-occur, it is difficult to obtain sizable samples of women who are only psychologically abused or only physically abused in order to examine unique effects. However, statistical control is an available alternative. There appears to be only one study that attempted to statistically control for the effects of physical abuse of women in determining the psychological impact of their psychological abuse. Kahn, Welch, and Zillmer (1993) administered the MMPI-2 to 31 battered women residing in a shelter and instructed them to indicate whether or not they had been subjected to each of nine psychologically abusive partner behaviors such as criticisms, threats, isolation, and intimidation, and nine physically abusive behaviors such as pushing, punching, hair-pulling, and use of weapons. Mean profiles revealed significant elevations (i.e., *T*-score equal to or greater than 65) on scales F, 4, 6, and 8, suggesting high levels of maladjustment and distress among the participants. Likewise, elevated mean *T*-scores emerged for the MacAndrew Alcoholism (MAC-R) and posttraumatic stress disorder (*PK* and *PS*) scales of the MMPI-2. Indeed, 68% of participants scored high on the *PS* and *PK* supplementary scales. Although physical abuse was not related, psychological abuse was significantly related to the average *T*-score. Further, the results of regression analyses indicated that when both forms of abuse were considered simultaneously, the experience of psychological abuse only emerged as a unique predictor of the average clinical *T*-score.

The results of investigations completed to date suggest that it is important to examine the impact of psychological abuse on women's psychological adjustment. Psychological abuse has been associated with negative psychological sequelae for women and their children, independent of the effects of any concomitant physical abuse. In addition to documenting the negative consequences of psychological abuse, it is important to determine mechanisms responsible for the negative impact. Although there are no studies directly assessing such mechanisms, Murphy and Cascardi (1993) offered a helpful heuristic. They hypothesized that three major pathways account for the destructive impact of psychological abuse–specifically, psychological abuse may instill fear, increase dependency on the abuser, and damage self-esteem. If this is accurate, the implications for relationship termination

and autonomous functioning are significant. Separating from an abusive partner necessitates ego strength that may frequently be lacking among victims
of psychological abuse.

Functioning, Coping, and Relationship Termination

To the extent that terminating abusive relationships is desirable, it is
important to specify variables, including psychological abuse, that facilitate
or hamper battered women's attempts to leave their abusers. Because women
have been shown to be more likely to leave their abusive partners as a function
of abuse severity and increases in abuse frequency and severity (Herbert,
Silver, & Ellard, 1991; Marshall, 1996; Strube, 1985), it is important to
control for the potential confounding effects of physical abuse when assessing the impact of psychological abuse on women's intentions to terminate
their abusive relationships. Further, it is important to specify conditions under
which severity of psychological abuse would and would not motivate women
to intend to terminate their relationships. Existing literature suggests that the
presence of PTSD symptomatology may be such a factor.

PTSD occurs frequently among battered women and has been shown to
be more likely to develop among victims who engage in dissociative strategies, such as distraction, to cope during and after a trauma (Bernat, Ronfeldt,
Calhoun, & Arias, in press). However, perceptions of control over stressful
events and using problem-focused coping strategies, such as developing a
plan of action, relative to the use of emotion-focused coping, such as fanta-
sizing about good outcomes, have been shown to be more effective in
reducing distress (Lazarus & Folkman, 1984). Specific to battering, Herbert
et al. (1991) found that battered women who remained with their abusers were
more likely to employ emotion-focused strategies to cope with their abuse
than women who terminated their abusive relationships. Thus, it seems
reasonable to expect that women who engage in ineffective, emotion-focused
coping and feel powerless or helpless may be more likely to develop PTSD
symptomatology in response to abuse.

A Study of Psychological Abuse

We conducted an investigation (Arias & Pape, in press) designed to assess
the extent to which psychological abuse would be a significant predictor of
battered women's psychological adjustment (i.e., PTSD symptomatology)
and their intentions to leave the abusive partner, controlling for the effects of
physical abuse. In addition to the unique effects of psychological abuse on
PTSD and intentions to terminate the relationship, we predicted that the
relationship between psychological abuse and intentions to leave the abusive
relationship would be stronger among women who did not suffer from high
levels of PTSD symptomatology than among those who did; and that the

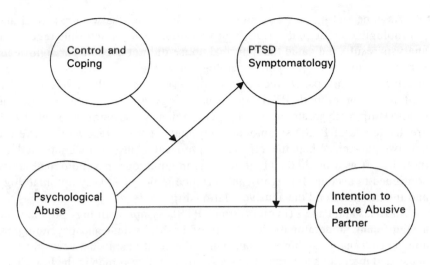

Figure 7.3: Hypothesized relationships among psychological abuse, coping and control, PTSD, and intention to leave abusive relationships (Arias & Pape, in press).

relationship between psychological abuse and PTSD symptomatology would be stronger for women who did not perceive themselves to have control over their partners' violence and for women who engaged in emotion-focused coping (see Figure 7.3).

Arias and Pape (in press) studied 68 women currently residing in battered women's shelters. On average, the women were 36 years old and had 12.6 years of education; 48% were White American, 43% African American, 3% Latino American, and 6% Native American. Over half of the women (56%) were employed outside the home, earning an average personal annual income of $22,000, and all had children living at home. In this sample, 84% of the women reported being survivors of severe violence such as being beaten, choked, and threatened or actually assaulted with weapons. Their average psychological victimization score on Tolman's (1989) Psychological Mal-treatment of Women Inventory was 202 out of a possible score of 290, indicating that participants in this investigation survived frequent exposure to abusive behaviors. Likewise, participants were characterized by fairly high levels of PTSD symptomatology: 60 participants (88%) had scores at or exceeding the cutoff point for suspected PTSD (i.e., .89) according to Saunders, Arata, and Kilpatrick's (1990) screening scale. Participants on average employed a moderate number of coping strategies in response to partner violence and were equally likely to rely upon emotion- and problem-focused coping. Women saw themselves as having little control over their partner's violence and expressed strong intentions to leave their abusive partners permanently.

As expected, there was a significant relationship between physical and psychological abuse in this study. Surprisingly, however, multiple regression analysis results indicated that physical abuse did not account for significant variance in either PTSD symptomatology or women's intentions to end their abusive relationships. On the other hand, psychological abuse was a significant predictor of both PTSD symptomatology and intentions to end the relationship, with greater levels of psychological abuse being associated with greater levels of PTSD symptomatology and a greater resolve to leave the abusive partner. When the effects of physical abuse were controlled by including it as a predictor in the regression equations, psychological abuse continued to account for significant variance in both PTSD symptomatology and intentions to end the abusive relationship.

In Arias and Pape's (in press) study, PTSD symptomatology proved to be a significant moderator of the effects of both physical and psychological abuse. The analyses showed that, while the relationship between physical abuse and intentions to terminate was significant for women in the low PTSD symptomatology group, there was no significant relationship for women in the high PTSD symptomatology group. Likewise, psychological abuse and intentions to terminate were highly related among women in the low PTSD symptomatology group, but there was no significant association for women in the high PTSD symptomatology group. Thus, it appears that the presence of high levels of PTSD symptomatology interfered with the intention to leave the abusive partner in response to both physical and psychological abuse.

Because of the significant association between physical and psychological abuse, a second set of regression analyses predicting intention to leave was conducted, examining the moderating effects of PTSD symptomatology while controlling for the remaining form of abuse. As was the case when main effects were examined, the interaction between PTSD symptomatology and physical abuse was no longer significant after controlling for the effects of psychological abuse. However, the interaction between psychological abuse and PTSD symptomatology continued to be significant even after controlling for physical abuse.

With regard to coping, emotion-focused coping and the ratio of emotion- to problem-focused coping strategies were significant predictors of PTSD symptomatology in this study. Greater use of emotion-focused coping and greater use of emotion-focused relative to problem-focused coping were associated with greater levels of PTSD symptomatology. While the ratio of emotion- to problem-focused coping strategies was no longer a significant predictor of PTSD symptomatology after controlling for the effects of psychological abuse, emotion-focused coping continued to account for a significant amount of unique variance. However, none of the three coping variables nor perceptions of control moderated the effects of psychological abuse on PTSD symptomatology.

CONCLUSIONS

The results of the studies described above underscore the importance of assessing and addressing psychological abuse among battered women. Psychological abuse of women appears to be a strong and significant predictor of poor psychological adjustment and poor physical health. More importantly, the results of our recent work indicated that the effects of psychological abuse appear to be significant even after controlling for the effects of physical abuse. Surprisingly, we found that physical abuse failed to account significantly for variance in women's psychological adjustment or their intentions to terminate an abusive relationship. In some studies, lack of variability in physical abuse scores among shelter samples like the one in our investigation could make it difficult to obtain significant associations between physical abuse and other variables of interest. However, samples employed by past investigators have included both shelter and community samples representing a wide range of victimization experiences, and the predictive properties of physical abuse appeared to be less robust than those of psychological abuse.

Rather than lack of variability being responsible for minimal associations, it is possible that the inability to obtain significant results for physical abuse was due to the method of measuring physical abuse in our work and that of others. The studies reviewed herein operationalized physical abuse by summing the product of frequency and severity of various forms of physical aggression for the year preceding the shelter contact or the assessment. However, women may be more likely to decide to leave their abusers, and/or to suffer PTSD and other maladaptive symptomatology, in response to the severity of the most recent violent event only, rather than in response to the cumulative frequency and severity of previous events. For example, a woman who has been slapped and pushed repeatedly during the preceding year and then is assaulted with objects and/or weapons may be more likely to take initial steps toward leaving her abuser, e.g., to reside in a shelter, and may be more committed to terminating the relationship in response to this event, than a woman would be who has been repeatedly threatened and assaulted with objects and/or weapons and then is slapped and pushed during the most recent violent incident. To state this notion in other words, women may respond to *changes* in severity and frequency of abuse, or to their own perceptions of dangerousness, rather than to absolute, objectively defined levels of frequency and severity.

The ability of psychological abuse to significantly and independently predict both women's psychological adjustment and their intentions to terminate the relationship may indicate that, relative to physical abuse, psychological abuse exerts considerable influence on these variables. There are several reasons why this might be the case. First, it is possible that women experienced psychological abuse more frequently than physical abuse. More frequent exposure to psychological abuse may allow it to have a greater impact on women's functioning than the relatively less frequent physical abuse. Unfortunately, measures of psychological and physical abuse typically employ response scales having a different metric, thus prohibiting direct examination of relative frequency. Second, relative to discreet episodes of physical violence, episodes of psychological abuse may be of longer duration. This may be particularly true in functional terms, if women internalize psychological abuse, especially emotional abuse and assaults on their self-esteem and self-concept such as humiliation. That is, a physically violent episode has a beginning and an end; physically violent acts commence and cease in occurrence during a dispute. Psychological abuse, on the other hand, may be prolonged, and especially so if events such as name-calling (e.g., "you're crazy/stupid") are incorporated into the self-concept (e.g., "I'm crazy/stupid"). Third, psychological assaults and trauma simply may have a greater impact on psychological well-being, at least in regards to PTSD symptomatology, than physical assault. By definition, psychological abuse is psychological in nature. Its targets are emotions and cognitions. The similar specificity and fundamental congruence between psychological abuse and psychological well-being may account for their significant association.

The results of our investigations and those of others point to the importance of recognizing the risk of PTSD among physically battered and psychologically abused women. Women in the studies reviewed typically completed the assessment within a short period after their arrival at a shelter, which, in turn, closely followed an abusive incident (i.e., a trauma). The short duration of the period following the trauma (i.e., less than one month) and the absence of standardized clinical assessment do not allow determination of the extent to which women scoring high on paper-and-pencil measures of PTSD symptomatology actually would meet DSM-IV criteria (APA, 1994) for the disorder. However, PTSD has been found to be quite prevalent among shelter residents even when assessed with standardized diagnostic interviews (Astin et al., 1995). Treatment for PTSD symptoms and the disorder *per se* during or after shelter residence should be considered and explored as an appropriate component of intervention.

In the Arias and Pape (in press) study, neither perceptions of control over the partner's violence nor coping strategies affected the probability that PTSD symptomatology would develop in psychologically abusive contexts in our sample of battered women. However, frequent and preferred use of emotion-focused strategies was predictive of PTSD symptoms. Women who frequently relied on ignoring the violence and focusing on less negative aspects of their lives were more likely to develop PTSD symptoms than women who focused on actions that could be taken to reduce, eliminate, or otherwise change the violence and its impact. It is not clear to what extent such actions were taken, but it did appear that focusing on potential actions buffered women against some of the negative effects of psychological abuse.

Of special note, Arias and Pape (in press) documented that PTSD symptomatology exerted a detrimental impact on women's responses to their victimization. That is, high levels of PTSD symptomatology significantly attenuated the impact of physical abuse and psychological abuse on women's intentions to terminate the abusive relationship. Termination of the abusive relationship appeared less likely in the context of PTSD and PTSD-like reactions, apparently no matter how badly a woman was treated by her partner. Women were able to conceive of termination of the abusive relationship as a viable option and were committed to that option in response to abuse *only* if they were not hampered by high levels of psychological distress. Women experiencing high levels of distress did not appear to be committed to terminating the abusive relationship and would be unlikely to attempt and succeed in leaving their abusive partners.

IMPLICATIONS FOR TREATMENT

This significant moderation of the main effects of physical and psychological abuse on intention to leave a partner suggests that women's experiences of their own victimization and their related decision-making processes may be more complex than typically assumed. Physical and psychological abuse frequency and severity alone may not provide sufficient motivation to disengage from a dangerous situation. Rather, women's feelings of psychological well-being may determine whether or not abuse is sufficient motivation. In our study, only women who were relatively unscathed psychologically strongly intended to disengage. It may be that when abuse produces significant psychological detriments, women feel less ready or able to terminate their relationship and to attempt self-sufficiency. Further, Arias, Street, and Brody (1996) illustrated that complications such as alcohol and drinking problems may set in as further obstacles. Interventions with battered women may have to take women's psychological well-being into account before expecting them to choose and attempt self-sufficiency. While women should not be dissuaded from attempting to leave their abusers, supportive services that are provided may have to vary as a function of women's psychological well-being. Future research should examine directly the extent to which psychological well-being has an impact on women's evaluation of their ability to carry out plans to terminate the relationship and their appraisal of being able to be self-sufficient. Ameliorating psychological distress or its effects by increasing social support, for example, appears to be important.

Because of the moderating effects of PTSD symptoms that were illustrated in our research, it seems prudent to attempt to reduce battered women's PTSD and related symptoms. Also, the negative impact of emotion-focused coping suggests that encouraging women to engage in problem-focused coping more frequently, and in preference to the use of emotion-focused strategies, may be productive. In addition to increasing or maintaining psychological distress in the context of abuse, emotion-focused coping may decrease women's ability to stay out of the abusive relationship even if they intend and do carry out plans and strategies for permanently leaving their abusive partners. Continued use of emotion-focused coping may increase the risk of developing psychological distress in response to the difficulties that may be experienced after leaving the abusive partner, such as financial, employment, and housing difficulties. High levels of psychological distress, in turn, may increase the probability of returning to the abusive partner.

The results suggesting that coping and distress have a negative impact on women's ability to terminate their abusive relationships underscore the need for shelter stays that extend beyond the common 30-day limit. It seems crucial to focus on the development of transitional housing and to design interventions that can be implemented over a longer period of time. Protective and supportive environments of longer duration would allow women to improve their self-esteem, decrease their psychological distress, and stabilize their improved affective and cognitive reactions enough to be able to focus on the complex task of independent living. Further, such interventions should increase the probability of maintaining constructive changes and independent living.

While the women who are the immediate victims of psychological abuse have received most research attention, the available data suggest that children are also at risk for psychological and behavioral dysfunction when exposed to interparental psychological abuse. The pattern of results is similar to that found in exposure to interparental physical abuse. Interventions for children residing in shelters with their abused mothers may need to address directly the potential consequences of exposure to interparental psychological abuse. Arias and Street (1996) documented the destructive impact on children of psychological abuse even after controlling for the effects of exposure to interparental physical abuse and child physical abuse. Because the relationship between women's physical victimization and their psychological adjustment appears to be nonexistent when the impact of psychological abuse is statistically controlled, it would be interesting and important to assess the extent to which children's exposure to interparental psychological abuse likewise accounts for the effect of their exposure to interparental physical abuse on their own psychological adjustment.

REFERENCES

Aguilar, R. J., & Nightingale, N. N. (1994). The impact of specific battering experiences on the self-esteem of abused women. *Journal of Family Violence, 9,* 35-45.

American Psychiatric Association. (1994). *Diagnostic and statistical manual of mental disorders* (4th ed.). Washington, DC: APA.

Arias, I., & Pape, K. T. (in press). Psychological abuse: Implications for adjustment and commitment to leave violent partners. *Violence and Victims.*

Arias, I., & Street, A. E. (1996, August). *Children of psychologically abused women: Effects of maternal adjustment and parenting on child outcomes.* Paper presented at the 8th International Conference on Personal Relationships, Banff, Canada.

Arias, I., Street, A. E., & Brody, G. H. (1996, September). *Depression and alcohol abuse: Women's responses to psychological victimization.* Paper presented at the American Psychological Association's National Conference on Psychosocial and Behavioral Factors in Women's Health: Research, Prevention, Treatment, and Service Delivery in Clinical and Community Settings, Washington, DC.

Astin, M. C., Lawrence, K. J., & Foy, D. W. (1993). Post traumatic stress disorder among battered women: Risk and resiliency factors. *Violence and Victims, 8,* 17-28.

Astin, M. C., Ogland-Hand, S. M., Foy, D. W., & Coleman, E. M. (1995). Posttraumatic stress disorder and childhood abuse in battered women: Comparison with maritally distressed women. *Journal of Consulting and Clinical Psychology, 63,* 308-312.

Babcock, J. C., Waltz, J., Jacobson, N. S., & Gottman, J. M. (1993). Power and violence: The relation between communication patterns, power discrepancies, and domestic violence. *Journal of Consulting and Clinical Psychology, 61,* 40-50.

Bernat, J. A., Ronfeldt, H. M., Calhoun, K. S., & Arias, I. (in press). Prevalence of traumatic events and peritraumatic predictors of posttraumatic stress symptoms in a nonclinical sample of college students. *Journal of Traumatic Stress.*

Burgess, E. W., & Locke, H. J. (1953). *The family: From institution to companionship* (2nd ed.). New York: American Book.

Carmen, E. H., Reiker, P. P., & Mills, T. (1984). Victims of violence and psychiatric illness. *American Journal of Psychiatry, 141,* 378-383.

Cascardi, M., & O'Leary, K. D. (1992). Depressive symptomatology, self-esteem, and self-blame in battered women. *Journal of Family Violence, 7,* 249-245.

Cascardi, M., O'Leary, K. D., Lawrence, E. E., & Schlee, K. A. (1995). Characteristics of women physically abused by their spouses and who seek treatment regarding marital conflict. *Journal of Consulting and Clinical Psychology, 63,* 616-623.

Cummings, E. M., Zahn-Waxler, C., & Radke-Yarrow, M. (1981). Young children's responses to expressions of anger and affection by others in the family. *Child Development, 52,* 1274-1282.

Dobash, R. E., & Dobash, R. P. (1979). *Violence against wives: A case against the patriarchy.* New York: Free Press.

Downey, G., & Coyne, J. C. (1990). Children of depressed parents: An integrative review. *Psychological Bulletin, 108,* 50-76.

Emery, R. E. (1989). Family violence. *American Psychologist, 44,* 321-328.

Fagan, J. A., Stewart, D. K., & Hansen, K. V. (1983). Violent men or violent husbands. In D. Finkelhor, R. J. Gelles, G. Hotaling, & M. A. Straus (Eds.), *The dark side of families: Current family violence research* (pp. 49-67). Beverly Hills, CA: Sage.

Fantuzzo, J. W., DePaola, L. M., Lambert, L., Martino, T., Anderson, G., & Sutton, S. (1991). Effects of interparental violence on the psychological adjustment and competencies of young children. *Journal of Consulting and Clinical Psychology, 59,* 258-265.

Fantuzzo, J. W., & Lindquist, C. U. (1989). The effects of observing conjugal violence on children: A review and analysis of research methodology. *Journal of Family Violence, 4,* 77-94.

Federal Bureau of Investigation. (1982). *Uniform crime reports.* Washington, DC: United States Department of Justice.

Ferraro, K. J., & Johnson, J. M. (1983). How women experience battering: The process of victimization. *Social Problems, 30,* 325-339.

Follingstad, D. R., Rutledge, L. L., Berg, B. J., Hause, E. S., & Polek, D. S. (1990). The role of emotional abuse in physically abusive relationships. *Journal of Family Violence, 5,* 107-120.

Forstrom-Cohen, B., & Rosenbaum, A. (1985). The effects of parental marital violence on young adults: An exploratory investigation. *Journal of Marriage and the Family, 47,* 467-472.

Gelles, R. J., & Cornell, C. P. (1985). *Intimate violence in families.* Beverly Hills, CA: Sage.

Goldberg, W., & Tomlanovich, M. C. (1984). Domestic violence victims in the emergency department. *Journal of the American Medical Association, 251,* 3259-3264.

Hammen, C., Gordon, G., Burge, D., Adrian, C., Jaenicke, C., & Hiroto, G. (1987). Maternal affective disorders, illness, and stress: Risk for children's psychopathology. *American Journal of Psychiatry, 14,* 736-741.

Hampton, R. L., Gelles, R. J., & Harrop, J. W. (1989). Is violence in Black families increasing? A comparison of 1975 and 1985 national survey rates. *Journal of Marriage and the Family, 51,* 969-980.

Haskett, M. E., Myers, L. W., Pirello, V. E., & Dombalis, A. O. (1995). Parenting style as a mediating link between parental emotional health and adjustment of maltreated children. *Behavior Therapy, 26,* 625-642.

Hastings, J. E., & Hamberger, L. K. (1988). Personality characteristics of spouse abusers: A controlled comparison. *Violence and Victims, 3,* 31-48.

Herbert, T. B., Silver, R. C., & Ellard, J. H. (1991). Coping with an abusive relationship: How and why do women stay? *Journal of Marriage and the Family, 53,* 311-325.

Heyman, R. E., O'Leary, K. D., & Jouriles, E. N. (1995). Alcohol and aggressive personality styles: Potentiators of serious physical aggression against wives? *Journal of Family Psychology, 9,* 44-57.

Hilberman, E., & Munson, K. (1977-1978). Sixty battered women. *Victimology: An International Journal, 2,* 460-470.

Holtzworth-Munroe, A., & Hutchinson, G. (1993). Attributing negative intent to wife behavior: The attributions of maritally violent men versus nonviolent men. *Journal of Abnormal Psychology, 102,* 206-211.

Hotaling, G., & Sugarman, D. (1986). An analysis of risk markers in husband-to-wife violence: The current state of knowledge. *Violence and Victims, 1,* 101-124.

Hotaling, G., & Sugarman, D. (1990). A risk marker analysis of assaulted wives. *Journal of Family Violence, 5,* 1-13.

Hughes, H. M. (1988). Psychological and behavioral correlates of family violence in witnesses and victims. *American Journal of Orthopsychiatry, 58,* 77-90.

Hughes, H. M., & Barad, S. J. (1983). Psychological functioning of children in a battered women's clinic. *American Journal of Orthopsychiatry, 53,* 525-531.

Jacobson, N. S., Gottman, J. M., Waltz, J., Rushe, R., Babcock, J., & Holtzworth-Munroe, A. (1994). Affect, verbal content, and psychophysiology and the argument of couples with a violent husband. *Journal of Consulting and Clinical Psychology, 62,* 982-988.

Jaffe, P., Wolfe, D. A., Wilson, S. K., & Zak, B. A. (1986). Similarities in behavioral and social adjustment among child victims and witnesses to family violence. *American Journal of Orthopsychiatry, 56,* 142-146.

Jezl, D. R., Molidor, C. E., & Wright, T. L. (1996). Physical, sexual and psychological abuse in high school dating relationships: Prevalence rates and self-esteem issues. *Child and Adolescent Social Work Journal, 13,* 69-87.

Jouriles, E. N., Murphy, C. M., & O'Leary, K. D. (1989) Interspousal aggression, marital discord, and child problems. *Journal of Consulting and Clinical Psychology, 57,* 453-455.

Kahn, F. I., Welch, T. L., & Zillmer, E. A. (1993). MMPI-2 profiles of battered women in transition. *Journal of Personality Assessment, 60,* 100-111.

Kalmuss, D. (1984). The intergenerational transmission of marital aggression. *Journal of Marriage and the Family, 46,* 11-19.

Kaufman Kantor, G., Jasinski, J. L., & Aldarondo, E. (1994). Sociocultural status and incidence of marital violence in Hispanic families. *Violence and Victims, 9,* 207-222.

Kemp, A., Rawlings, E. I., & Green, B. L. (1991). Post-traumatic stress disorder (PTSD) in battered women. *Journal of Traumatic Stress, 4,* 137-148.

Kempe, C. H., Silverman, F. N., Steele, B. F., Droegmueller, W., & Silver, H. K. (1962). The battered-child syndrome. *Journal of the American Medical Association, 181,* 105-112.

Leonard, K. E., & Senchak, M. (1993). Alcohol and premarital aggression among newlywed couples. *Journal of Studies on Alcohol, 11,* 96-108.

Levinger, G. (1966). Sources of marital dissatisfaction among applicants for divorce. *Journal of Orthopsychiatry, 36,* 803-807.

Lazarus, R. S., & Folkman, S. (1984). *Stress, appraisal, and coping.* New York: Springer.

Maiuro, R., Cahn, T., & Vitaliano, P. (1988). Anger, hostility, and depression in domestically violent men versus generally assaultive men and nonviolent control subjects. *Journal of Consulting and Clinical Psychology, 56,* 17-23.

Malone, J., Tyree, A., & O'Leary, K. D. (1989). Generalization and containment: Different effects of past aggression for wives and husbands. *Journal of Marriage and the Family, 51,* 687-697.

Margolin, G., John, R. S., & Gleberman, L. (1988). Affective responses to conflictual discussions in violent and nonviolent couples. *Journal of Consulting and Clinical Psychology, 56,* 24-33.

Marshall, L. L. (1996). Psychological abuse of women: Six distinct clusters. *Journal of Family Violence, 11,* 379-409.

Miller, B. A., Downs, W. R., & Testa, M. (1993). Interrelationships between victimization experiences and women's alcohol use. *Journal of Studies on Alcohol,* (Suppl. 11), 109-117.

Moffitt, T. E., Caspi, A., Krueger, R. F., Magdol, L., Margolin, G., Sylvia, P. A., & Sydney, R. (1997). Do partners agree about abuse in their relationship? A psychometric evaluation of interpartner agreement. *Psychological Assessment, 9,* 47-56.

Molidor, C. E. (1995). Gender differences of psychological abuse in high school dating relationships. *Child and Adolescent Social Work Journal, 12,* 119-134.

Murphy, C., & Cascardi, M. (1993). Psychological aggression and abuse in marriage. In R. L. Hampton, T. P. Gullotta, G. R. Adams, E. H. Potter, III, & R. P. Weissberg (Eds.), *Family violence: Prevention and treatment* (pp. 86-112). Newbury Park, CA: Sage.

Murphy, C. & O'Leary, K. D. (1989). Psychological aggression predicts physical aggression in early marriage. *Journal of Consulting and Clinical Psychology, 57,* 579-582.

O'Leary, K. D. (1987). The emergence of marital assessment. In K. D. O'Leary (Ed.), *Assessment of marital discord: An integration of research and practice* (pp. 1-11). Hillsdale, NJ: Erlbaum.

O'Leary, K. D., Barling, J., Arias, I., Rosenbaum, A., Malone, J., & Tyree, A. (1989). Prevalence and stability of spousal aggression. *Journal of Consulting and Clinical Psychology,57,* 263-268.

Pagelow, M. D. (1981). *Woman-battering: Victims and their experiences.* Beverly Hills, CA: Sage.

Parker, B., McFarlane, J., Soeken, K., Torres, S., & Campbell, D. (1993). Physical and emotional abuse in pregnancy: A comparison of adult and teenage women. *Nursing Research, 42,* 173-178.

Prince, J. E., & Arias, I. (1994). The role of perceived control and desirability of control among abusive and nonabusive husbands. *American Journal of Family Therapy, 22,* 126-134.

Ronfeldt, H. M., Kimerling, R., & Arias, I. (1998). Satisfaction with relationship power and the perpetration of dating violence. *Journal of Marriage and the Family, 60,* 70-78.

Rosenbaum, A., & O'Leary, K. D. (1981). Marital violence: Characteristics of abusive couple. *Journal of Consulting and Clinical Psychology, 49,* 63-71.

Rounsaville, B. J., & Lifton, N. (1983). A therapy group for battered women. In M. Rosenbaum (Ed.), *Handbook of short-term therapy groups* (pp. 155-179). New York: McGraw-Hill.

Saunders, B. E., Arata, C. M., & Kilpatrick, D. G. (1990). Development of a Crime-Related Post-Traumatic Stress Disorder scale for women within the Symptom Checklist-90-Revised. *Journal of Traumatic Stress, 3,* 439-448.

Silvern, L. Karyl, J., Waelde, L., Hodges, W. F., Starek, J., Heidt, E., & Min, K. (1995). Retrospective reports of parental partner abuse: Relationships to depression, trauma symptoms and self-esteem among college students. *Journal of Family Violence, 10,* 177-202.

Star, B., Clark, C. G., Goetz, K. M., & O'Malia, L. (1979). Psychosocial aspects of wife battering. *Social Casework: The Journal of Contemporary Social Work, 6,* 479-487.

Stark, E., Flitcraft, A., & Frazier, W. (1983). Medicine and patriarchal violence: The social construction of a "private" event. In V. Navaro (Ed.), *Women and health: The politics of sex in medicine* (Vol. 4, pp. 177-209). New York: Baywood.

Stets, J. E. (1990). Verbal and physical aggression in marriage. *Journal of Marriage and the Family, 52,* 501-514.

Straus, M. A. (1979). Measuring intrafamily conflict and violence: The Conflict Tactics (CT) Scales. *Journal of Marriage and the Family, 41,* 75-88.

Straus, M. A. (1980). Victims and aggressors in marital violence. *American Behavioral Scientist, 23,* 681-704.

Straus, M. A. (1986). Medical care costs of intra-family assault and homicide to society. *New York Academy of Medicine Bulletin, 62,* 556-561.

Straus, M. A., Gelles, R. J., & Steinmetz, S. (1980). *Behind closed doors: Violence in the American Family.* Andover Hills, MD: Anchor.

Strube, M. J. (1985). The decision to leave an abusive relationship: Empirical evidence and theoretical issues. *Psychological Bulletin, 104,* 236-250.

Terman, L. M., & Wallin, P. (1949). The validity of marriage prediction and marital adjustment tests. *American Sociological Review, 14,* 497-504.

Tolman, R. M. (1989). The development of a measure of psychological maltreatment of women by their male partners. *Violence and Victims, 4,* 159-177.

Vitanza, S., Vogel, L. C. M., & Marshall, L. L. (1995). Distress and symptoms of posttraumatic stress disorder in abused women. *Violence and Victims, 10,* 23-34.

Walker, L. E. (1979). *The battered woman.* New York: Harper & Row.

Walker, L. E. (1984). *The battered woman syndrome.* New York: Springer.

Wolfe, D. A., Jaffe, P., Wilson, S., & Zak, L. (1985). Children of battered women: The relation of child behavior to family violence and maternal stress. *Journal of Consulting and Clinical Psychology, 53,* 657-665.

8

Health Consequences for Victims of Violence in Intimate Relationships

Phyllis W. Sharps
Jacquelyn Campbell

Violence against women is a major public health problem that is at epidemic levels in this country and threatens the health and well-being of women. The most common form of violence that women experience is physical and/or sexual abuse in an intimate relationship. The 1992-1993 National Crime Victimization Survey reported that 29% of all violence perpetrated against women is committed by an intimate or former intimate partner (Federal Bureau of Investigation, 1993). Conservative estimates suggest that domestic violence (i.e., intimate partner violence) may occur in as many as one of every four families, and at least 2 million women are physically abused each year by a current or former partner (U.S. Department of Health and Humans Services, 1990; Novello, 1992). More recent reports suggest that, on average, for each year between 1992 and 1996, about 8 in 1,000 women, compared to 1 in 1,000, men experienced violent victimization inflicted by a current or former spouse, boyfriend or girlfriend (Greenfield et al., 1998). Research on emergency room visits has demonstrated that both physical and sexual

AUTHORS' NOTE: Correspondence concerning this article should be addressed to Phyllis Sharps, Ph.D., RN, Associate Director, Maternal Child Health Track, The School of Public Health and Health Services, The George Washington University, Washington, DC 20037, 202-994-0539; Fax 202-994-7893; email: sphpxs@gwumc.edu.

violence against women have significant consequences to the physical and mental health of victims, the most severe of which is femicide, the homicide of women.

This chapter examines the health consequences for female victims of intimate partner violence. This review of the literature will focus on (a) risk factors associated with violence against women, (b) physical health consequences of intimate partner violence, (c) physical health consequences of forced sex, and (d) the specific health consequences of violence during pregnancy. This chapter also includes a discussion of implications for health care providers who serve female victims of partner violence. Finally, the chapter will discuss implications for the future directions of health care research, with a particular focus on how such research might lead to new policies on violence and effective interventions for victims and perpetrators of violence and for family members of victims.

SCOPE OF THE PROBLEM

The U.S. health care system is burdened with costs for the treatment of women who are victims of intimate partner violence. Each year treatment costs to the health care system are estimated at $44,393,700. This represents 28,700 emergency room visits and 39,000 physician visits (McLeer & Anwar, 1989). Other research suggests that as many as 21% of all women seeking emergency surgical procedures require these services as a result of intimate partner abuse (Koss et al., 1994). Studies have found that between 3% and 35% of women seen in hospital emergency departments have been abused by an intimate partner (Dearwater, Campbell, Coben, McLoughlin, & Nah, 1998; Plichta, 1992, 1996a). The percentages vary according to the definitions used for identification (e.g., injury from abuse, abuse within the last year, ever abused), the type and location of the hospital, and the denominator used for calculations (e.g., all women, adult but not elderly women, trauma victims). Campbell, Pliska, Taylor, and Sheridan (1994) found that 63 of 74 shelter women had sought health care at a hospital emergency department as a result of injuries from abuse during the past 8 months. Among these women 40% reported physical health problems and 38% reported mental health problems (Campbell et al., 1994).

In addition to seeking out care for their immediate injuries, battered women use health care more often than nonabused woman. Over their lifetime, female victims of intimate partner violence use more primary care and mental health care services compared to nonabused women (Brendtro & Bowker,1989; Plichta, 1992; Rath, Jarratt, & Leonardson, 1989). In addition, battered women spend twice the number of days in bed due to illness as do nonabused women (Gelles & Straus, 1990).

Research has also documented that battered women perceive their own health status as worse than do nonabused women. In Rodriguez's (1989) descriptive study of 50 shelter residents, only 40% of the women rated their health as excellent or good. A national random survey conducted by the University of New Hampshire (Gelles & Straus, 1990) also found that abused women described their health as fair or poor. Similarly, Plichta's (1996b) study found that women who had experienced child abuse, violent crime, or intimate partner abuse were twice as likely to describe their health as fair or poor as were nonabused women.

There are also serious mental health problems associated with female victimization by an intimate partner, including increased depressive symptoms, lower self-esteem, posttraumatic stress disorder and increased use of alcohol and other illicit drugs (Campbell & Lewandowski, 1997; Plichta, 1992, 1996a). Although less frequently documented, the injuries abused women sustain affect their well-being in other ways. For example, McLeer and Anwar (1987) estimated that women victims lose a combined total of as many as 175,000 days from work each year.

VIOLENCE AGAINST WOMEN DEFINED

Many terms have been used in the arena of violence against women, including woman abuse, spouse abuse, domestic violence, domestic abuse, or simply abuse (Varvaro & Lasko, 1993). The U.S. Department of Justice (1990) defined *domestic violence* as abuse by an intimate other or close family member resulting in an intentional injury. Domestic violence against women is most often *battering*, which has been defined by Campbell and Humphreys (1993) as repeated physical and sexual assault by an intimate partner within a context of coercive control. In this definition, emotional abuse is considered to be almost always a part of the coercive control, but emotional abuse has not typically been measured in prior research related to physical health consequences. This chapter will describe the adverse physical health consequences of physical and sexual violence perpetrated against a women by a current or former intimate partner, and will use the terms "abuse," "intimate partner violence," and "battering" interchangeably.

RISK FACTORS ASSOCIATED WITH INTIMATE PARTNER VIOLENCE

The growing body of literature and research related to partner abuse has not identified a specific risk profile for victims (Crowell & Burgess, 1996; Hotaling & Sugarman, 1990). Any woman, regardless of her racial/ethnic group, age, marital status, education, or income may experience violence. However, prevalence rates of battering do vary by the age of women. For example, adolescent and young adult women are at high risk for battering, as are women over 60. Pregnancy is also a high risk period for battering (Stark & Flitcraft, 1996; Greenfield et al., 1998). Studies have also suggested other factors that increase a woman's risk for battering, including education less than high school, low income, and living in an urban area (Plichta, 1996a; Greenfeld et al., 1998). Across most studies, racial/ethnic background has not been found to be consistently related to intimate partner abuse, particularly once income is statistically controlled (Crowell & Burgess, 1996; Dearwater et al., 1998; Stark & Flitcraft, 1996; Plichta, 1996a).

PHYSICAL HEALTH CONSEQUENCES OF INTIMATE PARTNER VIOLENCE

Battering can produce a variety of physical health problems for women. Stark and Flitcraft (1996) described a battering syndrome resulting in repeated incidents of physical assault. In addition to the most obvious consequences of battering are acute and chronic pain (e.g., in the pelvic and genital area, abdomen, breast, and chest), bruises, broken bones, facial trauma, and other muscular and skeletal injuries (Grisso et al., 1991; McCauley et al., 1996; Mullerman, Lengahan, & Pakieser, 1996). For instance, a study by Varvaro and Lasko (1993) on 25 women revealed that more that one third of the abuse injuries were located on the face, head, and neck, and the most common type of injuries was contusion/soft tissue, abrasions, and lacerations. A study by Mullerman and colleagues (1996) showed that battered women were more likely to receive injuries to the head, face, neck, thorax, and abdomen than to other parts of their bodies. The authors identified at least 12 specific injury types, including ear drum damage, facial abrasion/contusion/laceration, neck abrasion/contusion, abdominal laceration/contusion, thorax abrasion/contusion, tooth loose/fracture, head abrasion/contusion, upper extremity abrasion/contusion, ankle sprains, knee sprains, eye abrasions, and back sprains.

The most severe traumatic injuries from intimate abuse can lead to death. Among African American women between the ages of 15 and 34 years, homicide is the leading cause of death, and it is the seventh leading cause of premature death for women overall (U.S. Department of Health and Human Services, 1992). From 1976 to 1996, more female homicide victims (44%) were killed by a spouse, ex-spouse, or boyfriend than by all other categories of perpetrator (Bureau of Justice Statistics, 1998). Death caused by another relative, stranger, acquaintance, or friend totaled 42.5%. (Because perpetrators who were ex-boyfriends were included in the friend or acquaintance categories, the rate of violence by those who have never been intimates is lower, and the rate by those who have been or are intimates is higher.) The remaining 13.5% were killed by an unknown perpetrator. In approximately two thirds of the cases of women killed by intimate partners, police-documented evidence of domestic violence existed (Campbell, 1992).

Beyond the immediate physical traumatic injuries, studies have documented other physical symptoms related to the abuse and the injuries. McCauley and colleagues (1996) studied 1,952 women in four community-based primary internal medicine practices in a large metropolitan city and found that the 108 abused women reported a variety of physical health symptoms at higher rates than did nonabused women. The reported symptoms that were associated with current partner abuse included loss of appetite, nightmares, vaginal discharges, eating binges, self-induced vomiting, diarrhea, fainting or passing out, frequent or severe headaches, difficulty passing urine, problems with sleeping, shortness of breath, and constipation. Other physical health symptoms that have been reported by battered women include chronic pain, gynecological health problems, neurological symptoms, and hearing loss (Cascardi, Langhinrichsen, & Vivian, 1992; Goldberg & Tomlanovich, 1984). Battered women also report more stress-related conditions such as irritable bowel syndrome (Campbell & Alford, 1989; Campbell & Lewandowski, 1997; Drossman et al., 1990; Stark & Flitcraft, 1988). Finally, studies have shown that abused women experience higher rates of mental health problems than nonabused women (Campbell, Sullivan, & Davidson, 1995; Plichta, 1996a), a topic discussed in more detail in other chapters in this volume.

PHYSICAL HEALTH CONSEQUENCES OF FORCED SEX

Women who experience intimate partner abuse also frequently are subjected to forced sex or unprotected sex, both of which can have negative physical health consequences. It is estimated that 40% to 45% of all battered women are forced to have sex with their partners (Campbell & Alford, 1989). In a large, randomly selected, national sample of women (Plichta & Abraham, 1996), 10% of women reported spouse abuse in the past year. Several gynecological problems were commonly found among the sexually assaulted women; one quarter reported severe menstrual problems and one sixth reported having urinary tract infections. Two fifths of the abused women were diagnosed with a sexually transmitted disease. Other studies provide corroborating evidence that forced sex is related to nonspecific pelvic pain, pelvic inflammatory disease, HIV/AIDS, vaginal and anal tearing, sexual dysfunction, and other genitourinary tract health infections (Bergman, Brismar, & Nordin, 1992; Campbell & Alford, 1989; Stark & Flitcraft, 1988). Other common aspects of forced sex by a male partner are his having multiple partners and refusing to use condoms (Plichta, 1996a; Eby, Campbell, Sullivan, & Davidson, 1995), which increases the partner's risk for sexually transmitted infections and diseases, unintended pregnancy, and pelvic, genital, and breast pain (Campbell, Pugh, Campbell, & Visscher, 1995; Gazmararian et al., 1995).

PHYSICAL HEALTH CONSEQUENCES
OF ABUSE DURING PREGNANCY

For many women, pregnancy is a time of increased risk for partner abuse (Campbell, Oliver, & Bullock, 1993; Gazmararian et al., 1996). Pregnancy may stimulate the first episode of abuse or escalate an already abusive relationship (Campbell et al., 1992). It is estimated that one in six pregnant women are abused during their pregnancy (Parker, McFarlane, & Soeken, 1994). In various studies, the prevalence rates of domestic violence reports during pregnancy ranged from 3% to 25% of woman seeking prenatal care, with the most frequent figure being between 8% and 19% (Amaro, Fried, Cabral, & Zuckerman, 1990; Gazamararian et al., 1996; Gielen et al., 1994). In one of the few ethnic-group comparisons of prevalence, Parker et al. (1994) found, in their study of 691 women, that 19% of African American and White women and 14% of Hispanic women reported abuse during the current pregnancy. These studies also indicated that across ethnic groups, the perpetrator was most often an intimate partner (McFarlane, Parker, & Soeken, 1995; McFarlane, Parker, Soeken, & Bullock, 1992). Evins and Chescheir (1996) studied 51 women who were self-referred to a university abortion clinic, and found that 31% had experienced physical abuse at some point in their life and 22% had been abused in the previous year. The highest prevalence rates were found when nurses conducted repeated face-to-face interviews (e.g., Helton, McFarlane, & Anderson, 1987; McFarlane et al., 1995).

Even severe abuse may occur during pregnancy. O'Campo, Gielen, Fadden, & Kass (1994) categorized violence into moderate violence ("throw objects at you," "push, grab or shove you," or "slap you") and severe violence ("kick, bite or hit you with a fist," "try to hit you with something else," "beat you up," "threaten you with a gun" or "use a knife or fire a gun") and found that 20% of women entering prenatal care reported moderate (11%) or severe (9%) abuse. Moreover, one study found that an even higher rate of women experienced moderate to severe abuse during the first 6 months postpartum (25% of women) than during pregnancy (19%; Gielen et al., 1994). Thus, not only pregnancy but birth may increase the risk for battering.

The risk factors identified for pregnant abused women are very similar to those described for abused women who are not pregnant. Abused pregnant women are at greater risk for becoming homicide victims than are nonabused pregnant women (McFarlane et al., 1995). In two recent studies of urban homicides, the leading cause of maternal mortality in Chicago and New York was trauma, with homicides constituting the largest proportion of traumatic deaths (Fildes, Reed, Jones, Martin, & Barrett, 1992). These findings suggest that pregnant abused women may be at greater risk for death due to abuse rather than due to complications of the pregnancy.

Battering during pregnancy has been associated with other hazards to the physical health of the mother. In addition to the direct effects of traumatic injuries, indirect effects of abuse include infections that may result from forced sex, and an exacerbation of other chronic medical conditions, such as hypertension, diabetes, or other stress-related conditions (Newberger et al., 1992). McFarlane, Parker, Soeken, (1996) studied 1,203 African American, Hispanic and White women, assessing them for abuse during the first prenatal visit and at two other prenatal visits during the pregnancy. They found that women who were abused during pregnancy tended to be younger than 17 years and unmarried; they also tended to have less than a 15-pound weight gain during the pregnancy, less than a 24-month interval between pregnancies, more infections, higher rates of anemia, higher rates of alcohol use and smoking, and higher rates of illicit drug use. Physical abuse during pregnancy has also been associated with late entry into prenatal care in at least three studies (Campbell et al., 1992; Parker et al., 1994; Sampselle, Petersen, Murtland, & Oakley, 1992), which increases the risk of less-than-optimal pregnancy outcomes for both the mother and developing fetus.

Research has shown that battering during pregnancy has been linked to poor neonatal and infant outcomes. The most common sites for battering is the head, however many women have reported being hit, kicked or having things thrown at abdomen and the torso (McFarlane, 1993). It is speculated that, blunt trauma to the abdomen, and back may be related to the high rates of miscarriage (Newberger et al., 1992). McCauley et al. (1996), in a study of 1,953 women in 4 community-based primary care internal medicine practices in a large urban city, found that the miscarriage rate was slightly higher in the abused group compared to the nonabused group

Women who report abuse have higher rates of unwanted and mistimed pregnancies, preterm labors and births, miscarriages, and low birth weight infants (American Medical Association, 1992; Donovan, 1995; Gazamararian et al., 1995; Helton et al., 1987). McFarlane et al. (1996) found that the abused women delivered a significantly higher percentage of low birth weight infants compared to nonabused women. The lowest mean birth weights were found among women abused during the current pregnancy, followed by women abused within the last year but not in the current pregnancy. Women who reported never having been abused gave birth to babies with the highest mean birth weight compared to abused women. Dye, Tollivert, Lee, and Kenney (1995) conducted a prospective study of 364 pregnant Appalachian women in West Virginia. Almost all of these women were White, and 15% of them reported abuse. Findings from this study revealed that perinatal abuse was associated with increased fetal distress and fetal death in utero, breech presentations, and poor fetal growth, as well as with a higher proportion of low birth weight and preterm infants. The researchers suggested that perinatal abuse and poor fetal and neonatal outcomes may be directly related to infant mortality.

Some studies have not found a direct link of abuse during pregnancy to low birth weight, when controlling for other factors (e.g., Amaro et al., 1990; O'Campo et al., 1994; Webster, Chandler, & Battistutta, 1996). However, these results are typically in samples of primarily poor women with many other complications of pregnancy (e.g., smoking) that can lead to low birth weight. Bullock and McFarlane (1989) found a stronger relationship between abuse during pregnancy and low birth weight in private patients than in public patients in Texas. Other possible mechanisms that may account for the connection of abuse and low birth weight are the increased substance abuse associated with abuse during pregnancy (Martin, English, Clark, Cilenti, & Kupper, 1996; McFarlane, Parker & Soeken, 1995), stress (Curry & Harvey, 1998), and late entry into prenatal care.

In addition to undermining the physical health of the mother and infant, battering during pregnancy has been associated with hazards to the mental health of the mother. One group of researchers (Sharps, Cepis, & Gering, 1997) examined perinatal abuse among military women. They studied 298 women who were on active duty (43%), wives of active duty men (43%), or dependent daughters of an active duty member (14%). Among these women, 9% reported never being abused, 9% reported being abused in the past year, and 3% reported being abused during the current pregnancy. On the Rosenberg Self-Esteem Scale, the nonabused women reported higher self-esteem scores compared to the abused women. On the Beck Depression Inventory, the abused women also reported a higher level of depressive symptoms compared to nonabused women. High self-esteem was negatively correlated with abuse and high depressive symptoms were positively correlated with abuse.

Several studies have reported that the rate of abuse is even higher for teens. Parker et al. (1994) found that 21% (73) of their teens reported abuse in the current pregnancy compared to 14% (120) among pregnant adult women. This represents one in five pregnant teens compared to one in seven adult women reporting abuse during pregnancy. Covington, Dalton, Diehl, Wright, & Piner (1997) studied the prevalence of abuse in adolescent pregnancy by comparing routine assessment procedures with a systematic assessment protocol. Their sample included 130 pregnant teens ages 12 to 19. They found an abuse prevalence of 5% with the routine procedure and 16% with the systematic protocol. The systematic protocol they used to assess for abuse was similar to Parker et al.'s (1994) protocol, and their obtained rate of 16% also supported Parker et al. in demonstrating that teens are at increased risk for abuse when compared to adult women. Both studies also found that teens were more likely to have multiple perpetrators of violence, which included partners, parents, and siblings. Teens also are more likely to enter into prenatal care late in the pregnancy, have poor weight gain, have preterm labor and birth, have increased first and second trimester bleeding, and give birth to infants that are small for their gestational age and low in birth weight. Abused pregnant teens, like abused adult pregnant women, are also more likely to smoke cigarettes and use alcohol (Parker et al., 1994). Finally, like abused adult pregnant women, abused teens entered prenatal care significantly later than did nonabused teen girls (Parker et al., 1994).

To summarize, across all ethnic backgrounds, both abused teens and abused adult women are at greater risk for delivering infants who weigh less, for having lower pregnancy weight gains and shorter intervals (24 months) between pregnancies, and for using substances such as cigarettes, alcohol, or drugs during the current pregnancy (Sampselle et al., 1992).

IMPLICATIONS FOR HEALTH PROVIDERS PRACTICE

Battered women use health care services and resources at a disproportionately higher rate than nonabused women. This gives health care professionals a unique opportunity to use their professional expertise to intervene in the lives of these women and their children

Limitations in Current Health Care System Responses to Abused Women

Most abused women are not identified as being abused by their health care provider even when their injuries are obviously due to battering (Dearwater et al., 1998; Goldberg & Tomlanovich, 1984; Plichta, 1996a; Rath et al., 1989; Stark & Flitcraft, 1996). Various reasons are given in the literature as to why physicians and nurses do not regularly ask about abuse. These include forgetting, being overwhelmed, fearing opening "Pandora's box," being uncomfortable about asking, or not knowing what to do with the information that the woman may disclose (Gerbert et al., 1996; McCauley et al., 1996; Sugg & Inui, 1992).

Both physicians and abused women find it difficult to communicate with each other about spousal abuse. Physicians tend to have a poorer quality of communication with abused women than with nonabused women. For instance, a study by Plichta's (1996a) revealed that only about 9% of abused women had discussed their abuse with physicians. The women reported that it was difficult to talk with physicians, that their physician was not a good listener, or felt that the physician did not take them seriously, talked down to them, or told them their medical problems were "all in your head." Another survey of 1,000 battered women found that the majority of these women stated that health care providers were the least helpful of all professional resources (Brendtro & Bowker, 1989). Abused women of color are also likely to find that the health care system is unresponsive to their plight (Campbell et al., 1994). This is partly related to the poverty, homelessness, AIDS, and substance use that are often more common in women of color in the U.S. Because health providers may not understand the complex interactions between these conditions and abuse, the health care system's response is especially likely to be one that blames a woman of color for her abuse (Richie & Kanuha, 1993).

One explanation of provider unresponsiveness is physicians and other health care providers may be handicapped by their lack of education and knowledge about intimate partner abuse and the resulting serious threats to the physical and mental health of women (Plichta, 1992). In addition, providers may have beliefs that prevent them from assessing for abuse in their patients, beliefs such as "violence is a private matter," "violence against women is not health problem," or "working with abused women is a hopeless cause" (Burge, 1989). It is discouraging that, as recently as 10 years ago, roughly half of U.S. medical schools included no formal educational experiences related to domestic violence in their curriculum (Holtz, Hames, & Safran, 1989).

Improving Health Care System
Responses to Abused Women

Comprehensive responses to violence against women require both primary and secondary interventions (Campbell & Humphreys, 1993; Plichta, 1996a). Primary interventions are those designed to prevent the onset of violence. Secondary interventions comprise additional efforts that aim to reduce existing violence.

Systematically educating all health care providers about domestic violence comprises one important primary prevention strategy. Education about domestic violence and its effects on victims could be included in the formal curricula for all health care providers (Campbell, 1995a). This education might include information on risk factors, indicators, estimated prevalence, and the physical and mental health sequelae of abuse. Upon incorporating domestic violence education in medical and nursing school curricula, health professionals' knowledge could be verified through accreditation procedures, certification, and licensure examinations. Professional organizations for health care providers should also take an active role in educating their members by including appropriate sessions and workshops in professional meetings and by endorsing incentives for self-learning (Plichta, 1996a). Several studies have demonstrated the efficacy of such training (Coeling & Harman, 1997; McLeer & Anwar, 1989; Tilden & Shephard, 1987).

A second important primary prevention strategy could involve the implementation by health care providers of efforts to educate women. Examples may include brochures, posters, media campaigns, and videos describing the cycle of abuse, the effect of injuries on the their health, and community resources for abused women. Women would benefit enormously from increased awareness about abuse and its effect on their health. Improving their knowledge might improve the quality of communication about their abuse with providers. Importantly, such awareness may also have an impact on safety behaviors. One group of nurses demonstrated that a brochure intervention with pregnant women that included information on the cycle of abuse, a safety assessment, and information about community resources, resulted in the women reporting a significant increase in adopting safety behaviors during and after their pregnancy (McFarlane, Parker, Soeken, Silva, & Reel, 1998). This study is the only published experimental educational protocol showing the effectiveness of an intervention for domestic violence in the health care settings.

Assessment of all women in health care settings is an important secondary prevention strategy. Studies described previously demonstrated that abused women use the health care system at a disproportionately higher rate than do nonabused women. Examples of secondary prevention strategies might include conducting routine screening in emergency departments, primary care settings, abortion clinics, and prenatal clinics, as well as providing referrals to appropriate community resources (Campbell & Lewandowski, 1997; Mullerman et al., 1996; Plichta, 1992). Health care professionals need opportunities to develop assessment skills that are culturally sensitive and appropriate, especially for women of color, who often believe that health care professionals are not sensitive to their plights. For example, nurse researchers (McFarlane et al., 1992) designed an abuse assessment instrument to be administered on pregnant women—the Abuse Assessment Screen (AAS)—that has been translated to Spanish, and has been found to be reliable and valid for Latinas as well as African- and Anglo-American groups (Soeken, McFarlane, Parker, & Lominak, 1998).

In addition to developing assessment skills, other secondary intervention efforts might focus on protocols to improve additional health care services for battered women (Sheridan & Taylor, 1993). For instance, in addition to primary prevention efforts (e.g., relaying definitions of domestic violence, facts and myths about domestic violence, common indicators of physical and nonphysical abuse) and improved assessments (e.g., by administering culturally sensitive assessment questions and techniques), hospital-based domestic violence programs could provide training on topics such as legal health care responsibility for reporting, criminal and domestic violence statutes, medical record documentation, forensic evidence collection (e.g., photographs of injuries, body map documentation), advocacy with police and court systems, safety issues for hospital or clinic staff, safety planning for victims, and effective community referrals (Sheridan & Taylor, 1993). Danger assessment and safety planning with the abused woman are particularly important aspects of programs for abused women. For instance, Campbell's (1995b) Danger Assessment uses a series of questions about the behavior of the woman's intimate abusive partner—for example, possession of a firearm, alcohol and drug use, frequency and severity of abuse, threats to kill her or himself, and his violence outside of the home. This assessment often increases the battered women's self-awareness of the potential risk for lethality in her relationship and can help her to make decisions about staying or leaving. Successful health care provider programs could also be modified to be suitable for community health settings where abused women may also go for help. For instance, intervention protocols have been useful in shelters for battered women and their children. These shelters have also offered additional services to women, including advocacy with the police departments and the legal system.

Additional secondary prevention efforts should aim to reduce the effects of violence on pregnant women and insure that they receive adequate prenatal care. The McFarlane et al. (1992, 1996) studies of pregnant women showed that abused pregnant adults and teens were likely to initiate prenatal care later in their pregnancy compared to nonabused women. Therefore, in light of the persistently high infant mortality rate in this country, and the injuries and poor outcomes associated with abuse during pregnancy, we need expanded efforts toward early initiation of prenatal care and community outreach programs to find and enroll adult and teen women into prenatal care and to provide screening and interventions for abuse as part of that care.

To effectively reduce and prevent intimate partner abuse, coordinated multidisciplinary efforts are optimal. A mechanism needs to be created that will coordinate the efforts of health care providers with the legal system, the social welfare system, and with community-based organizations where battered women seek help. It would be ideal for health care professionals to take the lead in coordination of these efforts (Plichta, 1996a).

IMPLICATIONS FOR HEALTH CARE RESEARCH

Recently there has been an accumulation of research on the health consequences of battering, particularly as a result of extensive research conducted by investigators in nursing. Despite the recent progress, there are several limitations in the existing body of research on intimate partner abuse. Campbell and Lewandowski (1997) cited the following limitations: (1) the lack of intervention research; (2) lack of systematic assessment of the extent of physical, sexual, and emotional violence against women; (3) lack of good measurement of health care costs and other costs to society (e.g., work productivity, entitlement payments to abused women and their children); (4) few investigations of the strengths and resiliency of battered women; (5) fragmentation of the literature and research studies along disciplinary lines; and (6) lack of attention to the complex relationship between ethnicity, gender, and poverty. These limitations provide directions for future health care research.

First, studies should include samples of diverse socioeconomic, educational, and ethnic backgrounds. In addition, although women are most often the victims of intimate partner abuse and are more seriously hurt in violent intimate relationships, more studies are needed on the health consequences for male victims. Very little is known about how men are affected by domestic violence or their health-seeking behaviors related to the abuse they experience (Campbell & Lewandowski, 1997). Investigators should also study the interactions between ethnicity, gender, and poverty—not merely describe the diversity of the study sample in terms of these sociodemographic characteristics.

More research is needed to substantiate the medical costs of abuse. Topics that need further study include: (1) the types and quantity of medical and mental health services used by abused and nonabused women and their families; (2) the number and types of temporary and permanent injuries suffered by victims as a result of battering; and (3) the number of days of productive functioning lost (i.e., time lost from work outside the home or household, or from attending career or job training; Plichta, 1996a). Systematic documentation of the economic and societal cost of abuse would provide compelling research-based evidence to help guide the development of policies to insure the safety and well-being of battered women and their children.

Clinical research is needed to test effective methods for assessing and identifying victims, to develop and test assessment tools, and to test and evaluate intervention models for victims. Attention should be given to standardizing definitions of physical, sexual, and emotional abuse. Investigators across all disciplines need to cooperate in developing standardized definitions and assessment tools—as is currently being spearheaded by the Centers for Disease Control. For example, McCauley et al. (1996) studied prevalence of domestic abuse among women attending community-based internal medicine practices and concluded that their identification model could help physicians to identify abused women more effectively. A strength of the model was the inclusion of nine sociodemographic, psychological, and physical characteristics related to abuse. The model consisted of demographic (e.g., age, race, education, marital status, income, medical insurance, household composition, family), psychological (e.g., emotional symptoms, alcohol/drug use, other medical history), and physical (e.g., symptoms such as nausea, vomiting, pain, headaches, etc.) characteristics. Using this model, the authors showed that a consistent increase in the prevalence rates of abuse was associated with an increase in the number of risk characteristics described above. They suggested that, if their model was validated with other populations, it could help practicing physicians to identify women experiencing abuse and to initiate appropriate treatment and referrals. More clinical research is also needed on the co-occurrence of physical health and mental health consequences of battering, including the role of alcohol and substance use, and subsequent injuries and diseases.

CONCLUSIONS

Intimate partner violence is a major public health problem. Injuries that result from partner abuse have significant consequences for the physical health and well-being of abused women. Health care providers are in a unique position to identify abused women and to intervene to help them. To be successful and effective, health care providers need to be educated about the significance of injuries, and how to routinely and effectively assess all women who enter any health care setting for signs of abuse. It is critical that health care providers increase and improve their research on: (1) injuries and physical health sequelae, (2) development of assessment and identification tools, (3) creation of reliable and valid culturally sensitive assessment techniques, and (4) systematic evaluations of existing assessment and intervention protocols and programs. Developing strategies that will effectively reduce and prevent battering and its physical health consequences will require the comprehensive combined efforts of health care providers, police, lawyers, judges, domestic violence workers, religious leaders, politicians, policy makers, and community activists.

REFERENCES

Amaro, H., Fried, L., Cabral, H., & Zuckerman, B. (1990). Violence during pregnancy and substance use. *American Journal of Public Health, 80,* 570-589.

American Medical Association (1992). American Medical Association diagnostic and treatment guidelines on domestic violence. *Archives of Family Medicine, 1,* 39-47.

Bergman, B., Brismar, B., & Nordin, C. (1992). Utilization of medical care by abused women. *American Journal of Public Health, 81,* 1486-1488.

Brendtro, M., & Bowker, H. L. (1989). Battered women: How nurses can help. *Issues in Mental Health Nursing, 10,* 169-180.

Bullock, L., & McFarlane, J. (1989). Higher prevalence of low birth weight infants born to battered women. *American Journal of Nursing, 89,* 1153-1155

Bureau of Justice Statistics. (1998). *Violence by intimates: Analysis of data on crimes by current or former spouses, boyfriends and girlfriends* (National Criminal Justice Publication No. 167237). Washington, DC: U.S. Department Of Justice.

Burge, S. K. (1989). Violence against women as a health care issue. *Family Medicine, 21,* 368-373.

Campbell, J. C. (1992). If I can't have you, no one can: Power and control in homicide of female partners. In J. Radford, & D. Russell (Eds.), *Femicide: The politics of woman killing* (pp. 99-113). Boston: Twayne.

Campbell, J. C. (1995a). Adult response to violence. *Violence: A plague in our land* (pp. 19-29). Washington, DC: American Academy of Nursing.

Campbell, J. C. (1995b). *Assessing dangerousness.* Thousand Oaks, CA: Sage.

Campbell, J. C., & Alford, P. (1989). The dark consequences of marital rape. *American Journal of Nursing, 89,* 946-949.

Campbell, J. C., & Humphreys, J. (1993). *Nursing care of survivors of family violence.* St. Louis, MO: Mosby.

Campbell, J. C., & Lewandowski, L. A. (1997). Mental and physical health effects of intimate partner violence on women and children. *Psychiatric Clinics of North America, 20*(2), 353-373.

Campbell, J. C., Oliver, C., & Bullock, L. (1993). Why battering during pregnancy? *Association of Women Health, Obstetric and Neonatal Nurses' Clinical Issues, 4*(3), 343-349.

Campbell, J. C., Pliska, M. J., Taylor, W., & Sheridan, D. (1994). Battered women's experiences in emergency departments: Need for appropriate policy and procedures. *Journal of Emergency Nursing, 20*(4), 280-283.

Campbell, J. C., Poland, M., Walker, J., & Ager, J. (1992). Correlates of battering during pregnancy. *Research In Nursing and Health, 15,* 219-226.

Campbell, J. C., Pugh, L. C., Campbell, D., & Visscher, M. (1995). The influence of abuse on pregnancy intention. *Women's Health Issues, 5*(4), 214-223.

Campbell, R., Sullivan, C. M., & Davidson, W. S. (1995). Women who use domestic violence shelters: Changes in depression over time. *Psychology of Women Quarterly, 19,* 237-255.

Cascardi, M., Langhinrichsen, J., & Vivian, D. (1992). Marital aggression: Impact, injury and health correlates for husbands and wives. *Archives of Internal Medicine, 152,* 357-363.

Coeling, H. V., & Harman, G. (1997). Learning to ask about domestic violence. *Women's Health Issues, 7*(4), 263-268.

Covington, D. L., Dalton, V. K., Diehl, S. J., Wright, B. D., & Piner, M. H. (1997). Improving detection of violence among pregnant adolescents. *Journal of Adolescent Health, 21*(1), 18-23.

Crowell, N. A., & Burgess, A. W. (Eds.) (1996). *Understanding violence against women.* Washington, DC: National Academy Press.

Curry, M. A., & Harvey, S. M. (1998). Stress related to domestic violence during pregnancy and infant birth weight. In J. Campbell (Ed.), *Empowering survivors of abuse: The health care system, battered women and their children.* Thousand Oaks, CA: Sage.

Dearwater, S., Campbell, J., Coben, J., McLoughlin, E., & Nah, G. (1998). Prevalence of intimate partner violence in community hospital emergency departments. *Journal of the American Medical Association.*

Donovan, P. (1995). Physical violence toward pregnant women is more likely to occur when pregnancy is unintended. *Family Planning Perspectives, 27,* 222-223.

Drossman, D. A., Leserman, J., Nachman, G., Li, Z., Gluck, H., Toomey, T. C., & Mitchell, M. (1990). Sexual and physical abuse in women and functional or organic gastrointestinal disorders. *Annals of Internal Medicine, 113,* 828-833.

Dye, D. D., Tollivert, R. V., Lee, R. V., & Kenney, C. J. (1995). Violence, pregnancy and birth outcomes in Appalachia. *Pediatric and Perinatal Epidemiology, 9,* 35-47.

Eby, K., Campbell, J. C., Sullivan, C., & Davidson, W. S. (1995). Health effects of experiences of sexual violence for women with abusive partners. *Health Care for Women International, 16,* 563-576.

Evins, G., & Chescheir, N. (1996). Prevalence of domestic violence among women seeking abortion services. *Women' Health Issues, 6*(4), 204-210.

Federal Bureau of Investigation. (1993). Uniform Crime Report. U.S. Department of Justice, Washington, DC.

Fildes, J., Reed, L., Jones, N., Martin, M., & Barrett, J. (1992). Trauma: The leading cause of maternal death. *Journal of Trauma, 32*(5), 643-645.

Gazmararian, J. A., Adams, M. M., Saltzman, L. E., Johnson, C. H., Bruce, F. C., Marks, J. S., & Zahniser, S. C. (1995). The relationship between intendedness and physical violence in mother's of newborns. *Obstetrics and Gynecology 85,* 131-138.

Gazmararian, J. A., Lazorick, S., Spitz, A. M., Ballard, T. J., Saltzman, L. E., & Marks, J. S. (1996). Prevalence of violence against pregnant women: A review of the literature. *Journal of Public Health, 275,* 1915-1920.

Gelles, R. J. & Straus, M. A. (1990). The medical and psychological costs of family violence. In M. A. Strauss & R. J. Gelles (Eds.), *Physical violence in American families: Risk factors and adaptations to violence* (pp. 425-429). New Brunswick, NJ: Transaction.

Gerbert, B., Johnston, K., Caspers, N., Blecker, T., Woods, A., & Rosenbaum, A. (1996). Experiences of battered women in health care settings: A qualitative study. *Women's Health, 24*(3), 1-15.

Gielen, A. C., O'Campo, P. J., Faden, R. R., Kass, N. E., & Xue, X. (1994). Interpersonal conflict and physical violence during the child-bearing years. *Social Science Medicine, 39*(6), 781-787.

Goldberg, W. G., & Tomlanovich, M. C.(1984). Domestic violence victims in the emergency department. *Journal of the American Medical Association, 251,* 3259-3264.

Greenfield, L. A., Rand, M. R., Craven, D., Klaus, P. A., Perkins, C. A., Ringel, C., Warchol, G., Matson, C., & Fox, J. A. (1998). *Violence by intimates* (National Criminal Justice-Publication No.167237). Washington, DC: U.S. Department of Justice.

Grisso, J. A., Wishner, A. R., Schwarz, D. F., Weene, B. A., Holmes, J. H., & Sutton, R. L. (1991). A population-based study of injuries in inner-city women. *American Journal of Epidemiology, 143*(1), 59-68.

Helton, A., McFarlane, J., & Anderson, E. T. (1987). Battered and pregnant: A prevalence study. *American Journal of Public Health, 77,* 1337-1339.

Holtz, H., Hames, C., & Safran, M. (1989). Education about domestic violence in U.S. and Canadian medical schools, 1987-1988. *Morbidity and Mortality Weekly Report, 38, 17.*

Hotaling, G. T., & Sugarman, D. B. (1990). A risk marker analysis of assaulted wives. *Journal of Family Violence, 5,* 1-3.

Koss, M. P., Goodman, L., Fitzgerald, L., Russo, N., Keita, G., & Browne, A. (1994). *No safe haven: Male violence against women at home, at work, and in the community.* Washington, DC: APA.

Martin, S. O., English, K. T., Clark, K. A., Cilenti, D., & Kupper, L. L. (1996). Violence and substance use among North Carolina pregnant women. *American Journal of Public Health, 86,* 991-998.

McCauley, J., Kern, D. E., Kolodner, K., Dill, L., Schroeder, A. F., DeChant, H. K., Ryden, J., Bass, E. B., & Derogatis, L. R. (1996). The "Battering Syndrome:" Prevalence and clinical characteristics of domestic violence in primary care internal medicine practices. *Annals of Internal Medicine, 123*(110), 737-746.

McFarlane, J. (1993). Abuse during pregnancy: The horror and hope. *Association of Women's Health, Obstetric and Neonatal Nurses' Clinical Issues, 4*(3), 350-362.

McFarlane, J., Parker, B., & Soeken, K. (1995). Abuse during pregnancy: Frequency, severity, perpetrator, and risk factors of homicide. *Public Health Nursing, 12*(5), 284-289.

McFarlane, J., Parker, B., & Soeken, K. (1996). Abuse during pregnancy: Associations with maternal health and infant birth weight. *Nursing Research, 45*(1), 37-42.

McFarlane, J., Parker, B., Soeken, K., & Bullock, L. (1992). Assessing for abuse during pregnancy: Severity and frequency of injuries and associated entry into prenatal care. *Journal of the American Medical Association, 267*, 2370-2372.

McFarlane, J., Parker, B., Soeken, K., Silva, C., & Reel, S. (1998). Safety behaviors of abused women after an intervention during pregnancy. *Journal of Obstetric, Gynecologic, and Neonatal Nursing, 27*(1), 64-69.

McLeer, S., & Anwar, R. (1987). The role of the emergency room physician in the prevention of domestic violence. *Annals of Emergency Medicine, 16*, 1155-1158.

McLeer, S. V. & Anwar, R. A. (1989). Education is not enough: A systems failure in protecting battered women. *Annals of Emergency Medicine, 18*(6), 651-653.

Mullerman, R., Lenaghan, P. A. & Pakieser, R. A. (1996). Battered women: Injury locations and types. *Annals of Emergency Medicine, 28*, 486-492.

Newberger, E. H., Barkan, S. E., Lieberman, E. S. (1992). Abuse of pregnant women and adverse birth outcomes: Current knowledge and implications for practice. *Journal of the American Medical Association, 267*, 2370-2372.

Novello, A. C., Rosenberg, M., Saltzman, L., & Shosky, J. (1992). The Surgeon General's Report: US Public Health Service. *Journal of the American Medical Association, 267*, 3132.

O'Campo, P. J., Gielen, A. C., Fadden, R. R., & Kass, N. E. (1994). Verbal abuse and physical violence among a cohort of low-income pregnant women. *Women's Health Issues, 4*(1), 1-9.

Parker, B., McFarlane, J., & Soeken, K. (1994). Abuse during pregnancy: Effects on maternal complications and birth weight in adult and teenage women. *Obstetrics and Gynecology, 84*(3), 323-328.

Plichta, S. B. (1992). The effects of woman abuse on health care utilization and health status: A literature review. *Women's Health Issues, 2*(3), 154- 163.

Plichta, S. (1996a). Violence and abuse: Implications for women's health. In M. Falik & K. Collins, (Eds.), *Women's health: The Commonwealth fund survey* (pp. 238-270). Baltimore: Academy Press.

Plichta, S. (1996b). Violence, health and use of health care services. *Women's health care seeking behavior* (pp. 237-270). Baltimore: Johns Hopkins University.

Plichta, S. B., & Abraham, C. (1996). Violence and gynecologic health in women 50 years old. *American Journal of Obstetrics & Gynecology, 174*, 903-907.

Rath, G. D., Jarratt, L. G., & Leonardson, G. (1989). Rates of domestic violence against adult women by men partners. *Journal of the American Board of Family Practice, 227*(4), 227-233.

Richie, B. E., & Kanuha, V. (1993). Battered women of color in public health care systems: Racism, sexism and violence. In B. Bair & S. E. Cayleff (Eds.), *Wings of gauze: Women of color and the experience of health and illness* (pp. 288-299). Detroit, MI: Wayne State University.

Rodriguez, R. (1989). Perception of health needs by battered women. *Response, 12*(4), 22-23.

Sampselle, C., Petersen, B. A., Murtland, T. L., & Oakley, D. J. (1992). Prevalence of abuse among pregnant women choosing a certified nurse-midwife or physician providers. *Journal of Nurse-Midwifery, 37*(4), 269-273.

Sharps, P. W., Cepis, L., & Gering, B. (1997). Abuse, depression, and self-esteem among military pregnant women. Paper presented at the International Family Violence Research Conference, July, 1997, University of New Hampshire.

Sheridan, D. J., & Taylor, W. K. (1993). Developing hospital-based domestic violence programs, protocols, policies and procedures. *Association of Women's Health Obstetric and Neonatal Nurses' Clinical Issues, 4*(3), 483-492.

Soeken, K. L., McFarlane, J., Parker, B., & Lominak, M. C. (1998). The abuse assessment screen: A clinical instrument to measure frequency, severity, and perpetrator of abuse against women. In J. C. Campbell (Ed.), *Empowering survivors of abuse: Health care for battered women and their children.* Thousand Oaks, CA: Sage.

Stark, E., & Flitcraft, A. (1988). Violence among inmates: An epidemiological review. In V. B. Van Hesselt, A. S. Morrison, A. S. Bellask, & M. Hersen (Eds.), *Handbook of family violence* (pp. 293-317). New York: Plenum Press.

Stark, E., & Flitcraft, A. (1996). *Women at risk: Domestic violence and women's health.* London: Sage Ltd.

Sugg, N. K., & Inui, T. (1992). Primary care physicians response to domestic violence: Opening Pandora's box. *Journal of the American Medical Association, 267,* 3157-3160.

Tilden, V. P., & Shepherd, P. (1987). Increasing the rate of identification of battered women in an emergency department: Use of a nursing protocol. *Research in Nursing and Health, 10,* 209-215.

U.S. Department of Health and Human Services. (1990). *Healthy People 2000: National health and promotion and disease prevention objectives.* Washington, DC: U.S. Government Printing Office.

U.S. Department of Health and Human Services. (1992). *Healthy People 2000: Update.* Washington, DC: U.S. Government Printing Office.

U.S. Department of Justice. (1990). *Criminal victimization in the United States.* Office of Justice Programs, Washington, DC: Bureau of Justice Statistics.

Varvaro, F. F., & Lasko, D. L. (1993). Physical abuse as cause of injury in women: Information for orthopedic nurses. *Orthopedic Nursing, 12*(1), 37-41.

Webster, J., Chandler, J., & Battistutta, D. (1996). Pregnancy outcomes and health care use: Effects of abuse. *American Journal of Obstetrics and Gynecology, 174*(2), 760-767.

9

Physical Aggression and the Longitudinal Course of Newlywed Marriage

Thomas N. Bradbury
Erika Lawrence

Physical aggression in marriage has been a topic of study for some time. However, only recently has attention focused on aggressive behaviors displayed early in relationships and the implications of those behaviors for how relationships develop and change. In making this shift investigators initially hypothesized, based on research on established marriages and on battered wives, that rates of physical aggression would be low prior to and early in marriage, and then would rise over the next several years (O'Leary, Malone, & Tyree, 1994). Evidence of markedly high prevalence rates among newlyweds quickly disconfirmed this expectation, however. O'Leary, Barling, Arias, Rosenbaum, Malone, and Tyree (1989) assessed couples one month before their wedding and found that either the man or the woman reported

AUTHORS' NOTE: Address correspondence to Thomas N. Bradbury, UCLA Department of Psychology, Box 951563, Los Angeles, CA 90095-1563. Direct electronic mail to bradbury@psych.ucla.edu.

Study 1 was supported by the Committee on Research of the UCLA Academic Senate. Study 2 and preparation of this chapter was supported by NIMH grant MH48674 awarded to the first author, and by a NIMH National Research Service Award to the second author. The authors thank Ximena Arriaga and Stuart Oskamp for the helpful comments on an earlier version of the chapter.

that at least one partner was aggressive in 57% of 272 couples in the previous year. Corroborating evidence for this finding was reported by McLaughlin, Leonard, and Senchak (1992), who observed that 36% of their 625 young couples reported at least one instance of husband-to-wife aggression in the past year. By comparison, on the basis of their national probability sample of 2,143 American families, Straus, Gelles, and Steinmetz (1980) reported that 16% of the couples had engaged in physical aggression in the past year; but they acknowledged that this probably underestimates the actual level of violence in these relationships. In a later survey, Straus and Gelles (1990) reported very similar rates of marital violence.

These results highlight the importance of distinguishing between different kinds of marital aggression (battering vs. escalated marital conflicts, or *patriarchal terrorism* vs. *common couple violence;* see Johnson, 1995; Chapter 2 (Straus) of this volume). Perhaps more importantly, they underscore the value of beginning to view aggression within the context of developing relationships.[1] The high rate of aggression in premarital and early marital relationships is also noteworthy because it draws attention to the needs (a) to develop interventions for couples entering marriage that will minimize or eliminate the physical aggression in their relationships, and (b) to conduct basic research in order to understand the role of physical aggression in developing relationships, which, in turn, could guide and inform prevention programs. Although it is certainly possible to develop useful prevention programs in the absence of a well-articulated understanding of aggression in marriage, the impact of these programs is likely to be greater to the extent that we know more about how marriages develop and deteriorate in relation to physical aggression (see Holtzworth-Munroe et al., 1995).

This chapter is intended to provide an overview of recent research on aggression in developing marriages. The first section is devoted to research linking physical aggression that occurs early in marriage to the longitudinal course of marriage. This research helps to document the consequences of physical aggression for the quality and stability of marriage, and it helps to clarify the characteristics of physical aggression that appear to have the greatest impact on marriages over time. The second section addresses longitudinal change in physical aggression itself in the early years of marriage. These data provide information about, for example, the degree to which aggressive spouses reduce or cease in their aggression over time. The chapter concludes with a summary and discussion of future directions.

THE ROLE OF AGGRESSION IN MARRIAGE

Before turning to the first section, it is worthwhile to consider how violence is viewed as a cause of marital dysfunction in the broader literature on marriage. Of course, the question of why some marriages are sources of support and satisfaction whereas others are sources of stress and despair has been examined for several decades. The motivation for studying this question derives from the fact that, despite stabilization in the rate of marital disruption since about 1980, about half of all first marriages end in separation or divorce (Cherlin, 1992); more than half of all divorcing couples have children under the age of 18 (Ahlburg & DeVita, 1992); and marital distress and disruption are associated with a host of adverse adult and child outcomes, including poor performance in work or school and poor physical and mental health (Amato & Keith, 1991a, 1991b).

In view of these statistics, it is plausible to expect that efforts to address the question of how marriages succeed and fail would incorporate the role of violence and aggression into their formulations. This expectation follows from what is known about the prevalence of violence in marriage, and from the hypothesis that aggression might be related to a number of factors that themselves might contribute to marital deterioration—including an inability on the part of spouses to manage their anger, deficiencies in problem-resolution skills, a lack of respect and appreciation between spouses, high levels of stress, various forms of psychopathology (e.g., alcohol and drug abuse, personality disorder), difficulties in managing intimacy, an imbalance of power in the marriage, and distance and distrust between spouses.

Despite these possible links, most psychological models of how marriages succeed and fail do not address explicitly the role of aggression in this process (see Bradbury, 1998; Karney & Bradbury, 1995a; Weiss & Heyman, 1997). Attention has been given to the interactional and cognitive variables that discriminate violent and nonviolent couples cross-sectionally (e.g., Holtzworth-Munroe & Hutchinson, 1993; Jacobson et al., 1994; Margolin, John, & Gleberman, 1988). This research demonstrates, for example, that among distressed couples important interactional differences emerge between those who are violent and those who are nonviolent. However, far less attention has been given to developmental analyses of how violence and marital outcomes (i.e., marital quality and stability) fluctuate over time, how nonviolent couples become violent over time, and vice versa. Thus, an analysis of the interplay between physical aggression and marital outcomes in newlywed samples holds the potential not only for refining our understanding of physical aggression in marriage but also for focusing attention on the role of aggression in broader psychological models of marital functioning.

PHYSICAL AGGRESSION DURING THE COURSE OF NEWLYWED MARRIAGE

Brief Review of Research

Relatively few longitudinal studies have examined marital outcomes in relation to physical aggression as assessed shortly before or after marriage. In one of the first studies conducted in this area, O'Leary et al. (1989)

assessed marital satisfaction and marital aggression in 272 couples 1 month before, and 18 and 30 months after, their wedding. All spouses were in their first marriage, and men and women were 25.3 years old and 23.6 years old, respectively. To increase the validity of the assessment of marital aggression, spouses reported on their own acts of aggression as well as those of their partner. As noted earlier, using this either/or method for assessing aggression, physical aggression was present in 57% of these couples in the first assessment. This figure dropped to 44% at 18 months and 41% at 30 months. At all three assessment intervals, wives were found to be more aggressive than husbands. The most common form of aggression for men and women at each assessment interval was "pushing, grabbing, and shoving," which was endorsed on average by approximately 25% of the couples. Across the three assessments and across all couples, nonreciprocal or unilateral aggression described 13%, 8%, and 9% of the men and 26%, 17%, and 16% of the women, thus indicating that both partners were engaging in aggression in many of these marriages.

O'Leary et al. (1989) also provided data on the stability of physical aggression through the first 30 months of marriage. For men and women who were not aggressive shortly before marriage, about 85% of them remained nonaggressive after 18 months of marriage whereas 15% became aggressive. For men and women who were aggressive at the initial assessment, about half remained aggressive at 18 months (51% for men, 41% for women) while the remainder became nonaggressive. Among couples who were not aggressive at 18 months, approximately 85% were not aggressive at 30 months, though this number was somewhat lower for men and women who were aggressive at the premarriage assessment. And among couples who were aggressive at 18 months, approximately 45% were not aggressive at 30 months and 55% were aggressive. Women appeared to be the more extreme in this condition, as 72% of those classified as aggressive at 18 months were also classified as aggressive at 30 months. In short, with some exceptions, these data indicate that about 85% of nonviolent spouses tend to remain nonviolent across 12 to 18 month intervals whereas about 50% of violent spouses tend to remain violent across this same span.

Thus, while there is (a) much continuity in nonaggression, and to a lesser extent, aggression, over the first 30 months of marriage, and (b) a general trend toward nonaggression over time, there is evidence that (c) couples' aggression status does change with time. The implications of these fluctuations are addressed in the next section of this chapter, but for now it bears noting that O'Leary et al. (1989) classified spouses on the basis of the stability in their aggression and examined these classifications in relation to marital satisfaction. Stable physical aggression (i.e., being physically aggressive at all three assessment intervals) characterized 8% of the men and 17% of the women, whereas stable nonaggression characterized 50% of the men and 39% of the women. (Thus it follows that 42% of the men

44% of the women changed their violence classification in this study at least once.)

The marital satisfaction of the *partners* of these two groups of spouses, over all three assessment intervals, was then compared. As one would predict, the partners of the stably aggressive spouses were less satisfied than the partners of stably nonaggressive spouses. When a cutoff score of 90 on the Locke-Wallace (1959) Marital Adjustment Test was adopted, 30% of the partners of stably aggressive men and 24% of the partners of stably aggressive women were found to be maritally distressed after 30 months of marriage, compared to 11% of the partners of stably nonaggressive men and 9% of the partners of stably nonaggressive women. These figures indicate that about 10% of the partners of stably nonaggressive partners will encounter marital discord through the first 2 $^1/_2$ years of marriage and that this degree of risk is 2.5 to 3 times greater for partners of stably aggressive mates. These figures are particularly noteworthy in that O'Leary and colleagues lost 121 couples to attrition; these couples were not more aggressive initially than the continuing couples, though it is typically the case that couples who drop from studies are more distressed than those who do not (Karney & Bradbury, 1995a). Thus, it seems likely that the general risk of marital disruption associated with physical aggression is actually greater than that reported by O'Leary et al. (1989).

Additional analyses with this sample involving severe physical aggression and wives' marital outcomes were reported by Heyman, O'Leary, and Jouriles (1995). The Marital Status Inventory (Weiss & Cerreto, 1980), which assesses steps taken toward divorce (e.g., "I have thought specifically about separation or divorce. I have considered who would get the kids, how things would be divided, pros and cons of such actions, etc."), was administered 1 month prior to marriage and 6, 18, and 30 months following marriage. An analysis was performed in which wives' MSI scores were predicted from wives' premarital satisfaction scores, husbands' premarital problem drinking, and husbands' severe premarital aggression. Severe aggression was defined as two or more acts of moderate physical aggression in the past year or one or more acts of severe physical aggression in the past year. Results indicated that wives who experienced severe aggression prior to marriage reported more steps toward divorce than wives who did not experience severe aggression, and that the wives who experienced severe aggression took more steps toward divorce from the 6- to the 30-month assessments. "Thus, serious premarital aggression . . . appears to be a significant risk factor for later potential dissolution, over and above any effects of premarital adjustment" (Heyman et al., 1995, p. 51).

Similar findings were obtained for wives' Locke-Wallace Marital Adjustment Test scores. Women married to men who were severely aggressive prior to marriage reported declines in satisfaction (from 125 premaritally to 106 after 30 months), whereas women married to men who were not seriously aggressive maintained their satisfaction over time (from 124 premaritally to 124 after 30 months). In neither analysis were there main effects or interactions involving husbands' problem drinking (cf. Leonard, Chapter 6 this volume). These findings help round out the picture provided by O'Leary et al. (1989) and show that wives of men who are severely aggressive prior to marriage are less maritally satisfied and more likely to take steps to end their relationship.

Physical Aggression and Marital Outcomes: Specifying the Relationship

The studies by O'Leary and colleagues provide initial evidence regarding the prevalence of physical aggression in the early stages of marriage, the stability of aggression over time and its association with marital satisfaction, and the association between severe aggression and marital functioning. These findings are important because they help to clarify the nature and possible consequences of physical aggression early in marriage and because they suggest that interventions that decrease premarital or early marital aggression could decrease the likelihood of adverse marital outcomes over the ensuing 2 years. With these data as a valuable foundation, we conducted a study that was designed to specify further the relationship between physical aggression and the longitudinal course of newlywed marriages (see Lawrence & Bradbury, 1998, for full details). This study differed from the O'Leary et al. (1989) and Heyman et al. (1995) studies in several important respects: (1) data were collected over 48 months of marriage rather than 30, thus examining the association between physical aggression and marital functioning over a longer span of time; (2) eight waves of marital data were collected rather than three, thus providing a more detailed portrayal of changes in marital functioning; (3) marital outcomes were known for 93% of our original sample as compared with 69% of the original sample studied by O'Leary and colleagues; (4) separated and divorced couples were retained in all analyses rather than dropped so that the full range of marital functioning could be examined; (5) distinctions were made between severe, moderate, and nonaggressive couples rather than severe and nonsevere aggression as in the Heyman et al study; (6) we examined couples' aggression in relation to couples' outcomes rather than husbands' aggression in relation to wives' marital outcomes, as in the Heyman et al. study; and (7) the present sample of 60 couples was much smaller than the 272 couples examined by O'Leary et al. (1989) and Heyman et al. (1995).

Sample and Design

Sixty couples in their first marriages were recruited from newspaper and media advertisements in Los Angeles County (see Karney et al., 1995, for details on the recruitment procedure used in this study). Husbands averaged 25.4 years of age and wives averaged 24.0 years of age; each averaged 15.6 years of education and a modal gross annual income between $11,000 and $20,000. Of the participants, 75% were Caucasian, 10% were Hispanic, 7% were Asian American, 5% were African American, and 3% indicated "other" for race. None of the spouses had children coming into the marriage and none of the couples were expecting a child at the time of the initial assessment. In a laboratory session held an average of 12 weeks following marriage, spouses completed a series of questionnaires including the Marital Adjustment Test (MAT; Locke & Wallace, 1959) and the Conflict Tactics Scale (Straus, 1979), were interviewed about their personal histories, and were observed engaging in various marital interaction tasks. At seven successive 6-month intervals, couples were contacted by telephone and, if they were not permanently separated or divorced, spouses were mailed a questionnaire packet that included the MAT. Four couples, all in the nonaggressive group, discontinued their participation prior to completing the study; the results reported here are therefore based on 56 couples.

The purpose of this study was to examine physical aggression assessed around the time of marriage in relation to marital outcomes over 4 years. Analysis of marital outcomes can be complicated by the fact that there are two outcomes of interest—dissolution and satisfaction—and that dissolution is a categorical variable (separated/divorced vs. intact) whereas satisfaction among continuing couples is a continuous variable. In order to define a single dependent variable that captured both of these aspects of marital outcomes, we used survival analysis[2] and considered a marriage to have failed if either spouse reported a score below 80 on the MAT (indicating a fairly significant degree of marital dissatisfaction) or if the couple ended their marriage in separation or divorce. As in the O'Leary et al. (1989) study, either/or reporting on the CTS was used to assess physical aggression, and spouses were classified as aggressive if they endorsed the item "threw something at spouse" or higher on the CTS (e.g., "slapped the spouse," "beat-up the spouse"). Spouses responded to the CTS based on the year preceding the laboratory session.

Preliminary Analyses

Consistent with the prevalence figures reported by O'Leary et al., 48% of the couples were physically aggressive around the time of marriage (n = 27), including 29% of the men and 46% of the women; the comparable figures reported by O'Leary et al. were 57%, 31%, and 44%, respectively. The most common form of physical aggression involved "pushing, grabbing, or shoving" the spouse, which was reported by 27% of the men and 39% of the women. More severe acts, such as beating-up the spouse, and threatening to use or using a knife or gun, were quite rare, although in more than 20% of couples there was evidence of "kicking, biting, or hitting the spouse with a fist" and "hitting or trying to hit spouse with something." Of the 56 couples (53.6%), 30 couples either experienced a permanent separation or divorce or had at least one spouse fall below 80 on the MAT over the 4 years of the study. Among physically aggressive (PA) couples, 19 of 27 (70%, including 12 dissolutions) encountered at least one of these outcomes, whereas in the nonaggressive (NA) group, 11 of 29 (38%, including 6 dissolutions) did so. These groups did not differ in their MAT scores at the time of the initial assessment.

Survival analyses conducted over the eight waves of data collection indicated that couples in the nonaggressive group achieved reliably better marital outcomes than did physically aggressive couples. A series of chi-square tests, conducted at each of the eight assessment points, further indicated that the two groups did not differ in marital survival rates until the third (18-month) assessment and that they differed consistently at all subsequent assessments. Thus it appears that the presence of any form of aggression around the time of marriage nearly doubles the likelihood of marital failure in the manner we have defined it here, that this is not an artifact of initial levels of marital satisfaction, and that this difference manifests itself reliably after about 18 to 24 months of marriage.

Nevertheless, distinctions among nonaggressive and physically aggressive marriages are rather crude, and they overlook considerable variability within the physically aggressive subsample of marriages (e.g., O'Leary, 1988; also see Holtzworth-Munroe, Chapter 3 of this volume). The analyses outlined next were designed to offer a more differentiated perspective on these couples and their marital outcomes.

Marital Outcomes and Direction of Aggression

Although there is little research to guide predictions about the longitudinal course of unidirectional versus bidirectional aggression, we hypothesized that marriages in which both spouses are victims of aggression would have poorer outcomes than marriages in which only one spouse was a victim of aggression, and these would in turn have poorer outcomes than marriages in which neither spouse was a victim of aggression. Classification of couples by their direction of aggression yielded 29 nonaggressive couples, 1 unidirectionally aggressive husband, 11 unidirectionally aggressive wives, and 15 bidirectionally aggressive couples. Husbands and wives in these three groups did not differ in their Time 1 MAT scores. To simplify the following analyses, the sole unidirectionally aggressive husband was no longer considered.

Analyses showed that the survival curves for these three groups, considered simultaneously, were significantly different. Pairwise comparison of groups using chi-square tests indicated that although nonaggressive couples differed from the unidirectional wife-to-husband and the bidirectional couples, there was no difference between the unidirectional and bidirectional groups. Couples having unidirectional wife-to-husband aggression failed in 82% of the cases and couples having bidirectional aggression failed in 67% of the cases. In short, couples in which there is unidirectional wife-to-husband or bidirectional aggression around the time of marriage are at increased risk for adverse marital outcomes relative to couples who are nonaggressive around the time of marriage.

Marital Outcomes and Severity of Aggression

To examine the association between marital outcomes and severity of aggression, spouses were classified as moderately aggressive based on either spouse's endorsement of one or more of CTS items k through m ("threw something at spouse," "pushed, grabbed, or shoved spouse," "slapped spouse") and as severely aggressive based on either spouse's endorsement of one or more of items n through r ("kicked, bit, or hit with a fist," "hit or tried to hit spouse with something," "beat-up spouse," "threatened with a knife or gun," "used a knife or gun"). This resulted in 13 moderately aggressive couples and 14 severely aggressive couples, who could be compared against each other and against the 29 nonaggressive couples. Husbands and wives in severely aggressive couples reported lower Time 1 MAT scores than the other two groups. Thus, although their average scores were in the nondistressed range of marital functioning, even within the first few months of marriage severely aggressive couples were far less satisfied with their relationships when compared to couples who were nonaggressive or moderately aggressive. Specifically, nonaggressive husbands reported an average MAT score of 120.9, moderately aggressive husbands averaged 124.8, and severely aggressive husbands averaged 107.4. Nonaggressive wives reported an average MAT score of 120.5, moderately aggressive wives averaged 126.2, and severely aggressive wives averaged 109.6. In view of these differences, MAT scores were controlled in the following comparisons.

The predictions for these analyses were straightforward in the case of severely aggressive and nonaggressive couples, but the projected marital outcomes for moderately aggressive couples were not as obvious. Would these marriages evolve more like the severely aggressive couples (in view of the fact that both groups are marked by at least some aggression) or more like the nonaggressive couples (in view of the fact that there is "at least some normative legitimacy" to milder acts of violence; Straus et al., 1980, p. 259)?

Survival analyses indicated that the moderately aggressive couples did not differ from the nonaggressive couples, whereas both of these groups differed from the severely aggressive couples. After 4 years, 93% (that is, 13 of 14) of the severely aggressive couples either separated or divorced or had at least one spouse reporting an MAT score below 80, whereas these same outcomes were encountered by 46% of the moderately aggressive couples and

38% of the nonaggressive couples. These results indicate that severe aggression around the time of marriage—defined as kicking, biting, or hitting with a fist and more severe acts on the CTS—is about as common as moderate aggression and that it approximately doubles the likelihood of marital dissatisfaction or dissolution in the following 4 years.

A Brief Digression: Communication, Aggression, and the Longitudinal Course of Newlywed Marriage

The argument was made earlier that the basic longitudinal research literature on marriage has not been well integrated with recent findings regarding aggression in marriage. To begin to address this gap, analyses were conducted on the sample described above in which marital outcomes as assessed at year four were examined in relation to the following data collected at the initial assessment: CTS violence subscale items, a measure assessing trait-like propensities toward anger (viz., the Multidimensional Anger Inventory or MAI; Siegel, 1986), and observational coding of the specific emotions (e.g., anger, contempt, humor) that spouses displayed in a 15-minute marital problem-solving discussion (using the Specific Affect Coding System or SPAFF; Gottman, 1994). Thus this set of analyses links a sample of communication behavior, a widely studied aspect of marriage commonly hypothesized to foreshadow marital declines, with anger propensities and physical aggression, in the service of predicting marital outcomes. Further details of this study are reported by Rogge and Bradbury (1998).

The results of this study were surprisingly simple. Actual aggression as assessed with the CTS and the propensity toward anger as assessed with the MAI formed one factor, and this factor discriminated between those couples that separated or divorced in the course of the study ($n = 18$) and those who remained married over the 4 years ($n = 38$). On the other hand, the specific emotions displayed in the problem-solving discussions formed a second factor, and this factor discriminated between those couples in intact marriages who were maritally satisfied after 4 years ($n = 22$) and those couples in intact marriages who were maritally dissatisfied after 4 years ($n = 16$). This factor was not associated with marital dissolution. Similar results were obtained when self-report measures of communication were substituted for the observational variables, and the results remained largely unchanged after controlling for initial levels of marital satisfaction.

These data highlight the value of incorporating assessments of aggression into the basic longitudinal research literature on marriage, which to date has focused heavily on communication behaviors as antecedents of marital dysfunction (for a review see Bradbury & Karney, 1993). They also suggest that the role of aggression in the longitudinal course of marriage will be underemphasized to the extent that researchers neglect dissolved marriages (which are commonly lost to attrition in longitudinal studies) and focus instead on intact marriages that vary in their level of satisfaction.

Finally, these findings raise the question of whether aggression emerges as a predictor of marital dissolution because of the importance of aggression itself, or whether aggression is a marker for a larger class of highly dysfunctional behaviors and patterns of relating (e.g., personality disorder, alcohol and drug abuse; cf. Chapters 5 and 8 in the volume by Lloyd and by Sharps). In any case, together with the results of the Lawrence and Bradbury (1998) study, these findings suggest that aggression or closely related factors are reliably linked to increased risk of marital dissolution. This in turn suggests that efforts to help young couples establish more satisfying and enduring marriages might be greatly enhanced by strategies that curtail interspousal violence.

Summary

Very little research has been conducted on the role of physical aggression in the longitudinal course of newlywed marriage. The available research indicates that physical aggression is common in this population, that husbands and wives both engage in physical aggression in marriage, that this form of physical aggression can be distinguished from more severe forms of aggression such as battering, and that physical aggression may contribute to the deterioration of young marriages. These initial findings draw attention to the potential value of intervening with young physically aggressive couples, particularly those who are severely aggressive, and they help to resolve a vexing question in the literature: Why do physically aggressive couples seeking marital therapy view their aggression as not being a problem in the marriage (e.g., Ehrensaft & Vivian, 1996)? One possibility is that the physically aggressive couples who have remained married for a significant length of time—about 10 years on average in the Ehrensaft and Vivian (1996) study—have actually survived the effects of aggression in their marriage and in this sense are correct in stating that the violence is not a problem for them. The couples for whom physical aggression is a problem, such as those examined in the analyses reported here, are likely to have ended their marriages, perhaps because of the aggression.

As with any developing literature, many important questions remain to be answered. For example, in the Lawrence and Bradbury (1998) study, why were nonaggressive couples and moderately aggressive couples comparable in their marital outcomes? Is it because moderately aggressive couples desisted in their aggression over time and thus, in effect, became nonaggressive couples? Or did some of the nonaggressive couples become aggressive, thus rendering them similar to the moderately aggressive subsample? And to what extent do couples classified as severely aggressive around the time of marriage persist in this level of violence? Do these couples remain severely aggressive, or is their relationship scarred by the violence that happens early in the relationship, even if the violence eventually subsides? Addressing questions such as these requires multiwave longitudinal data, not only on marital satisfaction but also on physical aggression. A review of research involving data of this sort is provided in the next section, along with preliminary findings from an ongoing study.

LONGITUDINAL CHANGE IN PHYSICAL AGGRESSION AND MARITAL QUALITY

Brief Review of Research

Questions about the nature and degree of longitudinal change in physical aggression are important to address for theoretical and applied reasons. With regard to basic research, our models of physical aggression would differ markedly if the degree of physical aggression enacted by a spouse or couple was assumed to be relatively stable over time (in which case, for example, biological and intrapersonal causes might be prominent) versus unstable over time (in which case causes within the relationship or within the environment might be important). With regard to preventive interventions, the view that aggression is stable might lead to interventions that focus specifically on aggressive individuals or couples or that focus on helping people select nonaggressive mates. In contrast, the view that aggression is relatively unstable would suggest interventions designed to clarify the temporal precursors to aggression so that it could be predicted and avoided. Although it is likely that there are stably aggressive and stably nonaggressive people in the population of young and recently married couples, the extent to which unstably aggressive people (i.e., people who would fluctuate into and out of an aggressive subgroup over time) are present in this population remains unclear.

A few studies do shed light on the extent to which physical aggression in young marriages changes over time. As noted earlier, the study by O'Leary et al. (1989) indicated that more than 80% of spouses who are classified as nonviolent tend to remain classified as such across 12 to 18 month intervals, whereas about half of the spouses who are violent tend to remain violent across this same span. Additional analyses indicated that the stability coefficients for aggressive versus nonaggressive classifications over time were .38 for men from prior to marriage to 18 months, .41 from 18 to 30 months, and .31 from premarriage to 30 months. Comparable figures for women were .44, .55, and .31 (O'Leary et al., 1989). These associations are noteworthy in their magnitude, but are not so high as to suggest that later aggression or nonaggression is fully accounted for by the same classification 12 or 18 months earlier. Stated in another way, 17% of the women and 8% of the men reported being physical aggressive toward the spouse at all three assessment intervals (i.e., prior to marriage and 18 and 30 months later), whereas 39% of the women and 50% of the men reported being nonaggressive at all three assessment intervals. Thus, 56% of the women and 58% of the men maintained their violence status through 30 months of marriage, but the large remainder changed their violence status at some point.

Quigley and Leonard (1996) examined the degree to which 188 husbands who were physically aggressive in the first year of marriage had desisted in their aggression over the next two years, as reported following the third year of marriage. Unlike the data just reported for the O'Leary et al. study (which relied solely on self-reports of aggression), in all cases physical aggression was defined as having occurred if *either* the husband or wife reported it. Results indicated that 24% of the husbands had desisted in their physical aggression for 2 years, but this figure varied as a function of the level of violence in the first year of marriage. Specifically, 35% of the husbands who had engaged in one minor act of physical aggression and no acts of severe aggression in year 1 had desisted over the next 2 years, 26% of the husbands who had engaged in more than one minor act of physical aggression and no acts of severe aggression had desisted, and 14% of the husbands who had engaged in one or more acts of severe aggression had desisted.

These data are important for several reasons. First, they show that most husbands did not desist in their physical aggression, although it can be argued that the criterion of desistance used by Quigley and Leonard—absolutely no acts of minor or severe aggression by the husband over 2 years as reported by either spouse—is somewhat strict. These data also indicate that husbands who were more prone to aggression early in the marriage were less likely to desist in their aggression over time. (For an analysis of desistance in couples with a battering husband, see Jacobson, Gottman, Gortner, Berns, & Shortt, 1996.) On the other hand, these data do not address the extent to which wives changed in their aggression, the extent to which husbands fluctuated from minor to severe levels of aggression over time, or the possible occurrence of aggression among couples who were not aggressive in the first year of marriage.

Some Preliminary Findings on the Stability of Physical Aggression

In view of the need for additional data on the temporal stability of physical aggression in the early years of marriage, we present some preliminary findings on changes in aggression from approximately 6 months after marriage to 18 months after marriage. These data were collected from a sample of 172 newlywed couples who are participating in an ongoing study of the longitudinal course of marriage (see Davila, Bradbury, Cohan, & Tochluk, 1997, for a full description). This sample, and the procedures used to study them, are quite similar to the 60-couple study described earlier in this chapter (Lawrence & Bradbury, 1998) with the exceptions that couples were recruited from public marriage records rather than with media advertisements and that physical aggression was measured at several points beyond the Time 1 assessment. Each spouse reported on their own physical aggression and on that of the partner on the CTS over the previous year at both 6 and 18 months. Whereas 48% of the couples in the aforementioned 60-couple study were physically aggressive, including 29% of the men and 46% of the women, 29% of the couples in this study were physically aggressive, including 18% of the men and 27% of the women. We attribute this discrepancy to the fact that recruiting couples from public records appears to produce a happier and psychologically healthier sample (see Karney et al., 1995, for a full discussion of this issue). Nevertheless, in both samples very severe acts of aggression were rare and acts such as pushing, shoving, and grabbing the partner were most common.

In the initial assessment, 71% of the couples ($n = 110$) were classified as nonaggressive using the CTS criteria outlined earlier for the Lawrence and Bradbury (1998) study, 17% were moderately aggressive ($n = 26$), and 12% were severely aggressive ($n = 19$). At the Time 2 assessment, 12 months later, 77% of the couples were nonaggressive ($n = 120$), 12% were moderately aggressive ($n = 18$), and 11% were severely aggressive ($n = 17$). A cross-tabulation of physical aggression classifications at these two time points was then examined. This showed that 87% (or 96 of 110) of the couples that were not aggressive initially were also nonaggressive 12 months later. However, 7% (8 of 110) were now classified as moderately aggressive and 5% (6 of 110) were classified as severely aggressive. Among the 46 couples who were moderately aggressive initially, 31% (8 of 26) remained moderately aggressive at Time 2, but 50% of them (13 of 26) had reduced their aggression and were nonaggressive. On the other hand, 19% (5 of 26) had increased in their aggression and were severely aggressive at the time of the second assessment.

Thus, the speculation offered earlier about whether nonaggressive and moderately aggressive couples are comparable in their 4-year marital outcomes because many of the moderately aggressive couples desist in their aggression seems to be only partially true. In this study, fully half of them reported maintaining or increasing their level of aggression in the year prior to the Time 2 assessment.

Finally, we have some indirect evidence to support the observation made about the Lawrence and Bradbury (1998) study, that severe physical aggression occurring around the time of marriage may have detrimental effects on the marriage even if the aggression desists after that point. Specifically, in this sample, 32% (6 of 19) of the couples classified as severely aggressive initially were again classified as severely aggressive at Time 2. However, 58% (11 of 19) were nonaggressive and 11% (2 of 19) were moderately aggressive.

These data show that whereas most couples who are nonaggressive around the time of marriage tend to remain nonaggressive from 6 months to

18 months of marriage, there is considerable reclassification of moderately and severely aggressive couples. Although substantial proportions of these latter two groups remained either moderately or severely aggressive, at least half of the couples in each group were nonaggressive at the later assessment. It is not yet clear whether these shifts toward nonaggression can be accurately viewed as desistance, but the presence of these shifts leads to questions about how they can be promoted and maintained.

For a variety of methodological reasons, these figures are difficult to compare directly with those of Quigley and Leonard (1996) and O'Leary et al. (1989). Nevertheless, all three studies do suggest that couples can fluctuate over time in the presence and degree of aggression in their relationships. Consideration of these studies also indicates that reliance on two waves of data in any given analysis provides a relatively vague portrayal of these fluctuations. One approach to addressing this problem is outlined below.

Toward a Trajectory-Based View of Marital Aggression

Constraints Imposed by Two Waves of Data

There are several reasons to consider how best to depict and study the longitudinal course of physical aggression in marriage. First, existing methods that make use of only two waves of aggression data for any given analysis, while certainly acceptable for simple descriptive purposes, provide relatively little information. Second, the degree of stability that does exist in aggression over time can create statistical difficulties. For example, O'Leary, Malone, and Tyree (1994) conducted analyses to examine the contribution of family of origin variables, aggression in childhood and adolescence, and personality variables to physical aggression early in marriage. These variables were examined as predictors of psychological aggression and marital discord after 18 months of marriage and of physical aggression after 30 months of marriage. As O'Leary et al. (1994, p. 597) noted, "we tried evaluating this model, including the measures of spousal violence at earlier points in the relationship (premarriage and 18 months after marriage). However, such a large percentage of variance in the CTS at 30 months was accounted for by previous physical aggression that we lost our ability to get stable estimates of the effects of concern to us. The best single predictor of physical aggression against a partner was physical aggression in the previous wave." One possible solution to this problem is to examine multiple waves of physical aggression data simultaneously for a given spouse or a couple, to define a line that captures these data (e.g., in terms of where it starts, how much it slopes upward or downward over time, whether the sloping is linear or nonlinear, how much fluctuation there is around the line), and to then use these parameters of the line as the dependent variables of interest and examine them in relation to other variables. Details of this approach are provided below.

A third reason for developing methods that go beyond two-wave analyses of physical aggression is that existing studies have not accounted for large proportions of variance in later aggression. For example, in a careful and comprehensive analysis of the contributions of a family history of violence, gender identity, hostility, perceived power, alcohol use, and marital conflict styles to changes in physical aggression over the first year of marriage, Leonard and Senchak (1996, p. 377) noted that "although the domains covered by the model predicted marital aggression, the overall amount of variance accounted for was only moderate. Without considering premarital aggression, the model accounted for 29% of the variance in marital aggression. This includes approximately 13% that was predicted on the basis of sociodemographic factors. Clearly, there may well be other factors that would improve the prediction of marital aggression." In addition to looking toward other predictive domains as a means of improving our capacity to predict changes in marital aggression, as Leonard and Senchak suggest, it may prove at least as informative to consider alternative approaches to collecting and quantifying longitudinal data on aggression.

Quantifying Marital Aggression Data as Trajectories

Several of the couples in the 172-couple study described above have completed the CTS twice annually at six or seven of the eight planned assessments. As a first step toward examining the longitudinal trajectories of aggression, we computed a score at each assessment interval by summing the wives' frequency ratings of the individual acts of physical aggression on the CTS. The resulting plot of these scores for seven wives' ratings on their own aggression is shown in Figure 9.1. Although these plots are not necessarily representative of the temporal patterning of aggression across this entire sample, they do illustrate that physical aggression can fluctuate over time and that it can fluctuate in different ways for different individuals.

These multiwave trajectories give a different impression of the nature of physical aggression than do two- or even three-wave plots; one can see that reducing any of the trajectories in Figure 9.1 to one or two data points results in an oversimplification and even a misrepresentation of the nature of aggression in these relationships. Our argument is that multiwave trajectories of this sort may have a great deal to offer researchers interested in change in relationships in general (Karney & Bradbury, 1995b) and change in physical aggression in particular. Moreover, these trajectories are likely to yield a better starting point for describing the longitudinal course of physical aggression, and subsequent efforts to quantify and account for variance in these trajectories are likely to enhance our understanding of the factors that give

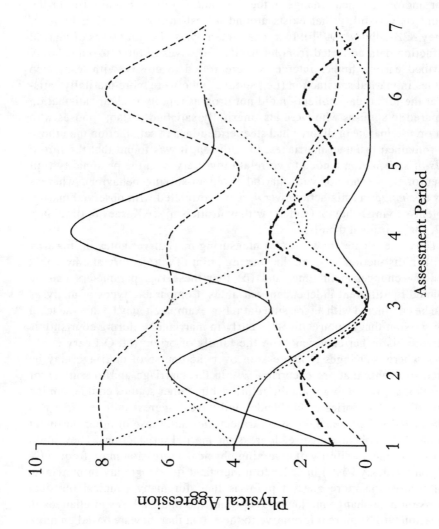

Figure 9.1: Trajectories of Physical Aggression: Wives' Reports of Wives' Aggression.

rise to (a) differences in aggression between spouses in different marriages and (b) changes in aggression over time for any given spouse.

How can data of this sort be quantified? Each of the lines in Figure 9.1 can be described by three main parameters: (1) the intercept, or the level of the variable at the beginning of data collection; (2) the slope, or the rate of linear and/or nonlinear change in the line; and (3) the residual term, or the amount of variability that exists around a best-fitting regression line (cf. Karney & Bradbury, 1995b). In a separate analysis of eight waves of marital satisfaction data collected from husbands and wives in the 60-couple study described earlier, higher intercepts were found to covary with less steep declines in marital satisfaction (i.e., spouses who were more maritally satisfied at the initial data collection did not drop as rapidly in their satisfaction compared to spouses who were less maritally satisfied). Also, spouses who went on to separate or divorce had steeper declines in satisfaction than those who remained in intact marriages. In addition, it was found that the *initial levels* of satisfaction tended to correlate inversely with the personality trait of neuroticism (and not with marital problem-solving behavior), whereas *rates of change* in satisfaction over 4 years correlated with observed marital problem-solving behavior (and not with neuroticism; see Karney & Bradbury, 1997, for additional details).

Thus, these data show that (a) measuring marital variables in this way permits a distinction between the starting point of a trajectory and how that trajectory changes with time, and (b) that these two parameters can be predicted by different independent variables. Comparable types of analyses could be conducted with aggression data. For example, it may be that the level of aggression that a spouse displays early in marriage or during courtship is related to his or her experiences in the family of origin (cf. O'Leary et al., 1994), whereas changes in aggression over the course of marriage may be related to events that are occurring within the marriage and to sources of stress that are impinging upon the relationship. Other studies could examine longitudinal trajectories of husbands' and wives' aggression over time and the covariation between aggression trajectories and those of other pertinent variables (alcohol and drug use, depression, marital satisfaction). They could also explore the possibility of assessing physical aggression more frequently (e.g., on a weekly basis) in order to understand its topography in marriage. In any case, the more general point is that, for many couples, physical aggression may change markedly over time, and that analyses of changes in aggression will be more informative to the extent that they are based on more rather than fewer waves of data.

SUMMARY AND CONCLUSION

In this chapter we have attempted to provide a review and analysis of the emerging literature on physical aggression in newlywed marriages. There is now clear evidence that physical aggression is quite common in this population, and in this chapter we have reviewed evidence to indicate that physical aggression early in marriage increases the likelihood of marital disruption in the ensuing years. Additional data are needed in this area, but severity of aggression appears to be more consequential for marital outcomes than does its direction, and aggression, more than marital communication, appears to increase the risk for marital dissolution. Although the larger longitudinal literature on marriage has not yet fully acknowledged that aggression may play a major role in the developmental course of young marriages, this oversight is becoming increasingly obvious. Recognition of the prevalence and impact of physical aggression in developing marriages is important, because further research on this topic should enhance the quality of interventions that are available for curtailing physical aggression and preventing marital dysfunction.

We have argued that further progress in understanding physical aggression in marriage will be facilitated by research that views aggression as a dynamic, changing phenomenon. Research on desistance of violence by Quigley and Leonard (1996) and others has begun to shed light on the extent to which aggression changes in the early stages of marriage. However, there is now a need to go beyond analyses that focus on two waves of data, so that a finer-grained portrayal of the longitudinal course of physical aggression in marriage begins to emerge. Here, we presented trajectories of marital aggression over the first 3 years of marriage to illustrate how such a portrayal might be derived, and we offered some suggestions about how these trajectories might be studied. Although there are undoubtedly many stably aggressive and stably nonaggressive young couples, we believe it is important to recognize that many of the stably aggressive couples are not uniform over time in their level of aggression, and that many other couples fluctuate a great deal over time in the amount, direction, and kind of aggression they display. The natural variability that exists across marriages and spouses in their levels of physical aggression, and the natural variability in aggression over time that exists within marriages and for individual spouses, may hold important clues for how aggression can be minimized and contained in developing relationships.

NOTES

1. A PsychInfo literature search conducted in March 1998 using the key words *marital* and *violence* yielded 678 papers, whereas *marital* and *aggression* yielded 254 papers. In contrast, *newlywed* and *violence* yielded just 3 papers and *newlywed* and *aggression* yielded 3 additional papers. *Dating* and *violence* turned up 167 papers, and *dating* and *aggression* turned up 77 papers. Thus it seems that aggression in relationships has been of interest to researchers up to the point that couples get married, and after that point newlywed couples have either not been of interest or are not differentiated from married couples more generally.

2. Survival analysis is a method by which investigators can describe whether and when some event (in this case marital dysfunction) occurs, and whether the likelihood of this occurrence differs between groups. Singer and Willett (1991) provide a valuable overview of this method.

REFERENCES

Ahlburg, D. A., & De Vita, C. J. (1992). New realities of the American family. *Population Bulletin, 47,* 3-44.

Amato, P. R., & Keith, B. (1991a). Parental divorce and the well-being of children: A meta-analysis. *Psychological Bulletin, 110,* 26-46.

Amato, P. R., & Keith, B. (1991b). Parental divorce and adult well-being: A meta-analysis. *Journal of Marriage and the Family, 53,* 43-58.

Bradbury, T. N. (Ed.) (1998). *The developmental course of marital dysfunction.* New York: Cambridge University Press.

Bradbury, T. N., & Karney, B. R. (1993). Longitudinal study of marital interaction and dysfunction: Review and analysis. *Clinical Psychology Review, 13,* 15-27.

Cherlin, A. J. (1992). *Marriage, divorce, remarriage* (2nd ed.). Cambridge, MA: Harvard University Press.

Davila, J., Bradbury, T. N., Cohan, C. L., & Tochluk, S. (1997). Marital functioning and depressive symptoms: Evidence for a stress generation model. *Journal of Personality and Social Psychology, 73,* 849-861.

Ehrensaft, M. K., & Vivian, D. (1996). Spouses' reasons for not reporting existing marital aggression as a marital problem. *Journal of Family Psychology, 10,* 443-453.

Gottman, J. M. (1994). *What predicts divorce?* Hillsdale, NJ: Erlbaum.

Heyman, R. E., O'Leary, K. D., & Jouriles, E. N. (1995). Alcohol and aggressive personality styles: Potentiators of serious physical aggression against wives? *Journal of Family Psychology, 9,* 44-57.

Holtzworth-Munroe, A., & Hutchinson, G. (1993). Attributing negative intent to wife behavior: The attributions of maritally violent versus violent men. *Journal of Abnormal Psychology, 102,* 206-211.

Holtzworth-Munroe, A., Markman, H., O'Leary, K. D., Neidig, P. H., Leber, D., Heyman, R. E., Hulbert, D., & Smutzler, N. (1995). The need for marital violence prevention efforts: A behavioral-cognitive secondary prevention program for engaged and newly married couples. *Applied and Preventive Psychology: Current Scientific Perspectives, 4,* 77-88.

Jacobson, N. S., Gottman, J. M., Gortner, E., Berns, S., & Shortt, J. W. (1996). Psychological factors in the longitudinal course of battering: When do couples split up? When does abuse decrease? *Violence and Victims, 11,* 371-392.

Jacobson, N. S., Gottman, J. M., Waltz, J., Rushe, R., Babcock, J., & Holtzworth-Munroe, A. (1994). Affect, verbal content, and psychophysiology in the arguments of couples with a violent husband. *Journal of Consulting and Clinical Psychology, 62,* 982-988.

Johnson, M. P. (1995). Patriarchal terrorism and common couple violence: Two forms of violence against women. *Journal of Marriage and the Family, 57,* 283-294.

Karney, B. R. & Bradbury, T. N. (1995a). The longitudinal course of marital quality and stability: A review of theory, method, and research. *Psychological Bulletin, 118,* 3-34.

Karney, B. R., & Bradbury, T. N. (1995b). Assessing longitudinal change in marriage: An introduction to the analysis of growth curves. *Journal of Marriage and the Family, 57,* 1091-1108.

Karney, B. R., & Bradbury, T. N. (1997). Neuroticism, marital interaction, and the trajectory of marital satisfaction. *Journal of Personality and Social Psychology, 72,* 1075-1092.

Karney, B. R., Davila, J., Cohan, C. L., Sullivan, K. T., Johnson, M. D., & Bradbury, T. N. (1995). An empirical investigation of sampling strategies in longitudinal research on marriage. *Journal of Marriage and the Family, 57,* 909-920.

Lawrence, E., & Bradbury, T. N. (1998). *Interspousal aggression and marital dysfunction: A longitudinal analysis.* Manuscript under review.

Locke, H. J., & Wallace, K. M. (1959). Short marital adjustment prediction tests: Their reliability and validity. *Marriage and Family Living, 21,* 251-255.

Leonard, K. E., & Senchak, M. (1996). Prospective prediction of husband marital aggression within newlywed couples. *Journal of Abnormal Psychology, 105,* 369-380.

Margolin, G., John, R. S., & Gleberman, L. (1988). Affective responses to conflictual discussions in violent and nonviolent couples. *Journal of Consulting and Clinical Psychology, 56,* 24-33.

McLaughlin, I. G., Leonard, K. E., & Senchak, M. (1992). Prevalence and distribution of premarital aggression among couples applying for a marriage license. *Journal of Family Violence, 7,* 309-319.

O'Leary, K. D. (1988). Physical aggression between spouses: A social learning theory perspective. In V. B. van Hasselt, R. L. Morrison, A. S. Bellack, & M. Hersen (Eds.), *Handbook of family violence* (pp. 31-55). New York: Plenum.

O'Leary, K. D., Barling, J., Arias, I., Rosenbaum, A., Malone, J., & Tyree, A. (1989). Prevalence and stability of marital aggression between spouses: A longitudinal analysis. *Journal of Consulting and Clinical Psychology, 57,* 263-268.

O'Leary, K. D., Malone, J., & Tyree, A. (1994). Physical aggression in early marriage: Prerelationship and relationship effects. *Journal of Consulting and Clinical Psychology, 62,* 594-602.

Quigley, B. M., & Leonard, K. E. (1996). Desistance of husband aggression in the early years of marriage. *Violence and Victims, 11,* 355-370.

Rogge, R. D., & Bradbury, T. N. (1998). *Till violence does us part: The differing roles of communication and aggression in predicting adverse marital outcomes.* Manuscript under review.

Siegel, J. M. (1986). The Multidimensional Anger Inventory. *Journal of Personality and Social Psychology, 51,* 191-200.

Singer, J. D., & Willett, J. B. (1991). Modeling the days of our lives: Using survival analysis when designing and analyzing longitudinal studies of duration and timing of events. *Psychological Bulletin, 110,* 268-290.

Straus, M. A. (1979). Measuring intrafamily conflict and violence: The Conflict Tactics (CT) Scales. *Journal of Marriage and the Family, 41,* 75-86.

Straus, M. A., & Gelles, R. J. (1990). How violent are American families? Estimates from the national family violence resurvey and other studies. In M. A. Straus

& R. J. Gelles (Eds.), *Physical violence in American Families: Risk factors and adaptations to violence in 8,145 families* (pp. 95-112). New Brunswick, NJ: Transaction.

Straus, M. A., Gelles, R. J., & Steinmetz, S. K. (1980). *Behind closed doors: Violence in the American Family.*New York: Anchor Books.

Weiss, R. L., & Cerreto, M. C. (1980). The Marital Status Inventory: Development of a measure of dissolution potential. *American Journal of Family Therapy, 8,* 80-85.

Weiss, R. L., & Heyman, R. E. (1997). A clinical-research overview of couples interactions. In W. K. Halford & H. J. Markman (Eds.), *Clinical handbook of marriage and couples interventions* (pp. 13-41). New York: Wiley.

Author Index

Abraham, C., 167
Adesso, V., 132
Adrian, C., 142
Aguilar, R. J., 145
Ahlburg, D. A., 183
Aldarondo, E., 142
Aldenderfer, M. S., 53
Alford, P., 167
Allen, B. A., 119
Amaro, H., 168, 170
Amato, P. R., 183
American Medical Association, 169
American Psychiatric Association, 154
Anderson, E. T., 168
Anglin, K., 64, 94, 96
Anwar, R. A., 163, 165, 172
Arata, C. M., 151
Arias, I., 6, 8-11, 13-14, 106, 139, 143-144,
    146-147, 150-152, 154-156, 181
Arriaga, X. B., 3
Astin, M. C., 141, 154
Atkinson, J., 98

Babcock, J. C., 92-93, 100, 103-104, 143
Bachman, R., 22, 24-25, 127
Balshfield, R. K., 53
Bandura, A., 10, 73, 74
Barad, S. J., 141-142
Barbour, L. S., 13
Bard, K. A., 127
Barling, J., 106, 143, 181
Baron, R. A., 73
Barratt, E. S., 63
Barrett, J., 168

Bartholomew, K., 62, 82
Barton, S. A., 65
Bates, J. E., 74
Battistutta, D., 170
Baumeister, R. F., 77
Berg, B. J., 144
Bergman, B., 167
Bernat, J. A., 150
Berns, S., 106, 193
Bird, G. W., 28
Black, D., 30
Bland, R., 28
Blane, H. T., 114
Bodnarchuk, M., 79
Bograd, M., 92-93
Boney-McCoy, S., 27, 50
Bowker, H. L., 164, 171
Bowlby, J., 80
Boyle, D. J., 95
Bradbury, T. N., 5-6, 8, 10, 11-12, 14, 181,
    183, 185-186, 190-191, 193-194, 196, 198
Brendtro, M., 164, 171
Brismar, B., 167
Brody, G. H., 146-148, 155
Bromet, E. J., 114
Brookoff, D., 25
Browning, J. J., 96
Bruun, K., 119
Bullock, L., 168, 170
Bureau of Justice Statistics, 127, 166
Burge, D., 142
Burge, S. K., 172
Burgess, A. W., 165-166
Burgess, E. W., 139
Burman, B., 92, 99-100

Burt, M. R., 65
Buss, A. H., 59, 119
Buzawa, C. G., 35
Buzawa, E. S., 35
Byrne, D., 73

Cabral, H., 168
Cahalan, D., 57, 118
Cahn, D. D., 92
Cahn, T., 143
Calhoun, K. S., 150
Calvert, R., 21, 32
Campbell, D., 144, 168
Campbell, J. C., 6, 8, 10, 12, 163-165,
    167-169, 172-175
Carmen, E. H., 140
Carrado, M., 19, 28,
Cascardi, M., 140-142, 149, 167
Castleton, A., 92
Cate, R., 13
Cepis, L., 170
Cerreto, M. C., 185
Chandler, J., 170
Chandler, T. A., 92, 95
Check, J. V. P., 64
Cherlin, A. J., 183
Chescheir, N., 168
Choice, P., 96
Christensen, A., 104
Cicchetti, D., 80
Cilenti, D., 170
Cisin, I. H., 57, 118
Clark, C. G., 141
Clark, K. A., 170
Clark, W. B., 114
Coan, J., 103
Coben, J., 164
Coeling, H. V., 172
Cohan, C. L., 193
Cole, A., 74
Coleman, D. H., 114
Cook, P. W., 26, 36
Cordova, J. V., 100
Cornell, C. P., 114, 142
Covington, D. L., 170
Cowen, E., 29
Cox, G., 100
Coyne, J. C., 142
Craven, D., 33
Crohan, S. E., 118
Crossley, H. M., 57, 118
Crowell, N. A., 165-166
Cummings, E. M., 141
Curry, M. A., 170

Dalton, V. K., 170
Das Eiden, R., 128
Davidson, W. S., 167
Davila, J., 193
Day, N. L., 114
Dearwater, S., 164, 166, 171
Demaris, A., 28
Denenberg, V. H., 82
DeVita, C. J., 183
Diehl, S. J., 170
Dobash, R. E., 25, 93, 140
Dobash, R. P., 25, 93, 140
Dodge, K., 74
Dombalis, A. O., 142
Donovan, P., 169
Downey, G., 62, 142
Downs, W. R., 141
Droegmueller, W., 139
Durkee, A., 59, 119
Dutton, D. G., 6, 7, 9-10, 12, 48, 57, 62, 73-74,
    77, 79-80, 82-83, 93-94, 96
Dye, D. D., 169

Eby, K., 167
Egeland, B., 76
Ehrensaft, M., 98, 191
Elias, B., 64
Ellard, J. H., 150
Emery, B. C., 92-93, 96
Emery, R. E., 141
English, K. T., 170
Evins, G., 168

Fadden, R. R., 168
Fagan, J. A., 114, 127, 140, 143
Falsetti, S. A., 57
Fantuzzo, J. W., 141
Federal Bureau of Investigation, 3, 21, 23, 140,
    163
Feld, S. L., 21
Feldman, S., 62
Felson, R. B., 35
Fenn, M., 74
Ferraro, K. J., 23, 93, 96, 140
Fiebert, M. S., 19, 33-34
Fildes, J., 168
Finkelhor, D., 60
Fisler, R., 80
Fitzgerald, H. E., 114
Flitcraft, A., 141, 166-167, 171
Folkman, S., 150
Follingstad, D. R., 143, 145
Forstrom-Cohen, B., 141
Foshee, V. A., 14

Foster, F. M., 119
Foy, D. W., 141
Frazier, W., 141
Fried, L., 168

Gage, R. B., 92, 102
Ganley, A., 74
Garfinkel, H., 30
Gazmararian, J. A., 168-169
Gelles, R. J., 3-4, 18, 19-21, 23, 30, 35-36, 45,
    91, 93, 96, 113-114, 125, 139, 142,
    164-165, 182
George, M. J., 19, 28
Gerbert, B., 171
Gering, B., 170
Gibson, B., 4
Gielen, A. C., 168
Giles-Sims, J., 35
Gilligan, C., 34
Gleberman, L., 91, 99, 143, 183
Goeckner, D., 132
Goetz, K. M., 141
Golant, S. K., 93-94
Gollan, J. K., 93
Goldberg, W., 140, 167, 171
Goldner, V., 92-94
Gonzales, D. M., 33-34
Gordon, G., 142
Gortner, E. T., 93, 106, 193
Gottman, J. M, 46, 51, 92, 93, 100-103, 106,
    143, 190, 193
Green, B. L., 141
Greenfield, L. A., 163, 166
Grisso, J. A., 166
Gryl, F. E., 28
Gunderson, J. G., 79

Hamberger, L. K., 51, 143
Hamby, S. L., 27, 50, 60
Hames, C., 172
Hammen, C., 142
Hampton, R. L., 142
Hansen, K. V., 114, 127, 140
Hare, R. D., 57
Harman, G., 172
Harrop, J. W., 21, 142
Hart, S., 79
Harvey, S. M., 170
Haskett, M. E., 142, 147
Hastings, J. E., 143
Hause, E. S., 144
Hawkins, G., 32
Helmreich, R. L., 119
Helton, A., 168, 169

Henderson, D. A., 93
Henton, J., 13
Herbert, T. B., 150
Herron, K., 6, 45
Heyman, R. E., 98, 121, 143, 183, 185-186
Hilberman, E., 140-141
Hilton, M. E., 114-115
Hiroto, G., 142
Holtz, H., 172
Holtzworth-Monroe, A., 6-7, 9, 11-12, 14,
    45-48, 55, 60, 62, 64, 66, 69, 93-96, 100,
    143, 182, 183, 188
Horn, J. L., 119
Horowitz, L. M., 62
Hotaling, G. T., 6, 13, 19, 23, 32, 142, 165
Hughes, H. M., 141-142
Humphreys, J., 165, 172
Hunter, R. S., 76
Huston, T. L., 98
Hutchinson, G., 64, 95, 143, 183

Infante, D. C., 92, 95-96
Innes, C. A., 23
Inui, T., 171

Jacob, T., 114
Jacobson, N. S., 46, 92-93, 96, 100-103, 106,
    143, 183, 193
Jacobvitz, D., 76
Jaenicke, C., 142
Jaffe, P., 141-142
Jarratt, L. G., 164
Jasinski, J. L., 142
Jezl, D. R., 145
John, R. S., 91, 92, 96, 99-100, 143, 183
Johnson, J. M., 23, 140
Johnson, M. P., 3-5, 7, 11, 14, 29, 91, 182
Jones, L., 19, 28
Jones, N., 168
Josephs, R. A., 132
Jouriles, E. N., 121, 141-143, 185

Kahn, F. I., 149
Kalmuss, D. S., 74, 76, 143
Kanuha, V., 172
Karney, B. R., 183, 185-186, 190, 194, 196, 198
Kass, N. E., 168
Kaufman, J., 76
Kaufman Kantor, G., 25, 32, 36, 121, 125, 142
Keith, B., 183
Kemp, A., 141
Kempe, C. H., 139
Kennedy, L. W., 30

Kenney, C. J., 169
Kihlstrom, N., 76
Kilpatrick, D. G., 57, 151
Kimerling, R., 144
Kirkpatrick, L. A., 80
Kirkwood, C., 93-94
Klein, D. F., 81
Kohn, R., 21, 23
Koss, M. P., 55, 164
Koval, J., 13
Krokoff, L. J., 101
Kropp, R., 79
Kupper, L. L., 170

Lampke, L. K., 96
Lang, A., 132
Langan, P. A., 23
Langhinrichsen-Rohling, J., 97-99, 167
Lasko, D. L., 165-166
Lawrence, E., 5-6, 8, 10-12, 14, 141, 186, 191,
    194
Lawrence, K. J., 141, 181
Lazarus, R. S., 150
Lee, R. V., 169
Lefcourt, H. M., 120
Lengahan, P. A., 166
Leonard, K. E., 6, 8, 10-12, 14, 113-114, 117,
    120-122, 127-128, 132, 143, 182, 186,
    193, 195-196, 199
Leonardson, G., 164
Levinger, G., 140
Lewandowski, L. A., 165, 167, 173-175
Lewis, H. B., 80
Lewis, M., 80
Lifton, N., 140
Lindell, M., 119
Lindquist, C. U., 141
Lloyd, S. A., 6-7, 9-11, 13, 91-94, 96-99, 104,
    191
Locke, H. J., 49, 139, 185, 187
Lominak, M. C., 173
Loseke, D. R., 4
Loxam, E., 19, 28
Luckenbill, D. F., 32
Lyons-Ruth, K., 81

Maguin, E. T., 114
Maiuro, R., 143
Malamuth, N. M., 64
Malone, J., 95, 106, 143, 181, 195
Margolin, G., 91-92, 96, 99-100, 119, 143, 183
Marlatt, A., 119
Marlatt, G., 132
Marshall, L. L., 93, 145-146, 150

Martin, M., 168
Martin, S. E., 127
Martin, S. O., 170
Martz, J. M., 13
Mathes, E. W., 62
Maynard, M., 93
McCauley, J., 166-167, 169, 171, 175
McFarlane, A. C., 79
McFarlane, J., 144, 168-170, 173-174
McHale, S. M., 98
McLaughlin, E., 164
McLaughlin, I. G., 182
McLeer, S., 164-165, 172
Meehan, J. C., 6, 45
Meyer, S. L., 99
Midanik, L., 114
Millon, T., 51
Miller, B. A., 141, 146
Miller, R. S., 120
Miller, S., 80, 102
Mills, T., 140
Moffitt, T. E., 145
Molidor, C. E., 144-145
Monson, C. M., 98
Moore, D. W., 32
Morse, B. J., 93
Mullerman, R., 166, 173
Munson, K., 140, 141
Murphy, C. M., 95, 99, 141, 144, 149
Murtland, T. L., 169
Myers, L. W., 142

Nah, G., 164
National Commission on the Causes and
    Prevention of Violence, 32
Neidig, P. H., 121
Newberger, E. H., 169
Nightingale, N. N., 145
Noll, R. B., 114
Nordin, C., 167
Novello, A. C., 163

Oakley, D. J., 169
O'Brien, M., 96
O'Campo, P. J., 168, 170
Ogloff, J., 79
Oldham, J., 57
O'Leary, K. D., 3-5, 9, 18, 59, 62, 65, 74,
    95-96, 99, 106, 114, 121, 140-144, 181,
    183-185, 187, 192-193, 195, 198
Oliver, C., 168
O'Malia, L., 141
Orn, H., 28
Orne, M., 22

Oros, C. J., 55
Oskamp, S., 3

Pagelow, M. D., 142-143
Pakieser, R. A., 166
Pan, H. D., 121
Pape, K. T., 13, 150-152, 154-155
Parker, B., 144, 168-171, 173
Parkinson, D. K., 114
Paschall, M. J., 35
Pearlstein, T., 21, 23
Penn, P., 92
Pernanen, K., 127, 132
Perris, H., 60
Perry, M., 59
Petersen, B. A., 169
Peterson, D. R., 96
Peterson, J., 21, 23
Peterson, K. S., 18
Petit, G. S., 74
Pillemer, K., 114
Piner, M. H., 170
Pirello, V. E., 142
Pirog-Good, M. A., 13, 93
Pittman, J. F., 96
Planalp, S., 92
Plichta, S. B., 164-167, 171-175
Polek, D. S., 144
Prince, J. E., 143
Ptacek, J., 32
Pugh, L. C., 168
Pynoos, R. S., 82

Quigley, B. M., 122, 127, 193, 195, 199

Radke-Yarrow, M., 141
Rath, G. D., 164, 171
Rathus, J. H., 62
Rawlings, E. I., 141
Reed, L., 168
Reel, S., 173
Reiker, P. P., 140
Reider, E. E., 114
Resick, P. A., 57
Resnick, H. S., 57
Retzinger, S. M., 80
Richie, B. E., 172
Riggs, D. S., 65, 96
Roberts, L. J., 121, 132
Robins, E., 98
Rodriguez, R., 165
Rogers, L. E., 92, 102
Rogge, R. D., 190

Rohsenow, D. J., 119
Ronfeldt, H. M., 144, 150
Rosenbaum, A., 59, 106, 141, 143, 181
Rosenfeld, B. D., 69
Rounsaville, B. J., 140
Roy, M., 113
Rudd, J. E., 92, 95-96
Runyan, D., 60
Rusbult, C. E., 13
Rushe, R. H., 46, 93, 100, 143
Rutledge, L. L., 144
Ryan, C. M., 114

Sabourin, T. C., 93, 95-96, 98, 102
Sacco, V. F., 32
Safran, M., 172
Saltzman, L. E., 22, 24-25
Sampselle, C., 169, 171
Sandin, E., 45
Santa-Barbara, J., 119
Saunders, B. E., 151
Saunders, D. G., 69, 82
Scanzoni, J., 28
Scheff, T. J., 80
Schlee, K. A., 98, 141
Schore, A. N., 81, 83
Schwartz, M. D., 93
Selzer, M. L., 57
Senchak, M., 117, 120-122, 128, 143, 182, 196
Severa, N., 62
Shannon, E. A., 95
Sharps, P. W., 8, 10, 12, 163, 170, 191
Shaver, P., 80
Sheinberg, M., 92
Shengold, L., 80
Shepherd, P., 172
Sheridan, D., 164, 173
Shortt, J. W., 46, 101, 106, 193
Siegel, J. M., 190
Silva, C., 173
Silver, H. K., 139
Silver, R. C., 150
Silverman, F. N., 139
Silvern, L., 141
Singer, J. D., 200
Skinner, H. A., 57, 119
Smutzler, N., 45, 95, 97
Soeken, K., 144, 168-170, 173
Sorenson, S. B., 28
Southwick, K., 119
Spence, J. T., 119
Spielberger, C. D., 59
Spielberger, C. R., 119
Steinhauer, P. D., 119
Spitzberg, B. H., 94

Stamp, G. H., 93, 95, 98
Stapp, J., 119
Star, B., 141
Stark, E., 141, 166-167, 171
Starzomski, A. J., 57, 80, 82
Steele, B. F., 139
Steele, C. M., 119, 132
Steinmetz, S. K., 4, 18, 21, 28, 35, 96, 139, 182
Stets, J. E., 9, 13, 21, 23, 26, 28, 91, 93-94
Stewart, D. K., 114, 127, 140
Stewart, J. H., 35
Stith, S. M., 28
Straus, M. A., 3-7, 11-12, 17-21, 23, 26-30, 32,
    35-36, 38, 40, 45, 49-50, 60, 91, 93, 96,
    114, 120-121, 125, 139, 140-145,
    164-165, 182, 187-189
Street, A. E., 146-148, 155-156
Strube, M. J., 13, 147, 150
Stuart, G. L., 6-7, 45-48, 55, 60, 66, 69
Sugarman, D. B., 6, 13, 19, 23, 27, 35, 50, 142,
    165
Sugg, N. K., 171
Suitor, J. J., 114
Sullaway, M., 104
Sullivan, C. M., 167
Summers, K. J., 100
Sweet, S., 21

Taylor, S. P., 132
Taylor, W. K., 164, 173
Telles, C. A., 28
Templar, D., 19, 28
Terman, L. M., 139
Testa, M., 141
Thoennes, N., 18-19, 23, 27
Tilden, V. P., 172
Tjaden, P. G., 18-19, 23, 27
Tochluk, S., 193
Tollivert, R. V., 169
Tolman, R. M., 55, 151
Tomlanovich, M. C., 140, 167, 171
Tompkins, S. S., 80
Torres, S., 144
Toth, S. L., 80
Turner, C., 74
Tyree, A., 95, 106, 143, 181, 195

U.S. Department of Health and Human
    Services, 163, 166
U.S. Department of Justice, 21, 165

Valente, E., 74
van der Kolk, B., 79-83
van Ginkel, C., 80
VanRooijen, L., 57
Varvaro, F. F., 165
Veroff, J., 118
Vinokur, A., 57
Visscher, M., 168
Vissing, Y. M., 21
Vitaliano, P., 143
Vitanza, S., 145
Vivian, D., 95, 97, 167, 191
Vogel, L. C. M., 145
Vuchinich, S., 97

Walker, G., 92
Walker, L., 77, 140-141, 143, 145
Wallace, K. M., 49, 183, 187
Wallin, P., 139
Waltz, J., 92, 93, 100, 143
Wanberg, K. W., 119
Ward, J., 53
Webster, J., 170
Weisaeth, L., 79
Weiss, R. L., 100, 183, 185
Welch, T. L., 149
Willett, J. B., 200
Wilson, S. K., 141-142
Wolfe, D. A., 141-142
Wright, B. D., 170
Wright, T. L., 145
Wurmser, L., 80

Yodanis, C. L., 35
Yllö, K. A., 4, 92-93

Zacker, J., 127
Zahn-Waxler, C., 141
Zak, B. A., 141-142
Zarrow, M. X., 82
Zigler, E., 76
Zillmer, E. A., 149
Zimring, F. E., 3,
Zlotnick, C., 21, 23, 28
Zucker, R. A., 114
Zuckerman, B., 168

Subject Index

Aggression in intimate relationships. *See*
    Violence in intimate relationships
Alcohol use:
    cognitive disruption hypothesis regarding,
        132
    effects of, 113, 186
    expectancy hypothesis regarding, 132
    measurement of, 119
    See also Correlates of intimate violence,
        alcohol use
Alcoholism, 113. *See also* Correlates of
    intimate violence, alcohol use

Batterers, characteristics of, 9, 45-69

Causes of violence in intimate relations. *See*
    Correlates of intimate violence
Centers for Disease Control (CDC), 175
Clinical fallacy, 29
Cluster analysis, 11, 53-55
Common couple violence, 4, 14, 91, 182
Communication perspective on intimate
    violence, 92-106
Conflict Tactics Scales (CTS), 10, 28, 49-50,
    53, 55, 60, 120, 187, 189, 190, 194-196
Consequences of physical abuse, 140-142,
    163-176
    death, 166
    divorce, 183, 185-191
    during pregnancy, 168-171
    for children, 141-142
    health consequences, 165-167
    injuries as, 3, 5, 28, 33, 36, 93, 127, 165-167
    mental health consequences, 165, 167

posttraumatic stress disorder (PTSD), 66,
    141, 150-155
relationship distress, 185-191. *See also*
    Correlates of intimate violence,
    relationship distress
See also Psychological abuse, consequences
    of; Responses to intimate violence;
    Sexual abuse, consequences of
Correlates of intimate violence, 9-11, 45,
    60-65, 79, 91-133, 165-166, 196
    alcohol use, 10, 113-133
    antisocial personality, 47-48, 52, 55-68
    attachment style, 62-63, 80-83
    between-subjects approach to assess,
        127-130
    borderline personality organization (BPO),
        46-48, 52, 54-68, 82-83
    communication problems, 6, 34, 94-106, 183
    cycle of abuse, 77-79
    dominance patterns, 102-104
    interaction patterns, 96-104, 126, 143, 183
    parental violence. *See* Violence in intimate
        relationships, intergenerational
        transmission of
    personality, 46-48, 51-52, 55-69, 77, 79-80,
        82-83, 119, 143
    physiological, 101
    proximal versus distal, 10, 46-48, 60-69,
        115, 123-125
    relational control, 102-103
    relationship distress, 10, 95-104, 183. *See*
        also Consequences of physical abuse,
        relationship distress
    self-esteem, 6
    sex-role attitudes, 6

social norms supporting violence, 6, 30-36
social skill and problem solving deficit,
    94-95
sociocultural, 142-143
within-subjects approach to assess, 130-131
Crime studies of intimate violence, 17, 19-20,
    22-26, 29
Criminologist perspective on intimate
    violence, 4
CTS. *See* Conflict Tactics Scales

Domestic violence:
    origins of interest in, 139
    See also Violence in intimate relationships

Family conflict studies, 17, 19, 22-24, 27-29
Feminist perspective on intimate violence, 4
    role of gender, 94

Growth curve analysis, 11, 196-198

Help-seeking behavior. *See* Responses to
    intimate violence, help-seeking
Homicide:
    rates of, 4
    violence resulting in, 166

Injuries resulting from intimate violence. *See*
    Consequences of physical abuse, injures
    as
Interventions and treatment of intimate
    violence, 5, 12, 69, 155-156. *See also*
    Prevention of intimate violence

Leaving a violent relationship. *See* Responses
    to intimate violence, leaving a violent
    relationship
Legal issues in defining violence, 21
Longitudinal research on violence, 11, 183,
    186-200
    Buffalo Newlywed Study, 117-131
    merits of, 68-69, 114
Los Angeles Epidemiological Catchment Area
    Study, 28

Marital distress. *See* Correlates of intimate
    violence, relationship distress;
    Consequences of physical abuse,
    relationship distress

National Crime Survey (NCS), 20, 22-25
National Crime Victimization Study (NCVS),
    20, 23-25, 127
National Family Violence Survey, 19, 28, 38,
    125, 144
National Survey of Families and Households,
    28
National Violence Against Women in America
    Survey (NVAW), 18-19, 22-24, 27, 39
NCS. *See* National Crime Survey
NVAW. *See* National Violence Against Women
    in America Survey
NCVS. *See* National Crime Victimization Study
Newlywed relationships. *See* Violence in
    intimate relationships, newlywed couples
    and

Patriarchal terrorism, 4, 14, 182
Physical abuse in intimate relationships. *See*
    Violence in intimate relationships
Physical assault in intimate relationships. *See*
    Violence in intimate relationships
Police statistics on violence, 20, 23, 25-26
Policy on intimate violence. *See* Social policy
    on intimate violence
Prevention of intimate violence, 12, 172-174.
    See also Interventions and treatment of
    intimate violence
Psychological abuse, 10, 14, 93, 139-156
    conceptualization of, 143-144
    consequences of, 145-155. *See also*
        Consequences of physical abuse;
        Responses to intimate violence
    co-occurrence of physical abuse and, 144,
        153-154
    disagreement over operational definition of,
        145
    responses to, 150-155

Rape. *See* Sexual abuse
Relationship distress. *See* Correlates of
    intimate violence, relationship distress;
    Consequences of physical abuse,
    relationship distress
Representative fallacy, 29
Responses to intimate violence, 13, 150-155
    coping mechanisms, 150-152, 155-156
    help-seeking, 13
    leaving a violent relationship, 13, 150-152,
        155
    limitations of healthcare system, 171-172
    self defense against, 28, 31, 33, 93
    See also Consequences of physical abuse;
        Psychological abuse, consequences of

Sexual abuse, 163
consequences of, 167-168
See also Consequences of physical abuse;
Violence in intimate relationships
Shelters for battered women, 29
Social policy on intimate violence, 12
Sociology of science, 37-39

Verbal aggression, 122-123, 126-132
Victims of violence:
economic dependence of, 13
emotional dependence of, 13
females as. See Violence in intimate
relationships, gender asymmetry in
perpetration of; see also Wife
battering
males versus females as. See Violence in
intimate relationships, gender
symmetry in perpetration of
risk factors for becoming, 165-166
Violence in intimate relationships:
causes of. See Correlates of intimate
violence
conceptualizations of, 4, 20-22, 37-39,
92-93, 165
consequences of. See Consequences of
physical abuse; Psychological abuse,
consequences of
correlates of. See Correlates of intimate
violence
costs to healthcare system as a result of, 164
crime defined as, 21, 22, 26-27
crime studies of. See Crime studies of
intimate violence
during pregnancy, 168-171
effect on children of, 21
ending, 13
etiology of, 14, 142
family conflict studies of. See Family
conflict studies
functions of, 9, 33, 93-94
gender asymmetry in perpetration of, 11,
24-27, 93, 140, 163

gender symmetry in perpetration of, 11, 18,
27, 30-36, 184, 191, 194
injuries resulting from. See Consequences
of physical abuse, injuries as
intergenerational transmission of, 6, 74-76
interventions. See Interventions and
treatment of intimate violence
measurement of, 17-20, 25-29, 50-51. See
also Conflict Tactics Scale
nature of, 4-6, 9-11, 17-87, 92-93, 186,
192-200
need for more research on, 13, 68-69, 174
newlywed couples and, 114-131, 182, 184,
186-190, 192-200
norms supporting. See Correlates of
intimate violence, social norms
supporting violence
prevention of. See Prevention of intimate
violence
psychological abuse. See Psychological
abuse
public perceptions of, 4, 91
rates of, 5, 19-29, 38, 45, 91, 139-140, 163,
182, 184-190, 192-200
responses to. See Responses to intimate
violence
self defense against. See Responses to
intimate violence, self defense against
severity of, 4
social learning models of, 73-76, 79, 83-85,
122
stability of, 182-200
trauma models of, 73, 77, 83-85
treatment of. See Interventions and
treatment of intimate violence
verbal aggression. See Verbal aggression
victims of. See Victims of violence
Violence targets. See Victims of violence

Wife battering, 4, 14, 45-69, 91-106, 139-156,
163-176. See also Patriarchal terrorism;
Violence in intimate relationships

About the Contributors

Ileana Arias, Professor of Psychology and Director of Clinical Training at the University of Georgia, received her doctorate from the State University of New York at Stony Brook. In addition to winning several teaching awards, she has been recognized by the Groves Conference on Marriage and the Family as a Marvin B. Sussman Family Scholar, and was honored in 1997 by the University of Georgia with a Creative Research Medal. Her main area of research interest and publication is spousal abuse. She is Associate Editor of *Behavior Therapy* and serves on the editorial boards of several leading psychology journals.

Ximena B. Arriaga, Assistant Professor of Psychology at Claremont Graduate University, received her doctorate from the University of North Carolina at Chapel Hill. She has been principal investigator of an NIMH-funded project to examine the development of commitment in intimate relationships, and recently received a grant to study interpersonal violence among Latinas. In addition to her research on commitment and relationship maintenance behaviors, her current interests focus on methods for studying interpersonal violence and coping strategies in abusive relationships.

Thomas N. Bradbury is Professor of Psychology at UCLA, where he conducts longitudinal research on marriage. He received his doctorate from the University of Illinois, after completing his clinical internship at the UCLA Neuropsychiatric Institute. He is the editor of *The Psychology of Marriage* (with Fincham, 1990) and *The Developmental Course of Marital Dysfunction* (1998), and also received the 1998 Distinguished Scientific Award for Early Career Contributions from the American Psychological Association.

Jacquelyn Campbell is the Anna D. Wolf Endowed Professor and Associate Dean for Doctoral Education Programs and Research at Johns Hopkins University School of Nursing, with a joint appointment in the School of Hygiene and Public Health. She has been the principal investigator of several major NIH- and CDC-funded research projects on battering and has authored or coauthored more than 80 publications on the subject. For nearly 20 years, she has worked with wife abuse shelters and policy committees on domestic violence, and is currently on the Board of Directors for House of Ruth, a shelter in Baltimore; the Family Violence Prevention Fund in San Francisco; the Institute of Medicine's Board on International Health; and the National Advisory Committee on Violence Against Women.

Donald G. Dutton is Professor of Psychology at the University of British Columbia. In 1974, he began to investigate the criminal justice response to wife assault, and subsequently developed and ran a training program for police on intervention techniques for cases of domestic violence. From 1979 to the present, he has been a therapist in the Assaultive Husbands Project, a court-mandated treatment program for men convicted of wife assault, and has served as an expert witness in civil and criminal trials involving domestic abuse, including the O. J. Simpson trial. Dutton has published over 80 papers and three books, including *Domestic Assault of Women, The Batterer: A Psychological Profile,* and *The Abusive Personality.*

Katherine Herron is a graduate student in the Clinical Science psychology program at Indiana University. She conducts research on husband violence, with a focus on coding the communication behavior of violent and nonviolent couples during marital problem discussions. She has also conducted research on parenting and the potential for child abuse among maritally violent couples.

Amy Holtzworth-Munroe is Associate Professor of Psychology at Indiana University, where she studies the problem of husband violence. Her research has compared the social information processing skills of maritally violent and nonviolent men, examined the marital interaction behaviors of violent and nonviolent couples, and more recently, sought to identify subtypes of maritally violent men. She has worked clinically with batterers and has helped to train therapists to identify and address husband violence.

Erika Lawrence is a PhD candidate in clinical psychology (with a minor in measurement and psychometrics) at the University of California, Los Angeles, where she is supported by an Individual National Research Service Award from NIMH. She is completing her dissertation, entitled "Understanding the Trajectories of Physical Aggression in Newlywed Marriage," and also conducting an outcome study on the prevention of physical aggression in marriage.

Kenneth E. Leonard is Senior Research Scientist at the Research Institute on Addictions and Director of the Division of Psychology in Psychiatry at the State University of New York at Buffalo Medical School. He is a Fellow in Division 50 of the American Psychological Association and an associate editor for the *Journal of Abnormal Psychology*. He has published numerous articles on alcohol and marital/family processes, and alcohol and violence.

Sally A. Lloyd is Professor and Director of Women's Studies at Miami University in Ohio. Her scholarship and teaching is centered around the study of physical and sexual aggression in courtship and marriage. Her recent work includes *Family Violence From a Communication Perspective* (co-edited with D. Cahn), which received the 1996 Distinguished Book Award from the Applied Communication Section of the Speech Communication Association; and a forthcoming volume entitled *The Dark Side of Courtship: Physical Violence and Sexual Exploitation* (coauthored with Beth Emery).

Jeffrey C. Meehan is a graduate student in the Indiana University Clinical Science psychology doctorate program. He is conducting research on the neuropsychological functioning of men who are violent toward their intimate female partners, including the possible influence of both impulsivity and head trauma on their violent behavior. He is also examining the relationship between husband aggression and the men's physiological reactivity during a marital conflict interaction.

Stuart Oskamp is Professor of Psychology at Claremont Graduate University. He received his PhD from Stanford and has had numerous visiting appointments at universities in other countries. He has served as the president of the APA Division of Population and Environmental Psychology and the Society for the Psychological Study of Social Issues (SPSSI) and as editor of the *Journal of Social Issues*. His main research interests are attitudes and attitude change, environmental preservation, and social issues and public policy. He has published nearly 100 articles and many books, including *Attitudes and Opinions* and *Applied Social Psychology* (both in their second editions).

Phyllis W. Sharps is Associate Professor and Codirector of the Maternal Child Health Track in the School of Public Health and Health Sciences at the George Washington University. She is the principal investigator of a Department of Defense grant to study domestic abuse and pregnancy outcomes among military women, and has collaborated with Jacqueline Campbell in studying risk factors for homicide in violent intimate relationships. She is the author or coauthor of numerous articles, chapters, and conference presentations related to violence against women and family violence. She is also involved with many community organizations that focus on adolescent pregnancy and educational initiatives concerning family violence.

Murray A. Straus is Professor of Sociology and Codirector of the Family Research Laboratory at the University of New Hampshire. He has also taught at Minnesota, Cornell, Wisconsin, Washington State, York (England), Bombay (India), and the University of Ceylon (now Sri Lanka). He has been president of three scientific societies, and received numerous honors, such as the American Professional Society on Child Abuse award for research contributions. Straus is the author or coauthor of more than 200 articles on the family, research methods, and South Asia; and 16 books, including *Stress, Culture, and Aggression, Beating the Devil Out of Them: Corporal Punishment in American Families, Physical Violence in American Families,* and *Four Theories of Rape.*

Gregory L. Stuart received his PhD in clinical psychology from Indiana University, and is currently a postdoctoral research fellow at the Brown University Center for Alcohol and Addiction Studies. He has conducted research in the area of marital violence, including study of batterer subtypes. His dissertation tested a mediational model in which impulsivity predicted marital violence among male batterers.